World Disasters Report

2001

Focus on recovery

International Federation
of Red Cross and Red Crescent Societies

The *World Disasters Report 2001* was edited by Jonathan Walter.

Thanks to all those who assisted contributors during travel and research, especially Aradhna Duggal.

Baseline maps by Geoatlas® – ©GRAPHI-OGRE, Hendaye, France
Typesetting by Strategic Communications SA, Geneva, Switzerland
Printed by SADAG Imprimerie, Bellegarde/Valserine, France
Production manager: Sue Pfiffner

For more information about the *World Disasters Report 2001,* contact: wdr2001@ifrc.org

To order the *World Disasters Report,* contact:

Kumarian Press Inc
1294 Blue Hills Ave
Bloomfield CT 06002
USA
Tel.: (1)(860) 243 2098
Fax: (1)(860) 243 2867
E-mail: kpbooks@aol.com
Web: http://www.kpbooks.com

Eurospan
3 Henrietta Street
Covent Garden
London WC2E 8LU, UK
Tel.: (44)(20) 7240 0856
Fax: (44)(20) 7379 0609
E-mail: orders@edspubs.co.uk
Web: http://www.eurospan.co.uk

International Federation of Red Cross and Red Crescent Societies
17, chemin des Crêts, P.O. Box 372
CH-1211 Geneva 19, Switzerland
Tel:. (41)(22) 730 4222. Fax: (41)(22) 733 0395
E-mail: secretariat@ifrc.org;
Web: http://www.ifrc.org

Contents

Section One Focus on recovery

Chapter 1 Relief, recovery and root causes   8

Chapter 2 The ecology of post-disaster recovery   34

Chapter 3 Somalia: programming for sustainable health care   58

Chapter 4 Trapped in the gap – post-landslide Venezuela   82

Chapter 5 Post-flood recovery in Viet Nam   102

Section Two Tracking the system

Planning recovery to minimize future risk

There were more disasters in 2000 than in previous years of the decade. The good news is that the year 2000 saw significantly less people killed by disaster. Some 20,000 as compared to the average of 75,000 per year during the decade. The bad news is that the number of people affected by disasters went up to 256 million compared with an average from 1991 to 2000 of 211 million per year.

A major cause in the increasing of number of people being affected by disasters is the increase in the number of hydro-meteorological disasters such as floods, wind storms and droughts.

Against this background, this year's *World Disasters Report* looks at the subject of, and the difficulties involved in, recovery from disasters. The overall picture, particularly for those in the most disaster-prone countries, is far from encouraging. Chapters in this edition of the *World Disasters Report* look at the way in which recurrent disasters from floods in Asia to drought in the Horn of Africa to wind storms in Latin America are sweeping away development gains and calling into question the possibility of recovery. Gaps between life-saving relief and longer-term development can leave disaster-affected people stranded. Technical solutions that do not adequately take account of community's needs may mean that reconstruction does not lead to recovery.

In the past, post-disaster reconstruction has focused too much on rebuilding physical infrastructure. But there is more to recovery than concrete. Local livelihoods, economies and institutions have to be strengthened and rebuilt. Volunteer networks, from Bangladesh to the Caribbean, are a critical part of many early warning and disaster preparedness systems. Investment in the social capital of disaster-affected communities is key to building sustainable recovery.

Too often those affected by disaster such as the families afflicted by floods in Viet Nam and mudslides in Venezuela are rebuilding their homes and communities the way they were before the disaster. They are literally 'reconstructing the risk', leaving them just as exposed to future hazards. They don't have the resources to do otherwise and they can't wait for the benefits of long-term development. This transitional period, which may start days or hours after disaster, is where humanitarian organizations need to play a more effective role. This role may include strengthening private homes against flood waters, encouraging the community to draw up a 'risk map' or establishing locally-based preparedness measures – all measures to improve the resilience of communities to catastrophe.

However, action at the local level alone will not bring genuine recovery from disasters. Root causes need identifying and tackling. In many cases, nature's contribution to 'natural' disasters is simply to expose the effects of deeper, structural causes – from global warming and unplanned urbanization to trade liberalization and political marginalization. The effects of man's action are often evident – many natural catastrophes are *un/*natural in their origins.

Macro-factors driving disasters are beyond the scope of aid. But not beyond the remit of humanitarian advocacy, which can champion solutions to these root causes with both national and international institutions. The ever-increasing risk posed by disasters will only be contained by putting the planet's vulnerable people at the centre of disaster response and of humanitarian advocacy.

I hope that this edition of the *World Disasters Report* – including the thematic and country chapters and the expanded commentary on disaster statistics – will promote debate, and the development of better practice in helping communities recover from disaster.

Didier J Cherpitel
Secretary General

chapter 1

Section One

Focus on recovery

Relief, recovery and root causes

Recent massive floods, wind storms and earthquakes from Latin America to south Asia have set back development in hardest-hit areas by a decade – leaving thousands of communities more exposed than ever to disasters now recurring every few years. Many of the world's regions at risk from disasters simply fail to recover before another catastrophe strikes. Shattered families, homes, schools, roads, livelihoods take years to repair, let alone to rebuild and recover in a way more resilient to the next disaster. Pernicious combinations of conflict and drought, from the Horn of Africa to central Asia, are perpetuating states of emergency which call into question the value of relief aid interventions. Emergency relief, although often life-saving, may fail to promote long-term recovery. Should relief be broadened, imbued with developmental elements to bridge the relief-recovery gap? Or should development take more account of the 'disaster dimension'? This chapter will examine how the gaps, not just between relief and development, but between front line and headquarters, leave thousands of disaster-affected people abandoned to an uncertain fate. And we will consider the limits of humanitarian action in tackling disasters' root causes.

If there is one thing you can rely on in the Bay of Bengal it is a cyclone. Almost a year after a super-cyclone tore into India's eastern state of Orissa in October 1999, killing anything between 10,000 to 40,000 people and devastating the lives of millions, the dawn of a new storm season brought panic.

For weeks, marginal farmers and fishermen had anxiously sought news from visitors to their isolated coastal communities. Was there talk in the state capital of meteorological developments? They had survived 300-kilometre-per-hour winds and a seven-metre tidal surge that had overwhelmed life up to 20 kilometres inland. Most had lost their livelihoods, and the return of still, hot, heavy air had made them fearful of further catastrophe.

They had reason to fear. Nowhere in the world do tropical cyclones wreak greater havoc than on the subcontinent. A major cyclone hits the eastern coast of India every two to eight years and 1999's has gone down as the country's worst natural disaster of the 20th century.

As in Bangladesh, where at least one severe cyclone and a number of lesser storms bring annual destruction, such disasters are far from 'natural'. Along densely populated coasts some of the poorest of Asia's poor are trapped in high-risk zones by social, political and economic circumstances. All too often abandoned by government, downtrodden and marginalized by the powerful, disregarded by the western world, they are the fodder of recurring calamity. An outpouring of global consternation in their most desperate moments dissipates with the retreat of CNN, leaving modestly funded non-governmental organizations (NGOs) and humanitarians struggling. The cyclone has gone; the human condition on which it fed remains. Worse, it has been aggravated.

The year 2000 saw Orissa's coastal population more vulnerable than ever, their defences low, coping mechanisms in near collapse. The 1999 cyclone had enjoyed an easy run inland, partly

Photo opposite page: Rebuilding a new life: what can be done to help disaster-hit communities recover from one catastrophe and become more resilient to the next?

Jerry Gulea/ International Federation, Papua New Guinea 1999

due to commercial depletion of tidal mangrove forests, which had once formed barriers to the tidal surges that often accompany cyclones. Unrestricted, the sea swept 20 km inland and the winds tore down man-made embankments, uprooted 90 million trees, most of the coast's green cover, and left communities exposed to a degree unprecedented in living memory. A year on, reports of rough seas, and low pressure in the Bay moving north-westerly towards Orissa or neighbouring Andhra Pradesh, terrified parts of the population.

The authorities remained calm. When asked what would happen if a cyclone struck again, Ajit Tripathy, Orissa state's former special relief commissioner said, "I am not saying we would be fully prepared. But we have arrangements with the meteorological department that they will give us at least 72 hours warning of a cyclone approaching, and give wind speeds and area of landfall...to be sure, people will take warnings seriously now." What would occur thereafter was less clear. Should word even reach remoter villages – an uncertain prospect given the inadequate lines of communication – what would people do? Where would they run? Roads, swept by flood waters and rutted by relief convoys, were impassable in the rains, hindering large-scale evacuation. Cyclone shelters were scarce and, crucially, except for areas with preparedness strategies, the people themselves would be defenceless.

The danger this time would subside but it refuelled a debate which had risen to fever pitch in the wake of the super-cyclone. Catastrophes in India during the 1990s killed or affected on average 56 million people a year and claimed US$ 1.9 billion annually in direct economic costs alone. Yet, according to the *India Disasters Report,* there has been an "absence of any clear national and state-level disaster preparedeness, management and mitigation strategy". The director of India's national disaster management division, S.K. Swami, argues this was not the case at the time of the super-cyclone, but acknowledges, "It is a fact that the state machinery took some time to gear up. This was firstly because of the magnitude [of the disaster] and secondly because most of the staff and officers of the state government were themselves victims."

Either way, Orissa's cyclone brought chaos. Power supplies and communications were severed, the state was cut off from the outside world, and, when thousands of tonnes of relief supplies did arrive, much remained undelivered. Public and media outrage at the apparent indifference and ineptitude of the government's response led to demands for rigorous structural change. Five months later, Orissa's administration was voted out of power.

International relief did get through, but so fast, furious and uncoordinated that the people in Orissa were overwhelmed. Some agencies – particularly those with a long-term presence in the state – were exemplary, but the United Nations (UN) later found evidence of extensive duplication. One after the other, agencies purified the same well on the same day, distributed food or blankets to the same villages, and channelled relief to media-covered hot spots rather than to those in greatest need. Having suffered from a natural cyclone, Orissa underwent a humanitarian one.

Rather like India with its satellites, humanitarians possessed the hardware. But did they make the most of the opportunity? Or did they put victims back in harm's way? Some would argue they did all that relief agencies are capable of in emergencies: saving lives fast and alleviating suffering. It may have been untidy, but mess is in the nature of a heavy, fast-moving beast.

Others would contend it was another prime example of band-aid relief, covering up wounds which would consequently fester, reconstructing long-term risk, and providing an alibi for political players unable – or unwilling – to nurture sustainable change. Humanitarian aid pours in but too often fails to define and address root causes, or create the environment in which others can.

Orissa is one of many examples where band-aid alone can do little more than patch over root causes. In August 2000, UN agencies reported that extreme drought and conflict had brought 13.4 million people in six East African nations to the brink of starvation. Again. Over 10 million of those were in Ethiopia. Daily, dozens of children were already dying from malnutrition, measles and tuberculosis (TB). Protracted hostilities between Ethiopia and Eritrea featured strongly in the equation. But after three decades of emergency aid pouring into the country, more was amiss than conflict. Failure by agencies and governments alike to address sectors other than food aid have made long-term recovery virtually impossible.

After emergency food aid in late 2000 averted near disaster, Catherine Bertini, special envoy of the UN secretary-general to the Horn of Africa, launched a fresh US$ 353 million appeal in January 2001 to cover the needs of the most affected. She argued that food aid alone was not enough and encouraged donors to support the health, nutrition, water, agriculture and livestock sectors of the new appeal. "If we want to make a real difference, we have to properly address these sectors," said Bertini. "They are key to the recovery process." Commenting on the appeal, Mark Bidder, a member of the UN country team in Ethiopia, said it had been launched "to bridge the gap between the relief operation and recovery". He added that signs of recovery included "improved weather conditions, animals getting fatter, IDPs [internally displaced persons] returning home and a peace agreement signed between Ethiopia and Eritrea".

Two years earlier, Tenna Mengistu, former secretary general of the Ethiopian Red Cross, had said, "Relief will save the day, but when people are living on the verge of disaster it isn't enough to return them to the status quo. If we can raise the quality of life, we may enable the most vulnerable not just to survive but to cope with, and prevent, disasters." Commenting on a Red Cross package to improve rural water and sanitation, housing and community disaster preparedness, he pointed out that conditions in 85 per cent of homes were below an acceptable minimum level.

Un/natural disasters threaten recovery

While the debate rages about the extent to which humanitarian aid may perpetuate or cover-up the underlying causes of disaster, a more practical question needs addressing. How do you break the cycle of recurring disaster? For of one thing there can be no argument: the devastating impacts of disasters are increasing and, unless root causes as well as symptoms are confronted, they will continue to inflict ever-greater human suffering and expense – relegating the idea of recovery to the slag-heap of pious hopes. Since the 1950s, according to reinsurance giant Munich Re, costs associated with 'natural' disasters have rocketed 14-fold. Each year from 1991 to 2000, an average of 211 million people were killed or affected by 'natural' disasters – seven times greater than the figure for those killed or affected by conflict. Towards the end of the 1990s, the world counted some 25 million 'environmental refugees' – for the first time more people had fled natural hazards than conflict.

While no one seriously doubts that political solutions are necessary for conflicts, 'natural' disasters are often considered unavoidable and stuffed into the 'act of God' pigeon-hole. But, as a proverb from the Horn of Africa says, "God makes drought. Man makes famine." So 'natural' can be a misleading description for disasters such as the droughts, floods and cyclones which afflict much of the developing world. Recognizing these disasters as often *un*/natural, identifying the many human-made root causes and advocating structural and political changes to combat them, is long overdue.

As *un*/natural disasters become ever-more frequent, aid dollars and development gains are being washed away. Catastrophe is no longer a brief dip on the curve of development but a danger to the process itself. The poorest of the poor are becoming more vulnerable, trapped in vicious cycles of structural poverty and marginalization beyond their power to change. Worse still, some places prone to continual *un*/natural disasters are becoming lawless and a threat to security (see Box 1.1). After considering last year's US government assertion that AIDS was a global threat to security, the UN Security Council might be wise to do the same with *un*/natural disasters.

The global community's commitment, meanwhile, is too little and too selective, both in development policy and economic planning. The Development Assistance Committee (DAC) of the Organisation for Economic Co-operation and Development (OECD) – the club of the world's richest nations – stumped up an average of just 0.39 per cent of their 1999 gross national product (GNP) in annual overseas aid, half the amount the UN considers necessary. Of this figure, a mere fraction is invested in the prevention and reduction of disasters. The United States Geological Survey has said that an investment of US$ 40 billion in disaster preparedness, prevention and mitigation would have reduced global economic losses in the 1990s by US$ 280 billion. Which is to say nothing of human suffering.

Developing countries provide most of the victims – 98 per cent of all those killed and affected by 'natural' disasters come from nations of low or medium human development. Globally during the last decade, over 665,000 people reportedly died in 'natural' disasters alone, excluding conflict, technological accidents and chronic public health crises. This averages out at nearly 1,300 deaths every week of every year. Of that total, less than 1 per cent were in Europe, while 86 per cent were in Asia. In reality the numbers may be much higher. Indian authorities maintain the Orissa cyclone's death toll was around 10,000, while many aid agencies believe it exceeded 40,000. Official wariness of compensation is one reason for the lower statistic. Another is the marginalization of some sections of the population. Unrecognized by the authorities, they do not appear in any census. Villages were swept away, whole communities wiped out that never featured in public records: the *un*/people of *un*/natural disasters. As we shall see, around the Bay of Bengal, Orissa is no exception.

In the face of such enormous numbers of people killed and affected by disasters, and with ever-greater pressure on resources targeted at humanitarian responses, how can recovery be coherently addressed? This chapter will examine four issues informing the recovery debate:

I.   Relief delivery can support or undermine disaster recovery.

II.   Risk-aware development can reduce the likelihood and effects of disaster, thereby enhancing recovery.

Box 1.1 *Un*/natural disasters threaten security

While *un*/natural disasters threaten economic and social development, they also undermine stability. They interrupt trade, oblige governments to borrow, devalue their currencies, and compromise security.

Human unrest has shadowed catastrophes since historical records began. The physical and economic consequences of a volcano that shattered the Aegean island of Thira around 1600 BC hastened the decline of Crete's Minoan civilization. The 464 BC earthquake that left Sparta in ruins incited rebellion. And when another destroyed ancient Antioch in 115 AD, Christians were blamed and persecuted. In China at the close of the 19th century, drought and famine helped to spark the Boxer uprising.

Still it continues. General Somoza's regime in Nicaragua fell after the Managua earthquake of 1972. The fall of Haile Selassie's regime in Ethiopia, and that of Gaafar Mohamed el-Nimeiri in Sudan in 1985, were in part related to famine. The defeat of Poland's government after the 1997 central European floods was thought to be influenced by the impression that it had mishandled the disaster. And, following 1999's super-cyclone in Orissa, the ruling Congress Party was swept from state office in subsequent elections by the rival Bharatiya Janata Party (BJP) of the Indian prime minister. Not that that dispensed with public unrest. Critics accused central government of milking the disaster, placing politics before humanity, delaying the flow of aid to opposition territory. Three months after the cyclone, the BJP was electioneering but the destitute still awaited the release of US$ 200 million of approved federal assistance. *Time* magazine commented, "The winged buzzards are gone: the human ones are starting to campaign amid ruined lives and ruptured families living beneath plastic sheets."

Across the Bay of Bengal, the final decades of the 20th century have seen age-old river erosion grow in its impact (see Box 1.2). A leading erosion authority, Sharif Kafi of the Bangladesh Development Partnership Centre, estimates that as a consequence, functional landlessness has grown from 37 per cent of the population in 1972 to 59 per cent today. He warns, "If nothing is done, the pauperization of the people will only continue. The gap between rich and poor will widen, extreme poverty will spread, and total chaos will envelop society." What he describes is an Asian Somalia, deprived of central government, awash with crime, drugs, prostitution and violence, dependent upon God for sustenance. "Every day we are moving backwards," he says.

Kafi isn't scaremongering. The anarchy he fears can already be found in Bangladesh's deltas among the *chars*, richly fertile new islands, laid down by disgorging rivers. The *chars* present an uncertain world. Dispossessed by erosion, pushed to the fringe of society by repeated loss of livelihood, their desperate inhabitants are prone to the whims and the control of powerful elites and gangsters.

III. Reforms of donor funding strategies can help bridge the relief-recovery gap.

IV. Aid alone cannot tackle the macro-factors driving disasters: advocacy of structural changes at political and economic levels is needed.

I. Relief can support or undermine recovery

The idea that relief delivery should support rather than undermine recovery would not appear to be contentious. But the way aid is delivered can prove counterproductive, and continues to raise disturbing questions about whose needs are best served by aid – those of donor agencies or their beneficiaries?

Prasant Naik, Oxfam's project manager in Orissa, describes what he saw when the humanitarian circus pulled into town in late 1999, "There was this huge influx into the most well-publicized areas. Agencies wanted maximum impact in 20 or 30 days in the places donors were familiar with from the television news. It wasn't what was needed. The highest wind speeds had been elsewhere, where casualties were less but loss of livelihood was more severe."

Most agencies concentrated on the Ersama area. It was truly horrific, awash with human corpses and animal carcasses. Helicopter pilots dropping relief said they could identify it blindfold by the stench, and in the first days help reaching it was inadequate. Not for long. Ersama made powerful and moving television and agencies wanted a piece of it. More discerning charities backed off and sought the immense unmet need beyond the media spotlight. Many aid workers still pull a face and speak of 'relief supermarkets', and how destitute villagers became choosy, comparing quality of blankets or grain before accepting what was offered.

A year later, the region hadn't recovered. Uprooted trees littered the landscape. Everywhere people were rebuilding, in many cases literally reconstructing the risk. While villagers were aware that at least community buildings should be cyclone-proof, there simply weren't the resources to achieve this. Only a handful of agencies, mostly local, remained and media interest was back to the provincial.

In the village of Khurantatuth, schoolteacher Bhabasankar Panda sat by the Red Cross cyclone shelter and chose his words carefully. The village was grateful, he said, but a strategy of *kum kum* ('little by little') would have been better. The relief had been so great the villagers had not known what to do with it. "It was more than a family could consume," said the teacher. Rather than all the rice, they would have preferred help later on, getting the land productive again. The saline water of the tidal surge had brought many problems, and the paddy wasn't growing as it ought to.

Had anybody asked them what they wanted? There had been consultation with local NGOs, with CARE who had helped the fishermen, and with the Indian Red Cross, the first people to have reached them. But most relief had arrived from people who didn't ask questions.

A year on Khurantatuth remained grateful. There were a few things missing. Panda mentioned housing, roads, the embankment, the school. The school? It was washed away with the rest of the village. He and his colleagues still taught when time could be found. An agency had brought school kits, and the cyclone shelter could offer classrooms. But no one had been paid since the cyclone.

Oxfam's Prasant Naik sees more than irrelevant aid in such scenarios. He sees *bad* aid. Where it is indiscriminately dumped it enlarges the recovery gap. "Later, it was difficult for other agencies to make progress in these places," he says, "because of the expectancy and dependency created." The daily wage rate reflected that. By the time relief operations ended, it had been inflated to two-and-a-half times the government's recommended figure. "After everything had been thrown at the people, to go in and talk about disaster preparedness and community participation was like beating your head against a wall."

As the disaster's first anniversary came around, agencies with longer-term vision had nurtured self-help programmes and mobilized communities. But Oxfam wondered aloud how many had been left self-help*less*.

Relief is a platform for recovery

Well-targeted and programmed relief, however, can provide a secure platform from which the disaster-affected and those assisting them can begin the slow process of recovery. The International Federation of Red Cross and Red Crescent Societies (International Federation) has pursued this strategy in Orissa by giving 1,000 farmers seeds – which thrive in soils left too salty by the tidal wave for usual crops – plus the tools, fertilizers and agricultural training needed to make them grow. These saline-resistant strains of rice, chillies, green vegetables and fruit saplings are now reaching markets, and helping regenerate the local economy.

The Red Cross is also helping build disaster-resistant private housing for the most vulnerable – platforms for recovery in the most literal sense. The houses' concrete walls and foundations are designed to withstand falling trees, high winds and even tidal waves. Communities themselves select who should receive a 'model' house – some beneficiaries are as young as 10 years old – and villagers are taught how to construct them by skilled local masons. Similar 'relief housing' projects are being implemented by the International Federation in conjunction with local communities and authorities in Viet Nam (see Chapter 5).

Further round the Bay of Bengal, the erosion of Bangladesh's deltas and river banks presents an even-greater, ongoing challenge. While cyclones and floods draw international attention, river erosion – bringing distress, displacement and destitution to hundreds of thousands of people every year – is scarcely mentioned (see Box 1.2).

A cynical world looks on with indifference, unwilling to commit to a grave, enduring but unspectacular crisis that produces little media interest. If help does come it mostly derives from other disasters, as it did in September/October 2000 when a surge of water from West Bengal, India, swept into Bangladesh, compounding the problems of monsoon flooding and erosion. Among thousands of people crowded on banks were many long-term erosion victims. Without floods they would have gone unnoticed.

Concedes John Bales, disaster preparedness delegate for the International Federation in Bangladesh, "They were found by default if we're honest about it. Over the years many people have looked at erosion but nobody seems to have noticed what it means in terms of sustainable development. It is probably the number-one issue, affecting 80 per cent of the country."

Is recovery from such an ongoing catastrophe possible? While root causes will take decades to address, relief is part of the answer, says Bob McKerrow, the International Federation's regional head for south Asia. In his mind the displaced are first in need of breathing space, time in which to make decisions about recovering on meagre resources. "Targeted relief is the basis of good development," he says. "If you can induce people not to move on for three or four months you can limit their vulnerability. You give them a chance to sell their labour, and find other sources of income, and you provide them with shelter until things settle down."

McKerrow's vision is that relief can act as a platform, stabilizing the lives of those caught up in disaster for long enough to plan their recovery. Relief buys them time to make the right decisions. But relief is just the beginning of a bigger commitment. When they do move on, they'll need longer-term support for rehabilitation. Jobs will be a priority. Some people can be retrained, new employment can be created. Housing projects can assist resettlement.

Box 1.2 River erosion – a movable disaster

In the morning who is rich
Becomes a pauper by the evening
Oh brother, a pauper by the evening
This is how the river plays
At that bank of the river with what faith oh you forgetful
Did you sleep in your happy home
When erosion came you couldn't even get a raft to cross
This is how the river plays
Breaking this river bank, yet building another
This is how the river plays

(Traditional folk song)

Where the brown, silt-filled waters of the seemingly boundless Meghna River pour out of Bangladesh and into the Bay of Bengal, Hatiya island is vanishing. Among just one group of villages, more than 10,000 people have been displaced. Abul Kalam, a 36-year-old farmer, is one of them. His family's land disappeared as the Meghna ate its way two kilometres inland over the past year, encouraged by unusually heavy monsoons. His home is now a makeshift shelter near the island's retreating edge, which drops three metres to the waterline. A protective embankment collapsed some time ago.

While Abul works on his palm-thatch structure, a visitor asks, "Are you leaving?" Hundreds of thousands are forced to move to safer ground each year in Bangladesh. "No, coming," replies Abul. His shanty is new, and he is strengthening it less than 100 metres from the crumbling waterfront. He knows he will be forced to move again soon, but here at the end of the earth there is a poor man's method in his madness. He has no money, so he occupies land already abandoned by its owner and therefore rent-free. Abul has located a more sensible site a kilometre further inland but today that is safe and occupiers pay for it. As the Meghna closes in, that plot too will become free, for only the most desperate will want it.

Along the banks of Bangladesh's great rivers and tributaries a movable disaster is unfolding. The nation's deltaic plain is shifting, the rivers consuming around 9,000 hectares of fertile land a year and spewing them out elsewhere. A million people are affected annually. Of those, 500,000 are made homeless and half never find adequate shelter. Fresh hovels appear in already overpopulated villages. Victims migrate to city slums or

endure deprivations on the *chars* – inhospitable new land rising mostly as islands from the river silt, which in turn will fall to erosion.

Despite the efforts of a few agencies, substantial international response remains absent. Bob McKerrow, the International Federation's regional head for south Asia, says, "It is the biggest problem in Bangladesh. It does more damage to the socio-economic condition of the country than anything else and hardly anyone has been shouting about it. It is an abrogation of humanitarian duty." McKerrow believes the vastness and complexity of the problem put donors and agencies off. There is no quick answer, only long-term commitment along a path fraught with political considerations. Nor is there fund-raising profile to speak of. The media isn't sure how to cover it. It is a slow, silent disaster and there isn't the obligatory body count, or babies being born in trees. How, they all wonder, do you sell it?

Clearly with patience. When leading erosion authority Sharif Kafi, of the Bangladesh Development Partnership Centre, produced a training manual for family and community preparedness, USAID funded its publication. But a definitive erosion study that contains six years of research lies unpublished on Kafi's desk for want of financial backing. McKerrow says, "You can raise millions of unearmarked dollars for all kinds of training programmes but 4,000 bucks for an advocacy video on river erosion is a very different story." McKerrow has made one anyway and is campaigning for recognition and action, along with the Bangladesh Red Crescent. There can be few more poignant examples of the 'gap' than the erosion of Bangladesh – it doesn't fit snugly into anyone's paradigm of emergency relief or development.

Yukiya Saito of the Japanese Red Cross (JRC) is gravely concerned by the poor humanitarian response. He sees years of community development literally being undermined. The JRC has supported the Bangladesh Red Crescent for more than 30 years, investing in community disaster preparedness programmes which target about 92,000 people around a string of coastal cyclone shelters. The JRC has funded 29 shelters, 22 of them on Hatiya, and encourages communities to make

➡

➡ the most of them. Schools occupy some, another is expanding its facilities thanks to a government grant.

But what cyclones cannot blow down, rivers can erode. From 1996 to 2000, six JRC shelters on Hatiya were lost to floods – one had been built in 1997 three kilometres from the nearest river and considered out of erosion's reach. It is not the loss of physical structures that worry the Japanese most, but the loss of disaster mitigation programmes that served the population in a three-kilometre diameter around each shelter.

While statistics show the nation's cyclone death toll has been dramatically reduced by disaster preparedness, those who flee erosion flee the security of early warning systems, coping procedures and cyclone shelters. Last October when the first cyclonic depression threatened the Bay, Bangladesh saw none of Orissa's confusion. The depression was mapped and its progress passed to the population. Along the 710-kilometre coastal belt, 8 million people inhabit the high-risk zone. The Red Crescent alone had 33,000 volunteers and 149 purpose-built shelters on standby, in 11 coastal districts covered by 2,742 community units. From the Red Crescent's headquarters, satellite information from the meteorological office was beamed to 120 radio stations and on by VHF to remoter islands and settlements. Radio Bangladesh was broadcasting updates simultaneously.

Meanwhile, uncounted legions of unregistered people clustered onto the many chars. Who they were, where they were, interested no one. Unprepared and physically defenceless, a cyclone would remove them from the face of the planet. The authorities would have to guess at how many. Nearly 3,000 people perished on Hatiya alone in a 1991 cyclone.

Life on Hatiya may be lived on the edge, but on Bhoyar char it is sought in the abyss. Lawless and uncaring, it is peopled only by the most desperate. Like all new land, Bhoyar is khash (government) land, resulting from a 1972 presidential order which sought to ensure that emerging territory would be distributed to landless farmers rather than acquired by the rich and powerful. As is the norm, it was designated for a ten-year afforestation programme to help stabilize it, after which human habitation would be allowed.

But the honourable intentions of char legislation have been compromised in recent years by corrupt landowners and the vulnerable alike. Long before the forestry mandate expired, the homeless were heading for Bhoyar. Today the inhabitants, mostly displaced from Hatiya, put their number at 25,000 – a figure that can't be substantiated since there is no register.

There is also no justice. Human brutality, as well as the weather, threatens. Police allegedly burned down the first settlers' houses. They fled to the forest and hid, until gangsters arrived, assumed control of the island, and forced them to pay or leave. Today, say the settlers, two gangs operate and a family can pay 150 taka (US$ 2.75) a month in protection money. It is a fortune for some, but inability to pay is not tolerated. Beatings and rape are not uncommon retribution. Who the thugs work for and whom they pay off is known but unproven, and undoubtedly libellous. A Bangladeshi journalist who investigated was beaten up and dumped in the delta.

Alongside intimidation, the absence of health care leaves inhabitants at risk. Without safe water, diarrhoea is commonplace and often fatal. Asked to list their most urgent needs, char dwellers place health, law and order, a protective embankment and cyclone preparedness first. Education follows. As children multiply, a straw school has been built, but there is no money to pay a teacher.

No one would stay, were there any alternative. A once well-to-do farmer who had owned 16 acres of prime land on Hatiya said, "There is no going back now. When I lost my fields I went to the embankment. When the embankment eroded I came here. This must be my home now because there is nowhere else. All I can do is work for the day when everything will be all right again." He 'bought' his present plot twice. The first enforcer he paid was jailed by police. A second took 2,400 taka (US$ 44) from him before he too was imprisoned. Today, like the others, the farmer goes on paying. The police visit occasionally, but the char dwellers are too afraid to talk. They grow crops, fish, raise ducks, sell their labour when they can on the mainland. Some of the cultivators are forming cooperatives. They are survivors and optimists. Maybe, they say, the char can develop. It is their last chance. They have to believe in it.

Relief: the bridgehead for increasing aid

The kind of relief McKerrow suggests for victims of river erosion could be seen by some as the thin end of a developmental wedge – anathema to many disaster relief professionals. 'Developmental relief' has its opponents, including, in the context of conflict, British emergencies consultant Mark Bradbury.

In his 1998 paper, *Normalising the Crisis in Africa*, Bradbury viewed attempts to make relief 'developmental' as providing an excuse for international disengagement and the running down of programmes. Today he says the argument was over simplistic but the questions it raised remain, and he cites Somalia. "What does it mean on the ground when we speak of 'sustainability'? Immediately after the American decision to pull out in 1993, after losing the battle with Aideed, there was a donors' conference to rethink their position. The timing, I believe, was more than coincidence. They decided the emergency was over, and they would move into a post-conflict, recovery/development phase. From that moment on, there was lots of talk about a relief-to-development continuum and movement to sustainability. Over a number of years the trend increased, as aid to Somalia declined. But if you are talking about development you should see aid resources increase."

So if relief interventions provide the bridgehead within exposed communities for an *increased* flow of resources into disaster recovery, preparedness and development, then such 'developmental relief' could prove enormously beneficial. But how can the very different cultures of relief and development integrate themselves into one seamless response which meets the ongoing and multifarious needs of disaster-affected people?

Jean Ayoub, director of the International Federation's disaster management and coordination division, takes up the challenge. He, too, is wary of a hybrid developmental relief but insists there must be an efficient interface between distinct relief and development cultures. "One team should provide the short-term response, remove the life-threatening factors as much as they can. The other comes in to assess, and to design the rehabilitation and longer-term programming. The expertise required for each stage is different, and I think it is wrong to assume that whoever can deliver on the first phase can objectively review what has been done and go on to design the second one." As far as timing goes, he believes both groups should be together from the outset.

Ayoub wants far more investment in ongoing disaster intelligence. "We need to be more and more knowledgeable, we need better country profiles and vulnerability analysis," he says. Close monitoring of slow- as well as fast-onset disasters – such as that maintained by the International Federation for food-insecure northern Russia – is essential, Ayoub argues. Sound and detailed analysis is a prerequisite for integrating external assistance with the ongoing reality of local-level recovery (see Chapter 3).

Matthias Schmale, head of the organizational development department at the International Federation, says building a consensus on the practical steps to take as disasters unfold is more important than drowning in the theory of what is, or is not, relief. There was initial resistance to this process in-house, he recounts. "But we have moved on from where the relief guys were yelling 'Let's go', and the development people were saying 'We can't have these rambos running around leaving us to clear up their mess'." Schmale refers to nine key factors which can ensure that relief supports recovery:

- Use the capacities of disaster survivors – do not assume they are helpless.
- Identify the needs and capacities of diverse groups among survivors.
- Involve survivors in the decision-making process.
- Be accountable to survivors as well as to donors.
- Adapt strategy to meet reality – do not rely on pre-packaged delivery.
- Decentralize control, so management decisions are taken as closely as possible to beneficiaries.
- Ensure assistance complements survivors' normal means of livelihood.
- Work with local institutions and build their capacities so humanitarian work can continue after interventions finish.
- Set standards of service and welfare systems that can be sustained beyond the relief period.

II. Risk-aware development reduces disaster

The key factors outlined above suggest a level of integration with local communities' efforts at recovery that foreign aid agencies flying into a disaster zone may find difficult to achieve. Where positive impact was seen in Orissa, for example, agencies involved were indigenous, or were already operating in the region, or were working closely with local partners. Which comes as no surprise to the development set. Says John Seaman, development director of Save the Children Fund's (SCF) food security unit, "It used to be our house rule that you only responded to emergencies if you had prior presence in that country. Most people are concerned with the technology of relief – speed, boxes of this, boxes of that. To do a good job what you really need are links and contacts, knowledge of political process, insertion into the system. The technology is straightforward. You can buy that off the shelf."

Seaman argues that relief should respond to interruptions in an ongoing process of development. It can never be an end, rarely a beginning. Relief done right, in any event, is done through and with local structures. "The people who dig people from the ruins of earthquakes are people involved in earthquakes. Aid agencies are subordinate, not as a matter of philosophy but as a matter of fact. We did not feed Ethiopia. Ethiopians fed most of it. We added a percentage to part of the food supply. Much of what happens in international relief is irrelevant at best. You know, the mercy dash of doctors to the latest catastrophe, milling around at the airport. What 50 foreign doctors have got to do with anything is a mystery to us all. Except that the press have a habit of taking their photographs. It's a nonsense."

Following the devastating earthquake that struck El Salvador in January 2001, Debarati Guha-Sapir, director of the Belgium-based Centre for Research on the Epidemiology of Disasters (CRED), speaks of her sense of déjà vu. "Past experience has shown that 8 to 12 hours is the maximum delay within which to extricate trapped persons, if they are to survive," she says. Yet international search-and-rescue teams still flew in to El Salvador from the US, Europe and Japan – arriving days after the disaster. The lesson which never gets learnt, according to Guha-Sapir, is that "community preparedness is the only practical solution for poor countries located in high-risk areas. The locals are the ones who can bring any effective help in the first few hours and it is their capacity that has to be strengthened. This is less heroic than flying in after the event waving fist-fulls of dollars," she says, "but it is cheaper and effective" (see Box 1.3).

Given donor pressure to spend money fast, short-termism is only growing, to the alarm of some observers. "The chronic hand-wringing over aid coordination at the disaster site is a direct result of too much money, too soon, to too many groups," says Guha-Sapir. "The urgency to spend money, preferably in the shortest possible time, seems to supersede rational thinking."

Seaman is equally dismissive. "Take disease in rural Africa. There is an awful lot of it, then something happens and for a while there is an awful lot more. Foreigners move in, and treat it until the exceptional disease moves on – often because of the natural progression of epidemics – and you are back to something like normal. Where do you fit in there? You are not establishing health care; you are providing an astonishingly expensive short-run service. What is this, to arbitrarily come out of the skies to provide three months' assistance for people you have never seen before, and then disappear again?" He questions the value and the economics. "Up to a point I accept that we don't count the cost of saving lives. Emergencies are costly to intervene in, but the idea that there are no economics is absurd. Money doesn't have to be spent badly on an emergency. It can be spent well in the long term."

Invest in local risk management capacity

The question is, how exactly can money be spent well, to save lives, fuel recovery and reduce the risk of future disasters? Investing resources in local partners, boosting their capacity to mitigate, prepare for and respond to disasters, is one clear path to take. To break the cycle of disaster requires adopting a dynamic approach to risk and disaster management, which only locally-based institutions can achieve. The 'fast-in/fast-out' response, as witnessed in Orissa and virtually every other disaster, cannot be an appropriate response to people whose needs and exposure to risk are ongoing.

Yet last year's floods in south-western Bangladesh, for example, saw many small community organizations sidelined, and some probably ruined, by donor policy. A great deal of relief was designed in such a way that only big players could participate. Gawher Nayeem Wahra, director of policy advocacy for ActionAid Bangladesh, saw in that the denial of community empowerment in a region traditionally geared to 'group' initiatives. Relief could have exploited social resources and strengthened them. Instead, the poorest of the poor were not reached and the organizations which supported them could not sustain their activities.

Much lip service is paid to partnership but genuine collaboration is hard to find. By definition, integrated aid interventions require an ongoing presence on the ground. It is the preferred *modus operandi* of the most effective agencies. The International Federation, for example, aims to work by supporting the preparedness and response of independent National Societies all over the world. Yet even so, there is a tendency to override the local presence when the chips are down and the sense of urgency to 'deliver the goods' seems irresistible. But those who merely 'dump and run' are wasting their donors' investment. As Professor Anup Dash, a sociologist from Utkal University, remarked following the Orissa tragedy, "A large number of international agencies have come in and done their relief and then everything falls away. Where there is no strategy, no long-term plan, very important opportunities are missed."

Box 1.3 Local response and coordination key to Gujarati recovery

Kiran Bhandre huddles with her two little girls under a blanket pulled out from under the rubble of her former home in Bhuj, in the Indian state of Gujarat. On 26 January 2001, a massive earthquake, measuring 7.9 on the Richter scale, killed around 30,000 people and devastated the lives of millions more. Meanwhile, the relief supplies she needs are piling up at ports and cities. Local authorities are having to ask well-meaning donors to hold off sending more aid until they can distribute what they have.

Clearly, national and international generosity is not at fault. A neighbouring state sends a delegation of three trucks full of basics like blankets, while the international community sends huge C-130 cargo planes full of sophisticated medical equipment. Some aid organizations flew in international assessment and coordination missions, which seldom bring their own supplies and impose a greater burden on already scarce local resources.

Sending foreign seismologists, doctors, logistics and communications experts to India should be unnecessary, since this country produces some of the world's best. Flying in and catering for expatriate manpower is both costly and inefficient, when India's own plentiful skilled human resources could be mobilized for a fraction of the cost. International donors should pay for local personnel to be mobilized during disasters.

Experience from past disasters repeatedly reveals the need for a strong, centralized coordination system to channel aid resources to those in most need. This did not happen quickly enough in Gujarat. Yet India has a large professional army, which could have coordinated relief. All the more so since the Indian military has no political colour and is well respected. Its highly skilled medical and engineering corps are currently active in crisis management in many parts of the world. If the army had taken up the reins of coordination from the start, it may have been possible to prevent the bottlenecks that have left Kiran and her children stranded.

Even after the emergency phase, problems persist. For example, property ownership is often the basis on which reconstruction aid or relocation homes are provided. In Nicaragua, wealthy slum landlords profited when aid poured in after 1972's Managua quake. Dirt-poor slum dwellers were left to watch, since they had no leases, much less any property rights. In India's Latur earthquake of 1993, illiterate widows, unaware of the laws, lost out on reconstruction or home replacement aid. Relief agencies should make specific efforts to ensure aid reaches those who do not ask – orphans, widows and the elderly.

As for addressing the earthquake's root causes, there is much talk of shoddy construction and dishonest builders. But in a state that is not a high-risk region for earthquakes, where annual per capita income is about 11,000 rupees (approx. US$ 250), imposing formal building codes to make homes earthquake-proof is not realistic. What is realistic is strengthening community-based preparedness routines to allow local inhabitants to mitigate and manage the aftermath of a disaster. We know from experience that families and neighbours are the main rescuers and rebuilders in such situations. Familiarizing neighbourhoods with extrication techniques and simple building skills may be a more cost-effective solution for poor communities where it is in any case difficult to enforce regulations.

In the longer term, India will need solid disaster management plans with clear lines of authority and responsibilities. The window of opportunity for changes to the system is still open.

N. K. Jain of India's Joint Assistance Centre says international NGOs must reassess relationships. They must search out indigenous development agencies, train them to respond to disaster and build capacity. If disaster preparedness becomes a component of ongoing agency activity, then relief and development will be linked naturally, he believes. "Working out linkages and providing training is not without risk," says Jain. "You must identify the right partners. But there has to be a change of attitude. It isn't enough to say, 'Here is a project and the funding for it'."

Jain's conviction is the dominant one: relief must consider development but development must be more disaster-savvy. Since relief is part of disaster management, it belongs in development, argues ActionAid's Gawher Nayeem Wahra. He defines relief as 'a developmental job' which requires knowing your target population. It is hard to deny that when life is intrinsically calamitous, a crisis induced by disasters cannot be distinguished from the day-to-day struggle for survival.

This was echoed in Orissa by Concern, among others, who operated through six local partners to provide relief and rehabilitation. Agency head Kwan Lee said a properly conceived development programme should slip into relief when required. As did Oxfam, which has operated in coastal Orissa since the 1980s and responded quickly to the cyclone, first with relief and then with a nine-month livelihoods and employment restoration programme. Shamsul Huda, director of the Association of Development Agencies in Bangladesh, insists development cannot be done without knowing how to handle disaster.

Donors need to take the notion on board. According to Huda, 50,000 to 60,000 NGO workers across Bangladesh have already had disaster management training and he is anxious to see an integrated intervention strategy evolve. A disaster, he points out, brings more than personal loss and suffering. The ruination of ordinary individuals drives them into debt and can cause the collapse of credit and other organizations essential to the recovery process.

A village in the Puri district of Orissa, devastated by 1999's super-cyclone.

Patrick Fuller/ International Federation, India 1999

Relief in Bangladesh should do more to close the recovery gap once a Union Disaster Action Plan is finished. Guided by the UN, the plan covers more than 600 unions (groups of villages) and was due for completion by June 2001. It charts disasters: who is threatened by what, and where. It details local resources, designates roles. So, in theory at least, when disaster strikes, everyone will know what to do.

In the wake of Orissa's super-cyclone, says India's disaster management director, S.K. Swami, "There is need for focused attention on community participation and public awareness besides strengthening the early warning system, alternative communication networks and setting up an adequate number of cyclone shelters and cyclone-proof structures." He adds that the state government has created the Orissa State Disaster Mitigation Authority to coordinate this process.

As well as investing in people, plans and partnerships, the evidence for building disaster-resistant infrastructure, as an integral part of the development process, is compelling. Before the disaster, Orissa had just 23 cyclone shelters, built by the Red Cross, each designed to hold at least 1,500 people (see Box 1.4). The Orissa government's new relief commissioner says the shelters saved around 40,000 lives during the super-cyclone. The budget for the shelter programme from 1994-2002, met by the German Red Cross, comes to DEM 6.8 million. This covers construction, maintenance, disaster preparedness training and the community development focused around each shelter. That works out at about DEM 170 (around US$ 77) per human life. After the cyclone, Orissa state's government promised next of kin 75,000 rupees (around US$ 1,600) for each dead relative.

As well as the strengthened homes mentioned earlier, the International Federation is now constructing ten new school-cum-cyclone shelters in Orissa's most risk-prone districts. But the state has a lot of catching up to do – neighbouring Andhra Pradesh has over 1,000 cyclone shelters.

III. Funding must bridge relief-recovery gap

Ensuring development becomes more risk-aware and making disaster relief more sensitive to recovery priorities are only part of the problem. Putting this into practice requires not only more resources, but radically reviewing the relationship between different funding pots. Donors are aware of their own shortcomings. The relief-recovery gap concerns them, and has long been the subject of major discussion. A recent UN workshop on the consolidated appeal process was told by donors that they wanted longer-term agency planning in which relief related to development. But the donors admitted they lacked the framework to cope with it. "They were quite up front about it," says one participant. "They knew *they* were the problem and that the UN and Red Cross had moved a long way forward in strategic planning. Governments had not kept up."

Central to the problem are donor governments' financial structures, which nearly all separate relief and development funding sources. Rarely do they work well enough in unison, making strategic coherence impossible. A 15-year TB campaign launched by the International Federation in eastern Europe is being run on six-month contracts with the European Community Humanitarian Office (ECHO). Peter Rees, acting head of the relationship management department at the International Federation, says, "ECHO knows long-term programmes need long-term planning. But ECHO does emergency funding. Isn't it possible for the longer-term money to come from another EU body? I have raised the question several times and they all agree the programme should be funded differently. But no one has an alternative."

The European Union (EU) is moving to solve such conundrums. Since last year, the commissioner for humanitarian aid, Poul Nielson, has become responsible for all development and emergency assistance, although budget lines remain separate. These are enormous steps forward, but not without their problems. As Nielson has discovered, one has to break down many vested interests and political structures. The process can be a painful one.

Box 1.4 Shelters save lives and livelihoods

The villagers of Khurantatuth, on India's Orissa coast, had doubts about the cyclone shelter. Some heavy storms blow in from the Bay of Bengal and they reckoned this structure, standing tall on its slender legs, would topple over. Maybe the Red Cross had misused the funds. Maybe they had skimped on building materials.

On an October night in 1999, seven months after the shelter's completion, they would learn if their suspicions were justified. India's worst disaster in living memory engulfed them. Wind speeds were said to have reached 250-350 kilometres an hour. Tidal waves up to 7 metres high crashed inland. Whole villages vanished. Khurantatuth was one of them.

There had been a warning and the young volunteers of the Red Cross rescue team had alerted the population. When the winds picked up and the seas got wilder, they turned on the red light and siren on the shelter's roof. They went door to door urging people to evacuate. Some refused to move from their houses and, as conditions worsened, the team tied a rope to a sturdy village tree and ran it all the way to the shelter. It was a lifeline that saved a few hundred stragglers. Without that to hold on to, they would have been blown away.

Visibility dropped to less than five metres. Team member Bibakar Kumar, a 25-year-old tailor, remembers, "It was like being in smoke. You lost your bearings. We stationed ourselves along the rope and waved red loincloths to be seen. When people reached us we had to physically help them. You had to pull yourself along and the wind was so strong the weaker ones collapsed from exhaustion. Some were unconscious by the time we reached the shelter."

Before the tidal wave engulfed the village, over 2,000 people were squeezed into a structure the Red Cross had meant for no more than 1,500. The main halls were full, everyone standing shoulder to shoulder. Outside, the flat roof was packed and more people lay on exterior walkways. When, at the height of the storm, the shelter began to sway, the villagers remembered their misgivings. But the legs held, 11 metres of them buried below ground. The designers described the legs' swaying ability as an 'emergency buffer'.

After the storm subsided the villagers looked out and saw nothing but water, and hundreds of floating corpses, among them the neighbours who had chosen to stay on their properties. Virtually nothing remained of Khurantatuth but the cyclone shelter.

Similar stories could be heard among the 22 other locations where the Orissa branch of the Indian Red Cross had provided safe havens. Supported by the German Red Cross and German government funding, they had constructed them in remote, high-risk communities. According to the Orissa government they saved 40,000 people.

How many shelters Orissa really needs is debatable. The state says 500, others say anything from 1,000 to 3,000. Whichever figure is correct, it was the Red Cross's 23 shelters that mattered. There were no others in Orissa.

German Red Cross delegate Britta Girgensohn-Minker is quick to point out, however, that numbers are just part of the equation. The role of shelter projects in between cyclones is equally important to communities. Red Cross shelters nurture rural disaster preparedness and social and economic development, inseparable elements of living with, and recovering from, natural hazards like cyclones.

The Khurantatuth shelter had been completed in 1999 but the programme had begun three years earlier. First, a disaster preparedness (DP) and shelter management committee had been established, and a task force of rescuers recruited. DP, health and first-aid training followed. Women were encouraged to start self-help savings and credit groups. Said Girgensohn-Minker, "You can't just build a shelter and consider the job finished. There has to be a long-term approach, and social mobilization. The community has to take ownership."

Shelters become community centres, housing schools, health centres, meeting places. Khurantatuth lost its school in the cyclone but the shelter's two halls provide ideal classrooms. Almost a year to the day after the Orissa disaster, the women of Tentuliya, a community of farmers and fishermen three kilometres from the coast, were gathered in their shelter for some informal banking.

Debt entraps the poor and the landless of this region. When mishap or illness befalls them, the fortunate may

➡ borrow from relatives or friends but most have nowhere to turn. The banks will not lend without collateral, so their only recourse is to moneylenders whose interest rates can exceed 400 per cent over the period of repayment.

The Red Cross provides alternatives, arguing that families who escape such debt burdens cope more easily with crisis, and recover faster from the consequences. With its support, the women of Tentuliya began a self-help savings and credit group in 1997. They contributed a modest monthly sum to the fund, and when in need borrowed on conditions the group itself had agreed to. Some used the fund to start businesses, acquired a cow and sold any milk that was surplus, or leased a little land and entered the betel-leaf business.

All had gone well with such schemes in Orissa. So well, in fact, that other women came forward and the groups began to snowball. Then came the cyclone. Cows were washed away, betel plots vanished, women who were widowed were left single-handed to support their families. They could no longer afford their repayments.

But these are honest, hard-working people. The debts were written off, the Red Cross provided more seed money, and the schemes took off again. On this morning in Tentuliya, the women had gathered for the first distribution of new credit. There was a tangible sense of purpose, and as each woman collected her money the group behind her applauded. Barely literate, or illiterate, older women signed their agreements slowly, or had literate friends guide their hands. A signature is required for the credit, and the group has literacy classes.

German support for the shelter projects will continue until 2003, fulfilling a commitment of almost ten years. But in light of the success so far, a second phase could then begin, for an application to the German government is likely to be looked on favourably. Up to 30 communities could benefit, with preparedness, relief and development again integrated into one continuous cycle of living with disaster.

Through the 1990s, humanitarian common sense sometimes enabled ECHO to widen its mandate beyond emergency funding. Where it had an extended stay – as in former Yugoslavia, Somalia, Afghanistan and Africa's Great Lakes – rehabilitation funds would sometimes be forthcoming. So in 1998, deep in the Bangladesh floods, ECHO's south Asia regional office in Dhaka started bridging the gap. On the back of emergency assistance, it funded shelter and income-generation programmes, and helped communities to their feet.

A precedent was set and, after the Orissa cyclone, ECHO made it known that rehabilitation would again be in the frame. A number of agencies responded with proposals for cyclone-proof housing, multipurpose shelters, wells, disaster preparedness and training. In May 2000, while being processed, a Brussels directive put these proposals on hold. A decision had been taken to bring ECHO back to its mandate of emergency assistance. Orissa, still desperately trying to emerge from disaster, didn't understand.

It made sense to the policy-makers. ECHO has been roundly condemned for 'straying' into development fields where political, democratic and human rights factors need to be weighed, rather than humanitarian ones. The effects of disasters are forever increasing and, they argued, ECHO needs all its emergency resources to respond as EU members wish. But if ECHO fails to bridge the gaps left by projects abandoned after the six-month contract expires, then who will step in? And how long will it take them to do so?

Some people say that by restricting ECHO as he has, Nielson has exerted more pressure on less efficient quarters, forcing them to sharpen up their acts. Bureaucracy is being streamlined after billions of development Euros sat unspent in Brussels bank accounts. According to David

Bryer, director of Oxfam, by January 2001, two-thirds of the GB£ 142 million aid package promised by the EU in the wake of 1998's Hurricane Mitch remained unspent in Brussels. Hondurans continue to live in temporary shelters over two years later.

There are other governmental constraints to coherent planning and funding. Funds are based on parliamentary budgets which, like parliaments themselves, are not by nature long term. Rees believes an 'indicative budget' could overcome many problems. "A funder could say: 'I will give you x-million francs a year for the next ten years but I can guarantee it only for two'. At least a written indication of future funding would change the way we plan."

Long-term funding is "golden money", says Rees. "It is worth so much more than annual top-ups even if they amount to the same in the end. The value is in the impact that long-term planning has." Three- or four-year funding lines, like those of the UK's Department for International Development (DFID) or the Norwegian Agency for Development Cooperation (NORAD), provide clout. When NORAD approved four-year funding for social welfare support in Bosnia, the Red Cross of Bosnia and Herzegovina could begin serious negotiation with its ministry of health. Rees says, "Underwritten by a four-year budget, they could say: 'We want to be a partner in social welfare'. They could start talking about entitlements for the vulnerable. With a one-year budget, the government might have said, 'This is not serious enough for us to really see you as a long-term partner'."

Aid spending fails to reflect field realities

Sometimes time constraints mean agencies can't spend money fast enough. The UK's Disasters Emergency Committee (DEC), a grouping of Britain's leading relief agencies, reflects another donor dilemma that can only widen the gap. Placing a six-month spending window on emergency funds, it was trapped by imposing a time limit on something that can't always be rushed.

The reason for doing so was its relationship with the British public. Says Mark Bradbury, "You announce there is a crisis, lives need to be saved, and money is required to do that fast. If a year or two down the line the appeal's proceeds haven't been spent, questions begin to be asked. Why? Was there really a crisis?" The fast-spending credo has dispensed with that and the DEC today is a phenomenally successful fund-raiser.

Agencies, meanwhile, have been unable to absorb all the cash. Kosovo and Orissa saw huge amounts handed back, and some money had to be reprogrammed, a procedure that proved problematic. Clearly agencies need to communicate to public and government donors alike the field realities of disaster response. The DEC is now reviewing its policy, one introduced with reluctance in the first place.

From Bob McKerrow's vantage point in south Asia, such pressures have turned the aid business on its head, and the gap is but a symptom of it. Accountability to donors and the public is a must, but where is the accountability to the people who need the help? Loudly trumpeted, enshrined in codes of conduct, it isn't much in evidence on the ground.

On his crumbling Bangladeshi embankments, McKerrow can't *get* money fast enough. For three months following 2000's very heavy summer monsoon, his application for rehabilitation funds had sat with a donor. By October, time was running out and there wasn't a hint of a result. "If some poor man on a river bank has lost all he had to erosion, he won't hang around for two months. He'll be gone and his family with him," he says.

Has the humanitarian world become bound up by process and methodology? McKerrow believes it has. "We are strategizing ourselves to death. We have taken humanitarian aid and turned it into something like rocket science. Yes, we need strategic plans, and if the humanitarian world wants to be a business, let it. But then make decisions like businesses. A business would decide in 30 minutes, not prevaricate for a couple of months."

He continues, "The gap I find worrying is the one between people in the field – who know the communities, their capacities and their vulnerabilities – and a wall of bureaucracy that wasn't there before. The gap frequently is one of credibility and communication. There is a widening gulf between field and major donors and you need to be a clairvoyant to follow the mood swings and policy changes. Now that is a science." He sees the humanitarian as a broker for the poor and the vulnerable, "We who are well fed have become the beggar for those who are not. Selective morality has crept into aid."

Clearly disasters provide an entry point for increasing humanitarian commitment to the world's poorest – but does this fit with the donors' agenda? Says Peter Hawkins, SCF's regional director for East and Central Africa, "An emergency is an opportunity to look at changing things in the medium and longer term. It is, however, a very complex human process. I thought we were getting there in the 1990s but I get a very strong sense of moving away from that now." Donors are showing reluctance. "Look at the level of investment in the Horn. A whole Marshall Plan is needed to turn Ethiopia around, and investment at the moment is minuscule. The money is just not there. It *is* if the military wants to invade Somalia, but not if you want to invest in human capacity."

The Horn's desperate ongoing disaster may, ironically, prompt less international assistance, not more. Why? Poverty reduction targets set for 2015 by the OECD's Development Assistance Committee are suspected of widening the gulf between humanitarian and development sectors. One senior European source argues, "You can tell by the strategies some donor governments have adopted that they are targeting countries where they feel they can achieve something by the deadline, and crossing off those where they think they can't. Ethiopia and Eritrea are among those losing out. Humanitarian aid is there but development funds are scarce. The thinking seems to be: why invest in a place where the targets are unobtainable? I see this emerging and I am afraid it is the tip of the iceberg."

This raises the spectre of selective humanity, a basket-case syndrome with the poorest of the poor beyond recovery. Some observers fear the European Union could exacerbate that. Reform is in the air, and Brussels has been shaken up. Where EU aid goes in future will partly depend on who is using it best. Need will remain a determining factor, but levels of aid will depend on results, annual country audits.

Strategic concerns may also dictate where aid goes. Says Mark Bradbury: "In the Cold War, aid was very politicized and you can see that trend happening again. It's not just putting money where you think it is going to work but where you have friends or want to influence the situation."

Clearly, there is too often a lack of accountability to the vulnerable, a trend reflected in the *Global Humanitarian Assistance 2000* report commissioned by the UN Inter-agency Standing Committee. Not only does support for appeals reflect political considerations, the report found, but appeals are slanted to indulge those interests. A critical observer could conclude that aid agencies are putting financial interests and a sense of what is fundable ahead of humanitarian principles.

Rather than courting donors and governments, agencies must advise and inform them, lead them to where the need is greatest, argue the case for assistance, and mobilize public opinion simultaneously. If donor or host government interest is misguided, agencies must be honest and courageous enough to say so. That is why NGOs mushroomed in the first place.

Livelihoods and local investment key to recovery

Donor resources alone may support but can never guarantee recovery. Better use of aid to kick-start local economies and support livelihoods at the community level is needed, according to the International Labour Organization (see Chapter 2). Research from the Krishna delta in eastern India suggests that sustainable livelihoods and access to resources play a more crucial role than physical location in determining the vulnerability of inhabitants to cyclones and floods. Those with a diverse resource base can protect themselves better from disasters and recover quicker. Meanwhile, the external resources which flood into an economy after a disaster can quickly leak away without leaving long-term benefits. Plugging those leaks by, for example, procuring reconstruction materials locally, is crucial in promoting disaster recovery (see Figure 2.1, Chapter 2).

Failure to address the issue of livelihoods can seriously undermine recovery efforts. In Venezuela, following the devastating mudslides in 1999, thousands of families were relocated inland, away from the disaster-prone coastal state of Vargas (see Chapter 4). But there were so few jobs available in the relocation areas that many Venezuelans have returned to the scene of disaster to rebuild their old homes – literally reconstructing the risk. So long-term recovery is unlikely without a strategy that tackles not only reduction of the risks posed by natural hazards, but less concrete issues such as livelihoods, schools, health care, early warning, awareness raising and preparedness measures – the web of factors that strengthen community resilience to disaster.

IV. Advocacy to tackle root causes

However skilfully humanitarian organizations succeed in blending the disparate cultures of relief and development, and however much donors reform their funding strategies, aid alone will never be able to combat root causes and break the cycle of disasters. As emergencies consultant Mark Bradbury points out, "By asking such questions as 'Has relief been wrongly used?', are you not by implication blaming the relief system for the recurrence? I am not sure that is fair. Not that relief agencies should be blameless for lots of different things, but is that what relief is for?"

Disasters are driven by, among other things: conflict; climate change; poorly planned development; structural poverty; and uneven globalization of economies and opportunities – 'macro-factors' clearly beyond the capacity of humanitarian organizations alone to confront.

The UN's Intergovernmental Panel on Climate Change (IPCC) announced in early 2001 that the Earth's atmosphere will warm twice as fast as was foreseen ten years ago. Within this century, temperatures could rise by six degrees Celsius and sea levels climb by at least one metre. An IPCC spokesman predicted more extreme weather events and said there is now "stronger evidence that these changes are due to humans". Unless the world responds forcefully to global warming by drastically reducing carbon dioxide and other greenhouse gases, coastal regions like Bangladesh could be obliterated.

Structural poverty is another macro-factor. Of Orissa's 36 million people, more than two-thirds live below the poverty line, and nearly 90 per cent subsist in deprived rural areas. Chances of escaping the poverty trap are slim: over half the population is illiterate, education is inadequate, and every fifth child does not attend school. Jagadish Pradhan, of the Orissan NGO *Sahabhagi Vikash Abhiyan* (Campaign for Participatory Development), fears that without radical change the state is heading for permanent disaster. "For the poorest of our people, vulnerability to disaster is increasing," he says, "although ironically in some ways the cyclone meant little to them. Many who survived lost nothing. Other than their lives they had nothing to lose in the first place. Things were already so bad they couldn't get more miserable. Pigs live better elsewhere in India."

The marginalization of people is among the political factors driving the planet's disasters. Where governments seek to suppress or abandon the bothersome, it is a common weapon. In one arid region of East Africa, that which long and devastating droughts have not destroyed, a freak flood has washed away. Cholera, diarrhoeal and respiratory disease, and a deadly haemorrhagic fever arrived in the water's wake. Aid has been forthcoming; millions of dollars over the past few years. The International Red Cross and Red Crescent Movement, the UN network and major agencies have all been there. But unsustainable relief programmes have reached their end and faded away. What remains is a region as vulnerable as it has ever been. Perhaps more so, as traditional coping mechanisms have weakened.

Some humanitarians have looked to the long term. The Red Cross and Red Crescent, anxious to support rehabilitation and development, has repeatedly appealed to the authorities to consider the region's options. In a depressing meeting to which the Red Cross and Red Crescent had brought a donor, a senior regional official lifted his hands in a despairing gesture. "I am sorry," he said. "The government has no plans." Nor did it want any. The ethnic group which lives there is not one the government favours.

In the face of such challenges, humanitarian organizations have a moral duty to put pressure on host and donor governments alike to tackle the environmental, political and economic root causes of recurrent disaster. Only by a combination of action and advocacy will genuine disaster recovery stand a chance.

Relief an opportunity for advocacy

The International Federation's greatest success in disaster response in Bangladesh was advocacy related, argues Denis McClean, then acting head of disaster policy. After the great 1970 cyclone saw half a million people perish, the International Federation persuaded the Bangladeshi government and the donor community to invest heavily in disaster preparedness. When commitment flagged, the International Federation reinforced it. A 1991 cyclone took another 140,000 lives, but half a million people who might have died survived because the Bangladesh Red Crescent's early warning system had alerted them – tragic but timely evidence with which to justify the strategy.

"Advocacy in the humanitarian context is about giving a voice to the poor, those who are abused by the status quo and tossed about on the economic tide of globalization like disposable garbage," adds McClean. "Natural disasters may well finish them off, but there are many other structural issues which contribute to their vulnerability. We are in a position to shine a harsh and critical light on those, not necessarily by launching appeals but simply by raising our voice and making sure the various stakeholders take note and act."

McClean has argued within the International Federation for its network of listening posts around the world to prime a rolling advocacy, making use of disasters to further core campaigns. "Come a humanitarian crisis," he says, "the path of least resistance is always to launch an appeal, when often we could make a more long-term contribution if we used relief as an entry-point for advocacy."

Orissa's cyclone exposed the endemic misery of this coastal region to the wider world. Some Indian observers strongly assert that the state's feudal governance is one of the main sources of its suffering. What Orissa needs isn't aid, they argue, it is structural reform and better governance.

International aid can alleviate suffering and, managed well, ease and support a development process. But the process depends on other factors. With the world looking on, and the cash taps open, the cyclone was the chance to spotlight disaster's root causes and advocate ways of dealing with them.

The UK's DEC responded by funding a hard-hitting documentary fronted by Mahesh Bhatt, a flamboyant Bombay film director. With *Orissa Cyclone; The Calamity That Was,* Bhatt was not taking prisoners. "I invite you to watch this documentary," he intoned, "for its mind-boggling revelations with regard to the incompetence of our system that decimated thousands of innocent lives and still has no clue how it can rebuild broken hearts, shattered lives and the totally collapsed economy." Millions remained without jobs and shelter, as vulnerable as ever, desperation even driving some to sell their daughters.

Bhatt, who has said despair should be marketed like cola, poured it on, and prime-time India listened. But this concerned more than poor Orissa. "Calamities and disasters are like a fashion in India. One wonders," the commentary continued, "how many more we need before we have a national-level disaster management policy and plan."

Orissa was scripted and directed by Ajay Kanchan, former communications manager with Oxfam. He had been in the team of the *India Disasters Report,* which profiles the nature and spread of the subcontinent's disasters, and outlines the road to a comprehensive response and mitigation policy. Says Kanchan, "The problem with India is that we are relief centred. We do not consider disaster can be managed. Disaster management means working with the people but our government works with bureaucrats and the bureaucrats with politicians."

Action and advocacy can break disaster cycle

The plight of Bangladesh puts the issues on the line. River erosion, as with many other natural hazards, isn't going away – so those at risk must learn to mitigate risks and damage, and those helping them must advocate for more resources to turn back the tide of disasters' effects. Dr Ali Ashraf, a senior programme officer with the UN Development Programme (UNDP) in Bangladesh, wants sufficient investment made for risk and disaster management to form an integral part of every development programme. "If you are working to enhance earning capacity, or living standards, you cannot accept that a flood can come along and destroy, say, five years' achievements. Where communities know how to protect themselves, the recovery period will be shorter and the pressure on government and donors less. We spend millions of dollars, only to see them washed away."

Major Ali Hassan Quoreshi, secretary general of the Bangladesh Red Crescent advocates a coordinated pooling of agency resources to confront the multiplicity of problems that river erosion presents. "What a family loses to erosion takes a lifetime to regain. The whole development clock is being turned back. We need an all-embracing assistance programme to

Orissa, India: Areas affected by floods and storm damage in the wake of 1999's super-cyclone.

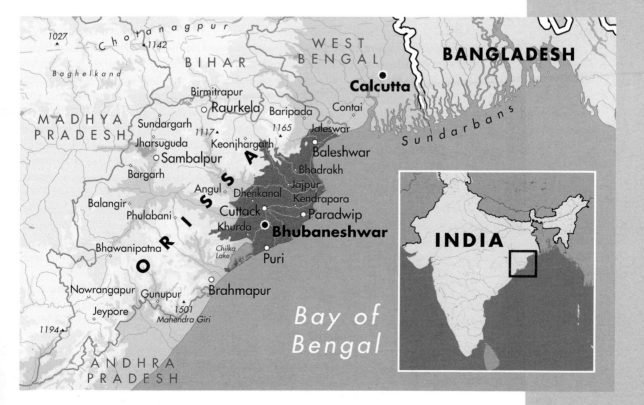

which all NGOs with something to offer can contribute, whether that be DP, health care or micro-credit," he says. "There are things like persuading the government that people who lose homes to erosion should be given priority when new land is allocated."

The challenges posed by complex emergencies such as river erosion in Bangladesh or drought in the Horn of Africa demand *concurrent action*, because disasters and needs endure on parallel levels. The homeless and threatened require *relief* while others are in the *recovery* phase or in need of *rehabilitation*. Where risk alone remains, *development* has to be paramount, prioritizing risk awareness, local disaster preparedness and low-cost mitigation. *Advocacy* towards governments, donors, agencies and communities must be unrelenting if action is to be maintained, root causes addressed, and the proper legal, political and economic tools employed.

With *un*/natural disasters recurring more frequently and recovery from them haphazard, the days of quick-in/quick-out relief are numbered. Short-term responses mean aid dollars and development gains are being swept away, the poor are becoming ever-more vulnerable and the security of countries and communities is increasingly at risk. The selective response of donors and the tendency of some humanitarian agencies to pursue the media spotlight don't help.

Three things must happen simultaneously, if the cycle of disasters is to be broken and recovery is to take root:

- **Inject the 'risk dimension' into development in all disaster-prone regions.** Risk and disaster management must become part of the development process. The opportunities to mitigate future disasters future will never be grasped unless governments analyse risks and develop disaster management plans. International agencies need to forge true partnerships with local NGOs and build their capacities to respond swiftly and effectively to their own disasters. To provide the necessary resources, donors need to reform their funding structures to integrate relief and development, and to prioritize investment in risk reduction.
- **Programme emergency relief as the beginning – not the end – of increased commitment.** In an ideal world, every exposed community would benefit from a development process which incorporates the 'risk dimension'. In reality, catastrophes often strike regions where sustainable development has barely begun, where government services are minimal. Emergency relief in such settings can provide the platform for recovery – to go beyond band-aid and reduce the risk that future disasters pose. But to ensure that relief integrates with local recovery efforts, better analysis and greater coordination with indigenous aid agencies are needed.
- **Seize the opportunity for advocacy that relief provides.** Disasters present the chance to seize the media spotlight and shine it towards root causes. Sustainable recovery is a task way beyond the capacities of humanitarian organizations alone. Aid cannot be blamed for failing to solve all the structural root causes of disaster. But neither must it be used as an alibi for inaction on the macro-factors driving disaster. Since aid alone will never be enough, humanitarian agencies have a moral duty to engage with donors, host governments and the public in an honest dialogue about the limits of humanitarian action and the responsibilities of politicians and economists in tackling root causes and root solutions.

With the exception of Box 1.3, John Sparrow, an independent writer who has been regional information delegate for the International Federation in Africa and Europe, was the major contributor to Chapter 1 and boxes. Box 1.3 was written by Debarati Guha-Sapir, director of WHO's Centre for Research on the Epidemiology of Disasters, and professor at the Department of Epidemiology, Université Catholique de Louvain, Belgium.

Sources and further information

Baqee, Abdul. *Peopling in the Land of Allah Jaane (Power, Peopling and Environment: The Case of Char-Lands of Bangladesh).* The University Press Limited, 1998.

Bradbury, Mark. "Normalising the crisis in Africa" in *Disasters*, Vol. 22, No. 4, December 1998.

Braun, Elke. *Living with Cyclones (Disaster Preparedness in India and Bangladesh).* German Red Cross, 1999.

Kafi, Sharif A. *What people can do to reduce the disastrous effects of river erosion.* PACT-Bangladesh/PRIP, November 1993.

Kreimer, Alcira and Arnold, Margaret (eds.). *Managing Disaster Risk in Emerging Economies.* Washington, DC: The World Bank, June 2000.

Parasuraman, S. and Unnikrishnan, P.V. (eds.). *India Disasters Report.* Oxford: Oxford University Press, 2000.

Winchester, Peter. *Cyclone Mitigation, Resource Allocation and Post-disaster Reconstruction in South India: Lessons from Two Decades of Research.* Blackwell Publishers/Overseas Development Institute, 2000.

Web sites

ActionAid http://www.actionaid.org/home.html
Care International http://www.care-international.org.uk
German Red Cross http://www.drk.de/weltweit/asien/zyklon/index.html
International Federation http://www.ifrc.org
OECD http://www.oecd.org/dac
Oxfam International http://www.oxfam.org
Save the Children http://www.savethechildren.org

Section One

Focus on recovery

The ecology of disaster recovery

"Most of us have lost what little land we had, many have lost our houses and everything we owned. But worst of all, we have lost our means of livelihood. River erosion is breaking up our traditional way of life. We have nowhere to go, no work."

Hasan Mollah from Bangladesh, August 2000

The planet's poorest are becoming ever more exposed to the risk of disaster – aggravated by the volatile effects of climate change and economic globalization. From 1991 to 2000, over 600,000 people were reported killed by hydro-meteorological catastrophes alone, an average of 1,100 every week. Each year, 210 million people are affected by 'natural' disasters. A single flood, earthquake or wind storm can set back development in the afflicted area by decades. Of the 3 million people reported killed by disasters and conflicts from 1991 to 2000, 73 per cent were from countries of 'low human development', while just 2 per cent of victims came from highly developed nations. Speaking in March 2001, Bangladesh's environment minister said that if official predictions about sea-level rise are fulfilled, one-fifth of her nation will vanish underwater, creating 20 million 'ecological refugees'.

Since the 1950s, costs associated with 'natural' disasters have rocketed 14-fold. Estimates for the costs of climate-related disasters over the next 20 years range from US\$ 6 to 10 trillion, ten times likely aid flows. Financial resources available from conventional aid for recovery remain low and static. Aid going to the world's 48 least developed countries (LDCs) has fallen by over one-third in real terms since 1991, accounting for just 20 per cent of official development assistance (ODA) in 1999. Other sources of income, such as foreign direct investment, concentrate on exploiting natural resources in LDCs. Meanwhile, the side effects of trade liberalization are undermining sustainable recovery and development in some of the world's most disaster-afflicted nations. If these trends continue, the ambitious international development targets of 2015 will recede into the distance.

In such a pessimistic scenario, post-disaster recovery efforts will increasingly be judged not by how quickly structures are rebuilt – only to be destroyed again the next time disaster strikes – but by how reconstruction contributes to the long-term disaster resilience of communities. Case studies in disaster-prone areas demonstrate that people with access to sufficient resources are better able to protect themselves. Yet still, damage to livelihoods barely features on the disaster response radar screen.

After 2000's floods in Mozambique, numerous statistics described damage to infrastructure, loss of life and injury, but no information could be found about lost livelihoods. Later estimates put the figure close to 350,000 lost jobs, undermining, through the impact on households, the livelihoods of up to 1.5 million people. Failure to focus on disasters' impact on livelihoods indicates and perpetuates misplaced aid priorities. Governments, media and non-governmental organizations (NGOs) tend to worry most about what is measured.

Photo opposite page: To help disaster-stricken people rebuild their lives and their livelihoods, strategies for post-disaster recovery must grow out of the 'ecology' of the affected community.

Caroline Hurford/ International Federation, Ethiopia 2000

Material infrastructure investments are easily measured, however, and have proved a popular form of disaster response. According to the World Bank's Alcira Kreimer and Margaret Arnold, an assessment was carried out of 198 disaster-related projects funded by the Bank from 1980 to 1998. It found only 10 per cent of projects had 'economic recovery' as a key component, against 53 per cent primarily focused on rebuilding infrastructure.

Is such a hardware-only approach even safe, let alone rational? More than just resilience to 'natural' disasters is at stake; security is under threat. Lack of economic recovery and of "income earning programmes is... arguably the cause of ongoing conflict in Somalia, Sudan, Colombia, Cambodia and Burundi", wrote Steve Hansch and Leslie Barcus recently.

A key question is how to increase the value of every reconstruction dollar in order to maximize aid's long-term contribution to sustainable livelihoods and local economies. Practical solutions include more community involvement in the design and implementation of reconstruction, more local procurement and new measuring tools to ensure aid interventions sustain rather than undermine local economies.

Experience from hurricanes in Central America and floods in south Asia suggests that to boost disaster recovery and resilience, poor countries and their communities need highly diverse economies, built on small-scale enterprises, sustainable resource use and indigenous knowledge. But this often conflicts with macroeconomic advice championed by international financial institutions.

Strategies for post-disaster recovery must grow out of the cultural, economic and social character of affected communities – their ecology. Just as vibrant ecosystems are created by diverse biological processes, so healthy communities and local economies are fed by a wealth of diverse social and economic activities. Diversity is the key to retaining resources and crucial in mitigating disaster. This counter-narrative to globalization can be termed 'localization' – a word that sums up how reconstruction resources must be circulated locally to have lasting effect.

This chapter will examine four key themes central to post-disaster economic recovery:

I. **Investing in sustainable livelihoods** will increase the speed of recovery and reduce vulnerability of the poor to disasters. People's livelihoods are as important as physical defences.

II. **Plugging the leaks:** Ensuring that post-disaster resources recirculate within the local economy, rather than leaking out of it, will help boost longer-term recovery.

III. **Diversified local economies** which maximize employment and respect economic, social and environmental priorities will be more disaster resilient than agricultural or industrial monocultures.

IV. **Impacts of globalization and climate change** are draining the resources of poorer nations that are needed to deal with disasters. Prevention will prove more cost-effective than recovery.

I. Sustainable livelihoods: key to disaster resilience

"Poverty... plays a big role in keeping people vulnerable to disasters. And in the same fashion, disasters keep the poor in poverty by consistently wiping out the few resources they have."

World Bank, 2000

It is common currency that poor people suffer more in disasters. Poverty drives them to live in environmentally vulnerable areas less popular with the wealthy, where disasters strike more often and cause more damage.

Yet the response of governments and donors tends to steer the economic benefits of post-disaster reconstruction towards civil engineering companies based in rich countries, more than to the people affected. If poor people are threatened by the forces of nature, the argument runs, the answer is for engineers and experts to build barriers between nature and the poor.

In the past few decades, millions of dollars have been spent on flood relief programmes – often as controversial in their consequences as they were huge in scale. Sixty per cent of the funds spent on the Bangladesh Flood Action Plan between 1990 and 1995 did not stay in Bangladesh, leading one commentator to describe it as "just another vast income-generating scheme for assorted experts, foreign consultants and commission-seeking bureaucrats".

Often schemes either simply did not work or made the impact of floods worse. The World Bank, which was centrally involved in the Bangladesh project, commented on the "extraordinary absence" of evaluation from past experience and "continuing pressure for large-scale capital intensive solutions" to environmental problems, despite evidence of their poor value.

The logic of planners was well-meaning. Extreme weather caused physical vulnerability so they set out to contain the weather through infrastructure. But this approach has been consistently challenged.

Cooperatives promote self-help and access to resources

After reviewing two decades of post-disaster reconstruction in the Krishna delta of south-eastern India, Peter Winchester, of the Flood Hazard Research Centre at Middlesex University in the UK, says that a major reason for the continuing vulnerability of poor people is the bad design of past aid efforts, and the failure to create dynamic and inclusive local economies. Economic vulnerability is a more important factor than physical vulnerability. His findings confirmed that, following cyclones, people who had "two or three income-earning occupations sustained fewer losses than landless labourers" who had only a single source of income. People with sufficient resources could protect themselves in spite of the "absence or failure of defence systems".

Winchester adds that, "The degree of people's vulnerability to and ability to recover from cyclones and flooding were directly related to... the underlying power relations within the local political economy." He continues, "The best way to reduce vulnerability is to improve the socio-economic standing of the most vulnerable and for this to happen, these people must have an assured income based on assets that will enable them to acquire social and economic credit-worthiness within the local economy."

The poorest usually have least political leverage and, following disaster, may suffer from either official negligence or outright discrimination. Says Winchester, "Resources intended for the benefit of all have been diverted by alliances of powerful people to a small minority." The difference between life and death in this case could be not just having your labour to sell, but having a cow or goats, savings and a plot of land to generate independent income.

Clearly issues of status and access to resources will not be solved by an infrastructural approach to post-disaster recovery. Winchester's research argues that the best way to achieve these ends is through local cooperative enterprises that promote self-help and self-employment schemes.

When floods in 1980 hit Gudari, in Orissa state, Oxfam intervened for eight months to "transcend the immediate rehabilitation programme and steer it towards long-term development", wrote Tushar Bhattacharya in the *India Disasters Report 1999*. The NGO introduced several new ideas to the community: minimum wages; equal wages for men and women; the saving of every sixth day's wage in a bank to build up a local credit facility; the creation of the villagers' own organization (called *Jaagarana* or 'Reawakening'), which was supported by Oxfam for eight years; and a cost-benefit and cultural analysis of using local materials and labour to rebuild 352 homes destroyed by the floods. Twenty years on, reports Bhattacharya, "Bonded labour is a nightmarish memory... the people had fought tooth and nail to disband the system and establish equal and minimum wages." Meanwhile, the savings scheme had enabled villagers to amass more than 150,000 rupees (US$ 3,800). The scheme continues to be run by the villages' women and most of the money is still in circulation, providing credit for those needing help with health or food emergencies.

If poverty plays an even-greater role than physical location in terms of exposing people to risks, then the 'before and after' of disaster preparedness and reconstruction should concentrate on creating the right conditions for building resilient, sustainable livelihoods at the individual, household and communal levels. That means analysing and improving the access of the poorest to jobs and resources – and not just to new land.

But this approach is not currently prioritized in post-disaster interventions. Following 1999's devastating landslides in Venezuela, for example, government officials attempted to relocate people to safer areas inland from high-risk zones. People were tempted away by houses replete with domestic appliances. However, many new homes were quickly abandoned by resettled people because there were no jobs in the new neighbourhoods; a local economy did not spontaneously materialize. The experience showed that the economic fabric of a community took time to weave and was dependent on many factors, something that planners had not understood. Many relocated people returned to their shattered homes on the coast and rebuilt the risks they used to live with, because that was where their friends and jobs were (see Chapter 4).

According to Alfredo Lazarte Hoyle, senior officer for socio-economic integration in the International Labour Organization's (ILO) recovery and reconstruction department, "No specific attention is given to solving the urgent needs of vulnerable sectors, whether in Venezuela or Mozambique." Hoyle adds that the priority should be "recovering jobs, reactivating the local economy and reducing people's economic vulnerability". Without such an approach even small businesses that survived the initial disaster will "go bankrupt because there is no money to be spent". The ILO believes that reconstruction plans should aim to be both labour intensive and to purchase rebuilding materials as much as possible locally.

Income generation boosts chances for peace

The failure to address livelihood issues properly can hamper attempts to break cycles of conflict as well as recovery from 'natural' disasters. In post-conflict situations, creating diverse income-generating opportunities is an essential element of successfully demobilizing troops. In Uganda, access to land was crucial to the successful reinsertion and reintegration of ex-combatants.

But while simple access to resources like land is important, ignoring the full dynamics of a successful local economy can be disastrous. According to a country case study on post-conflict reconstruction in El Salvador, published last year by the World Bank's operations and evaluations department (OED), "A substantial number of ex-combatants who have been provided land under the accord-mandated Land Transfer Program abandoned their land for a variety of reasons including poor land quality, lack of supporting services and credit, and lack of aptitude and interest." Soft infrastructure, such as training and work-and-life support services, acquires an equal if not greater importance than its hard equivalent of buildings, roads and bridges.

The lessons are still not being learnt, however. During 2000, a 70 per cent unemployment rate in East Timor was a major obstacle to peace and reconciliation, says the ILO, but employment programmes failed to be implemented due to lack of donor funding. Unemployment, both perceived and real, is often at the heart of tension between different social and ethnic groups. Investment that generates maximum employment opportunities is therefore a priority.

II. Plug leaks to maximize benefit of incoming resources

The post-disaster period can see hundreds of millions of reconstruction dollars pouring into often very poor economies. But how can the value of these incoming resources be maximized to promote long-term livelihoods and reinvigorate the local economy? A strong local economy is like a watertight bucket capable of catching and keeping resources that are poured into it. A weak local economy allows incoming resources to leak away leaving little continuing benefit – like a fractured bucket full of holes (see Figure 2.1).

"The strategy of plugging the leaks means mapping how different parts of the local economy link together and how money leaks out of an area, followed by finding ways of keeping the money within the community," says Bernie Ward of the London-based independent think tank, the New Economics Foundation (NEF). It is a long-term strategy to develop local economies capable of retaining resources, based on principles of local ownership and control.

A way to test the value of inputs in regenerating a community is to develop new ways of measuring how those inputs are taken up and used. NEF is creating ways to measure what it calls the 'local multiplier effect' of aid or investment going into an area. In this analysis, aid or investment cannot be assumed to make a genuine contribution until they can be demonstrated to have expanded the basis for sustainable livelihoods, and not displaced other local activities. Aid and investment have to earn their names by showing a significant multiplier effect. Local-development expert, Jane Jacobs, calls for a similar measure of the value of inputs to the local economy, which she describes as an 'import stretching ratio'. This is calculated by dividing the value of a settlement's production of goods and services by the value of the inputs it receives (see Box 2.1).

chapter 2

'Leaks' from the local economy	'Plugs' to stop the leaks
Aid staff use foreign-owned hotels and services	**Ensure staff localize spending on services**
Payments to foreign consultants and contractors	**Support local NGOs and businesses**
Purchase of foreign reconstruction materials and agricultural/medical inputs	**Localize purchase of recovery materials and inputs**
Crop and business losses	**Introduce disaster insurance against crop and business losses**
Profiteering and corruption	**Work with governments, NGOs and communities to stop corruption**
Economic markets lost to competitors during recovery	**Provide small enterprises with flexible credit during recovery period**
Long-term development aid redirected to disaster response	**Ensure fresh funds for disaster recovery**
Long-term commodity-price decline	**Commodity-price support for primary commodity-dependent regions**
Higher risk-related returns expected on investment	**Ensure 'investment measures' are not undermined**
Post-disaster flight of capital	**Introduce controls in high-risk areas to prevent destabilizing capital flight**
Costs of flying aid in rather than procuring locally	**Establish targets for local procurement**
Local initiative and ownership of recovery undermined by donor-driven aid	**Rebuild social economy through community-designed reconstruction**

Figure 2.1: Plugging the leaks: ensuring that post-disaster resources recirculate within the local economy, rather than leaking out of it.

Box 2.1 Measuring best value of aid to local economies

National governments, local governments and relief agencies all bring resources to the scene of post-disaster recovery. Exactly how they purchase services and materials can have very different effects. To create maximum long-term benefit to the local economy, the more spending that stays and keeps circulating, the better.

There are ways to measure this. The crucial determinant is the degree of local procurement. The more services and materials that are bought locally, the more there will be a multiplying effect on the local economy. In some cases, even if local suppliers are more expensive initially, their tendency to recirculate earnings locally will translate into a more significant long-term contribution to redevelopment.

In a hypothetical example, say US$ 100,000 is to be spent on water engineering. Company A is an international contractor and, through its presence in the community for a limited period, US$ 10,000 may recirculate. But Company B is local and its greater linkages to the disaster-hit area mean that US$ 25,000 recirculates. With the right measuring tools, the local multiplier factor could be used in procurement decisions to improve aid effectiveness.

Aid that embraces local procurement can benefit the post-disaster community in three related ways: competitive local prices for services and materials will mean aid dollars go further; aid procurement can stimulate the local economy; and a stronger local economy will strengthen social capital.

Similar exercises looking at the impact of 'visitor' spending on local earnings and employment have long been used to plan sustainable tourist development around the developed world. These, for example, indicate that travellers staying in 'chain' hotels contribute less to local economies than those staying in local guest houses.

Currently, developing countries use 'investment measures', such as specifying that new economic ventures must employ a certain proportion of local labour, in order to negotiate host-country benefits from foreign investment. Following the same model, disaster-afflicted nations and those who aid them could apply 'reconstruction measures', such as guaranteeing that a given proportion of post-disaster spending is directed according to local people's wishes and focuses on the purchase of local services and materials.

In addition to measuring the recirculation of money in the economy, there is the challenge of creating maximum economic space for local enterprises. This could be called the 'full ecology' of disaster recovery. Micro- and small enterprises, even more than medium-sized enterprises, have been shown to create the largest number of jobs. Yet such small producers and service providers would find it hard, for many reasons, to fit into the business formula of large-scale contractors. So maximizing the opportunities for micro- and small enterprises to participate in reconstruction is crucial to the successful rebuilding of a sustainable local economy. In this case, too much reliance on major contractors and foreign consultants will at best constrain recovery and at worst preclude it.

In disaster-afflicted areas, plugging the leaks means paying for labour and resources locally, instead of buying-in ready-made replacement infrastructure, housing and services from outside contractors. The use of inappropriate food aid and food-for-work schemes is notorious for undermining local producers, who cannot compete with what are, in effect, hugely subsidized imports. If people don't buy locally produced food, farmers will become unemployed, increasing their vulnerability to disaster, while the absence of a market will dissuade others from working the land.

The sheer financial presence of aid interventions – agencies' demands for hotel and office space, food, fuel and local employees – has a major impact on the local economy which can be either positive or negative. However, the vast spending power of international aid workers and peacekeepers based in East Timor, for example, benefits not locals, but mainly Australian and Singaporean entrepreneurs (see Box 2.2).

Box 2.2 East Timor diary, 20 April 2000

The sky is grey at six o'clock when I walk sleepily with my radio and its five-metre wire to a cup of coffee on the terrace of the hotel. At half past six, the sky is blue with patches of white. The sun is shining, palm trees waving in the breeze, children shouting, "Hello Mistar", on my morning run, sitting in front of green banana groves while their mothers smile at me, cooking something in iron pots over charcoal fires. They wear green sarongs and smile at me. They recognize me by now. I run on. An old man greets me in a language I do not understand. I answer in a language he doesn't understand.

Most of the houses in the suburban neighbourhood still lie in ruins. Walls blackened by smoke. Roofs destroyed. No repairs are going on. They are waiting for the UN to do it for them, say some. Others say it is because of lack of money. The UN administration has levied a 10 per cent tax on timber used for roofing beams. Aid organizations active in reconstruction are exempt. Private repairs are not encouraged. It's cheaper to wait and let a foreign organization do it for you for free.

I arrive at the sea. The sea is singing a homesick song of beaches I used to spend time on. The sea is gentle and loving with a slow swell. The sea caresses the shore as a lover caresses his loved one in the early morning hours. Far out in the bay waits a ship. It has been there for some weeks. On board are things normal people need, like soap, to be sold in the shops. But the ship has to wait for an opportunity to offload. All harbours to East Timor except the harbour of Dili are closed. Supplies for the 10,000 or so peacekeepers, UN officials and other humanitarians have priority. The East Timorese will have to wait.

The sun starts imploring everyone to go inside and hide. Another morning runner comes towards me, sweating with the sun on his back. We wave as runners in the morning do. I become sweaty and hot. At the second cape I see the statue of Christ blessing the sea. I touch the statue and return to my hotel, the Paximus Lodge, 'Hilton in Dili', a bunch of white containers huddled together on an empty car park.

I live in container 79. I enter my cupboard-size room where air-conditioning and four iron walls block any impression of a tropical atmosphere. I do my sit-ups and my push-ups. The floor gets wet with the sweat of my hands. I bathe, shave and brush my teeth.

Outside the dining container, I drink one last cup of watery coffee. I listen to the Australian owner negotiating with a fisherman selling him a huge fish over a metre and a half long. The fisherman wants 12 Australian dollars. The owner is good at negotiating. They settle on the price: AS$ 6. Fish-steaks will be sold over lunch at AS$ 12 a piece. I figure 40 steaks could come out of this fish.

➡

The cost of transporting aid supplies into a disaster-affected country is another drain on aid resources. Following two earthquakes which devastated parts of El Salvador in early 2001, the US aid-coordinating body, Interaction, discouraged donors from sending food and clothing. "Whenever possible, donate cash...," it told donors, "most essential relief goods can be purchased locally. Unlike material donations, cash donations entail no transport costs."

Plans for disaster mitigation, adaptation and reconstruction need to be employment-rich and locally rooted, rather than flying in every component and participant from abroad. Small, locally-based enterprises will be at the heart of rebuilding infrastructure and services. They also help absorb and retain incoming financial assistance. According to Jayasankar Krishnamurty, senior economist for the InFocus programme on crisis response and reconstruction at the ILO, "The process of reconstruction, starting from the clean-up of sites to the rebuilding of infrastructure and shelter, must be employment-creating for the communities involved. This means that employment is an immediate issue, not just a long-term aim."

If all the aid going into a post-disaster region is spent on externally supplied goods, services and consultants, then new money will quickly leave the area. If it is spent on services that are locally supplied, then aid will continue to circulate in the local economy. Only better measurement can

➡

The sky is light blue with specks of white when I get into the office. A Georgian sits behind one desk, writing e-mails. An Australian with a beard sits behind another, writing e-mails. An English woman sits behind a third desk, writing her doctoral thesis.

The sky is lapis lazuli when I leave the office at eight. After dinner of beer and lamb dumplings in soy sauce at the Hotel Dili, I join Gus, an Australian ex-soldier, and his mates for a drink by the beach – whisky, which they sell here mixed with cola in beer cans. The sea is quiet now. The mangrove trees by the sea are dark shadows against a sky which seems upside down. Small lights dance over the sea at night. They are the ramshackle catamarans of the fishermen, who are fishing by the light of oil lamps on the bow.

On the way home, in Gus's small Toyota pickup, we pass a sea of light, with a host of four-wheel-drive vehicles parked in front of it. It is a ship the size of a serious oil tanker; white, huge, towering over the white-washed Portuguese waterfront houses, dwarfing the palm trees, dwarfing life. It is the UN hotel, where guests are catered to by staff from Singapore. International staff serve, manage and cook. The food comes from Singapore and Australia. It serves 600 guests, UN guests, paying AS$ 150 a night. Not a dime, not a cent gets into the local economy. That is, if you exclude the shy girls, who look small and humiliated sitting next to overweight aid workers.

We pass the Chinese restaurant, where a Chinese from Singapore serves food to the epicurean aid community. It sits in a rented, emptied shop. The terrace is in the ruins of the shop next door on the corner. Bricks, pylons, plastic chairs, Australian beer and aid workers. Catering for the aid community has become a business. It is new and worrying. In my bleakest, most cynical days I always thought that even if we screwed up completely, we could at least claim that we spent our money in the local economy. With spending power of around US$ 10 million a month in East Timor, that would make a significant contribution. Now it goes all to Singapore and Australia. Only some shy girls get their share. Those aren't imported from elsewhere. They're cheaper here.

highlight potentially perverse effects whereby aid, export-led trade and investment can actually drain local resources, displace local enterprises and hamper reconstruction.

Tied aid handicaps recovery

The continued practice of tied aid (where donors make aid conditional on using their own nations' companies and resources) has been shown to significantly reduce aid value to the recipient country. The ILO highlights a reconstruction project for a bombed district of Djibouti, following 1997's peace agreement, which was to be managed by a French subcontractor importing most construction materials from abroad. The impact on the local economy in this situation, says the ILO, "would be absolutely zero".

Some disaster-affected nations are now rejecting aid they view as too expensive or too tied to donor conditions, aid which in effect undermines indigenous capacities. In autumn 1999, floods destroyed a coastal lagoon in central Viet Nam, whose prawn farms were vital to the local economy. Foreign donors offered technical and financial assistance, which would have involved Dutch engineers building a Dutch-designed sea wall. A third of the project's cost would have been a grant, with Viet Nam having to raise the rest through a loan. The Vietnamese government, however, turned down the foreign scheme, preferring to build their barrier, even if their initial solutions were not to the same technical specification as the Dutch design. The loan, design and foreign consultants were turned away and the repair work finished by local people in autumn 2000 at half the cost. In the process, Viet Nam's domestic capacity to respond to recurrent disasters was improved (see Chapter 5, Box 5.2).

✚C

After years of tied aid being commonplace, major donors like the World Bank now recommend that "procurement should be flexible", to allow for greater local sourcing. In December 2000, the United Kingdom took a stand on untying aid. And a proposal to untie aid to the 48 least developed countries gained the provisional support of the European Commission early in 2001. But, dependent on difficult consensus and omitting important types of aid such as food, the proposal has serious weaknesses.

III. Diversified local economies stronger than monocultures

While physical factors can aggravate the risk of disasters, people are also vulnerable because of the nature of their local economy and how they fit into it. If a person has only one income source, which is badly affected by disaster, they will find it more difficult to recover than someone who has several sources of income. As with diversity in ecosystems, diverse economies tend to be more resilient and to recover more quickly than economies dependent on single, specialized activities.

In the aftermath of disaster, aid needs to make a long-term contribution to rebuild sustainable local economies and livelihoods.

Christopher Black/ International Federation, Mozambique 2001

Hurricane Mitch's impact on the Honduran economy in 1998 was estimated at equivalent to three-quarters of annual gross domestic product (GDP). Banana farming was a major agricultural sector and its annihilation cut off the chief source of income for many farmers and plantation workers, revealing the fragile dependency that many households had on that single crop. While

this may seem an unexceptional insight, it runs counter to two centuries of economic convention that emphasizes economic specialization as the accepted route to prosperity.

Yet the story is not a simple one; according to the ILO, "Labour phenomena, such as unemployed banana workers, can be directly attributed to the hurricane. But the real problem to be addressed is the incapacity of the national economies to generate sufficient employment for the population as a whole, as well as the propensity in the banana sector to maintain much of the workforce in highly precarious conditions of employment." Least developed countries are heavily dependent on just a handful of cash crops for export, often produced on large-scale farms worked by insecure wage labour.

This means they are doubly vulnerable, both to crop loss in extreme weather, and to volatile commodity prices. Diversification rather than specialization, production for consumption rather than export, and redistribution of good-quality land would all increase food and economic security. Greater self-reliance reduces dependency and vulnerability to disaster.

Maximize employment through micro-businesses

Micro- and small businesses, the keys to an employment-rich economy, were seriously affected by the commercial disruption wrought by Hurricane Mitch. The highest post-disaster priority, said the ILO, was the "design and implementation of employment maximization policies" at the local level. Focusing more widely than mere 'wage employment', policies should identify small business opportunities, chances for cooperatives and make credit available to farmers. Special arrangements also need to be designed to accommodate women's needs in employment such as "day care and collective arrangements for dependants".

Creating diverse employment opportunities is a foundation stone of recovery. And micro-credit is an important tool for creating entrepreneurial opportunities. In Bangladesh, a network of micro-credit groups across the country helps the poorest recover from disaster, pioneered by the Grameen Bank. Community-guaranteed micro-credit schemes add to social cohesion because of the participatory way they are organized, allowing flexibility in the post-disaster phase, and because they provide cheap credit to people whose only other option would be to rely on extortionate local moneylenders.

According to the ILO's Krishnamurty, "Occupational diversification has to be viewed as a risk reduction strategy for not only the economy, but the individual household." One approach, which the ILO is piloting in the Indian state of Gujarat, following January 2001's devastating earthquake, is "to help women to go back to the craft activities they undertook before the quake. Home-based activities are particularly hard hit when the home and equipment in it are destroyed." In addition, he adds, risk-prone populations need micro-insurance and savings systems, tailored to their special needs.

Rebuilding the social economy

Non-conventional economic factors are as important in motivating recovery as creating jobs in the formal economy. Often in the post-disaster phase, there is the double problem of skilled people left jobless at exactly the moment when recovery work is needed. When money is not available at the local level, communities around the world are turning to 'Time Banks' to solve this problem. Time Banks connect people with time on their hands to work that needs doing, and create a cash-free means of exchange. For every hour of work done, the person is paid in a unit of 'time currency'. These units can then be exchanged for other goods and services. Time Banks have the double benefit of rebuilding connections and trust in the social economy and creating new liquidity in cash-poor areas.

Citizens' juries and forums are a new local initiative being used to solve everything from housing problems in Russia to farming dilemmas in India. They allow local people to pass judgement democratically on development strategies otherwise imposed from above. They could prove a powerful tool in designing plans for pre- and post-disaster programmes.

At a national level, research by the United Nations Development Programme highlights new techniques for setting budget priorities in participatory ways. In disaster-prone regions, this means proper resources can be earmarked for disaster adaptation, mitigation and recovery. Meanwhile in the business sector, there are moves to introduce stakeholder councils. Instead of firms and corporations only answering to shareholders, in this system they have to consider all the groups affected by what they do.

All these ideas point towards strengthening the fabric of community, building trust and reinvigorating the social economy – never more necessary than in the aftermath of disaster. As Noemi Espinosa of the Honduran Christian Commission for Development said following Hurricane Mitch, "The project of reconstruction must focus on the people, not just the infrastructure. We have to learn from this disaster. We have to change the way power is distributed and exercised, so that the poor and forgotten can participate in rebuilding their lives, and not just be spectators as international assistance is used to rebuild an economy for the wealthy."

Ecology of local economies

The economic problems facing communities after disasters are not new or isolated phenomena. The dynamics of reconstruction have been studied in rich and poor countries alike. Sometimes there is little relation between the amount of resources going into an economy shattered by war, disaster or the death of old industries, and successful regeneration.

The analogy between ecosystems and economies may help explain why. Local-development expert Jane Jacobs asks, "Can the way forests maximize their intakes of sunlight teach us something about how economies expand wealth and jobs?" Such a question has profound implications for planning post-disaster recovery. Jacobs criticizes conventional approaches as embodying a 'Thing Theory' which "supposes that development is the result of possessing things such as factories, dams, schools, tractors". But these "don't mysteriously carry the process along with them. To suppose that things, per se, are sufficient to produce development creates false expectations. Worse it evades measures that might actually foster development".

The tendency of conventional macroeconomic adjustment strategies pursued by many poor and post-conflict countries is to restore as soon as possible an outward orientation of the economy and export-led development strategies. The economy-ecology analogy, however, sees exports as 'discharges of economic energy' like clear-felling timber from a forest. Successful regeneration, rather, is built upon maximum ecological or economic diversification.

"In an ecosystem, the essential contributions made within the [natural] conduit are created by diverse biological activities. In the teeming economy, the essential contributions made within the [socio-economic] conduit are created by diverse economic activities," says Jacobs. Diversity is the defining characteristic to help form stable, resilient local economies that can successfully absorb and make maximum use of incoming resources, whether investment or foreign aid.

Taking the analogy further, development and disaster responses which do not respect economic, social and environmental priorities will become self-defeating. As Peter Winchester reports, recent development in the Krishna delta has aggravated the area's environmental vulnerability to climate-related disasters, while also increasing the economic vulnerability of the poorest. Mangrove forests, which once broke up cyclone-force winds and slowed storm surges, have all been removed. Since the 1970s, the 'blue revolution' (prawn and fish farming) has grown at the expense of rice cultivation. Trees and bushes that used to divide fields were dug out and cleared.

Land reform in the delta was intended to benefit small-scale fisher people and farmers. But because they could not get access to credit for tools and inputs, major landholders took advantage. Public investment and infrastructure work in response to past disasters benefited the larger landowners. As the new aquaculture displaced former farming practices, the number of landless labourers grew. And as their number grew, access to low-lying common land was cut. Small-scale farmers who had become trapped by debts to moneylenders were forced to sell their own land and moved on to the former commons. Then, the inherent vulnerability of single-crop economies became apparent in the mid-1990s when fish farms were devastated by a virus.

IV. Impacts of globalization and climate change

Local economies are only part of the disaster recovery picture. The adverse effects of globalization and climate change are draining the resources of the world's poorest. The continuous threat to vulnerable nations of climatic and economic disasters means that prevention, mitigation and recovery must combine in a broader, dynamic response to risk reduction.

The representative of the alliance of 43 small island developing states, speaking at a major summit in February 2000 on economic globalization, characterized this double problem. "Small island developing states have long been vulnerable to the forces of the seas and of natural and environmental disaster," he said. "But they are now having to brace themselves against forces of a different nature... the pace and terms of globalization and trade liberalization are dramatically altering their economies and hampering their efforts at sustainable development."

In an increasingly integrated and deregulated world economy, global fashions in economic policy-making among aid-giving nations and the institutions they control have a huge impact on what is possible at national and local levels. Since whatever strengthens diversified local economies reduces vulnerability to disasters, policies for aid, trade, investment and debt must be reassessed for how they influence the resilience of local economies to external shocks.

The local manifestations of climate change in poor countries place an enormous responsibility on the major aid-giving nations. The latter commonly both create the problem and set the terms by which the problem will be managed. Their responsibility is to identify appropriate and commensurate policies and resources. As the World Bank notes, "Global warming is primarily a result of the industrialization levels in the OECD [Organisation for Economic Co-operation and Development] countries, on whom the main onus for mitigation presently lies." The challenge is both to take appropriate action prior to disasters and to ensure coherence between macroeconomic policies and local recovery strategies.

Trade and investment liberalization threaten poorest

Virtually all post-disaster efforts to improve local economies and livelihoods place faith in a long-term trickle down from general economic recovery. But in a climate of increasing international competitiveness and decreasing resource flows to the poorest countries, general recovery cannot be guaranteed (see Box 2.3). Even when macroeconomic indicators improve, as happened following Asia's economic crisis in the late 1990s, they masked a lasting and disproportionately negative impact on the poorest people: jobs and poverty levels responded more slowly than total measures of economic activity.

Regarding investment, the vast majority of regulatory changes during the last decade have made it easier for investment to flow across national boundaries. This makes it harder for host countries to keep the profits of enterprises in the place where they are created. In the past, host countries used 'investment measures' to negotiate domestic benefits from foreign investors, such as specific proportions of local staff employed or local inputs purchased. However, these once-standard policy tools are being eroded under the jurisdiction of the World Trade Organization (WTO) in the name of open markets. Also, the poorer and more risk-prone a country is, the higher is the rate of return demanded by investors to compensate. Perversely, then, even if the poorest countries are successful in attracting foreign direct investment (FDI), they will see a higher proportion of profits from businesses drained out of their economies to pay back the investor, than would wealthier countries. Expected rates of return on FDI in sub-Saharan Africa can be from 24 to 30 per cent.

Latin America attempted to end the high cost and dependency of relying on imports of expensive manufactured goods by making things domestically. But this model of 'import substituting industrialization' failed, finally discredited by the debt crisis of the 1980s. It only benefited a small group of private investors. Failure was guaranteed by rigid economic strategies, bad deals with foreign companies supplying factory technology, corruption and an inappropriate focus on producing luxury goods which developing country markets could not support. However, a new model of import substitution that focused on guaranteeing basic needs, rather than fridges and luxury saloon cars, could well succeed in creating, keeping and distributing wealth and capacity where it is most needed – locally.

Recent research from the United Nations Environment Programme (UNEP) highlights how trade liberalization and export-led production have displaced local, community-serving

Box 2.3 Aid and investment to poorest nations slump

"Prospects for the developing countries could rapidly deteriorate if the major industrial countries continue to set their policies without regard for their global repercussions." UNCTAD, September 2000

At the same time that rich countries increase their consumption of global resources, the share of global wealth reaching the poorest is shrinking. The economic fate of the least developed countries illustrates the unequal consequences of globalization. Poverty is the prime indicator of vulnerability to disasters, so the impact of global economic trends is crucial. Adverse economic conditions restrict the ability of the poorest countries to invest in risk and disaster reduction. The greater damage then done by disasters makes it harder for them to compete in the global economy, pushing them into a lethal downward spiral of poverty and vulnerability.

In Latin America, conditions "deteriorated further" in 1999, according to the United Nations Conference on Trade and Development (UNCTAD). Asia recovered superficially from its crisis of 1997-98 but the aftermath included persistent, ingrained poverty, long-term damage to employment and to vital small and medium-sized businesses. Observers say that "strategic rather than closer integration with the global economy" will be the way forward for the region. Africa was stagnant and "neither the domestic nor the external conditions are yet right" for an African revival.

All the major resource trends seem geared to undermine, rather than maximize, aid effectiveness. Aid levels are low and stagnant with less going to the poorest countries, the trade picture for the same country group is bleak, private capital is negligible (and concentrates on exploiting natural resources), while debt remains a real drain on resources and deters development-friendly investment.

Trade trap: Unable to compete in other areas of the global economy against established nations, most poor countries depend heavily on exporting primary commodities like food, tea, coffee, tobacco and cotton for income. But commodity prices are unpredictable and have fallen over a long period. According to UNCTAD, "the terms-of-trade of the LDCs worsened in 1998 and 1999", and the "breadth and depth of commodity price declines" were "unprecedented" since the early 1980s. Closely linked is the fall in real per capita GDP.

Falling aid to LDCs: The impact of a decades-long overall fall in aid giving by donor countries is exaggerated by the shrinking share going to the poorest countries. The share of aid going to the LDCs fell from 0.09 per cent of donors' gross national product (GNP) in 1990 to just 0.05 per cent in 1998.

Failed investment: Most private investment going to developing countries crowds into just a handful of nations, dominated by China. The share of foreign direct investment flowing to all developing countries that is captured by the LDCs fell from an average 3.6 per cent two decades ago to 1.4 per cent in recent years. Some absolute increases in private capital inflows obscure the fact that most investment has gone into oil and gas exploitation in just four LDCs: Angola, Equatorial Guinea, Myanmar and Yemen. UNCTAD points out that FDI "remains highly focused on natural resource exploitation", with its associated environmental degradation and highly questionable contribution to sustainable development. Measured in terms of its purchasing power for foreign goods, real per capita long-term capital inflows into the LDCs have fallen 39 per cent since 1990. Also, most FDI goes into buying-out or 'acquiring' companies rather than investing in new economic ventures.

Debt deepens: Despite the political success of the international campaign to cancel foreign debts of poor countries, campaigners say around US$ 300 billion of outstanding unpayable debt remains to be cancelled. In many indebted countries, more is being spent servicing foreign debt than on health or education services – even after debt relief. According to UNCTAD, the debt situation for countries following IMF/World Bank-sponsored programmes was "worse in 1998 than at the start of the decade".

economic activities and created social instability. Employment, more than just insecure wage labour, is central to the coping strategies of people in poverty. The poorest in Asia and elsewhere are still suffering from the crisis linked to financial liberalization. There are 20 million more unemployed today than when the crisis began in 1997.

UNEP points to the danger of "serious negative environmental, and related social, impacts" from expanded trade activity. These include problems of land degradation, water pollution, obstruction of policies to mitigate environmental damage, social instability and loss of common property rights. In India, argues trade analyst Devindra Sharma, the combination of drought and trade liberalization is threatening millions with economic ruin and food insecurity (see Box 2.4).

Structural adjustment hampers recovery

According to a recent study on the implications of climate change for development in Pacific island countries, strong health and education systems, coupled with diverse and dynamic local economies, are the foundations for effective disaster resilience and recovery (see Box 2.5).

Conversely, the social and economic patterns that hamper post-disaster recovery are the opposite, for example, the loss of traditional knowledge, coping strategies and the breakdown of extended families. Informal settlements, poor transport and communications, weak health and education services and overcrowding also make recovery more difficult. Most importantly, a narrow economic and agricultural base, over-exploitation of natural resources and loss of diversity provide the weakest foundations for recovery.

A worrying trend is that many of these strategies for disaster resilience are contradicted by the types of development promoted for poor countries to integrate in the global economy. The economic restructuring championed by the World Bank and International Monetary Fund (IMF), common to many poor countries in recent decades, has shared certain characteristics. Firstly, as a consequence of budgetary pressures brought on by structural adjustment programmes, health and education services have suffered severe funding constraints. Secondly, strategies for economic development have concentrated on specialization and primary commodity production for export.

The same is the case for post-conflict recovery, where health and education are considered important components. They are often the first services to be disrupted, hitting the poorest and most marginalized people hardest. However, the World Bank's OED, assessing activities in Uganda, Bosnia and Herzegovina, and El Salvador, found that social sector, health and education work was "not generally a priority in the Bank's post-conflict projects". And in only one country had the Bank made a "specific operational effort to address the particular needs of women". Social sectors such as health, education, clean water and sanitation received between 4.2 and 7.4 per cent of total lending. The OED said that the Bank's support to agriculture and industry was only indirect. Its involvement in the areas crucial to livelihoods (e.g., micro-enterprise and participatory local development) was "mixed", at best only "relatively satisfactory" in one country. It was in the areas of economic "stabilization" and big infrastructure that the Bank's key energies were directed.

The Bank believes that "macroeconomic stability as soon as possible in a post-conflict setting is crucial to economic recovery", and should be an aim of the "highest priority". Yet measures for "stabilization" typically worsen conditions for the poorest and can threaten social stability during the sensitive post-conflict phase. The IMF's involvement in Rwanda was criticized by a Danish review for undermining stability. The OED recommends that "economic reforms" should only be pursued "incrementally" and adapted to the target country's very specific conditions.

Box 2.4 Impact of world trade on disaster recovery

Give India food security, argues Devindra Sharma, a respected journalist and trade analyst, and the floods, droughts, cyclones and earthquakes troubling the subcontinent can easily be taken care of. The problem, he says, is that free trade has undermined it.

India spent half a century shaking off dependence on food imports. A 'green revolution' saw agricultural production outpace domestic demand: in 1987, the century's worst drought affected 155 million hectares but there were no reports of starvation. Yet there were last year. As the coastal region of Orissa struggled to recover from 1999's super-cyclone, drought spread through the west of the state, reportedly damaging 90 per cent of crops there. Marginal farmers and labourers migrated.

The green revolution has slowed as problems related to intensive agriculture have grown, problems that Sharma says are aggravated by trade liberalization, "As the focus of policies shifts to agro-processing, foreign investments and exports, the critical connection between agricultural production and access to food has been ignored." Hunger increases yet Indian crops are exported for cattle feed.

Sharma says India last year had surplus grain stocks of 44 million tonnes, made available for export, while 320 million people went to bed hungry. He points to the convoluted economics of global trade, "The World Bank and the IMF discourage government support for agriculture, and the World Trade Organization says we must buy food at market prices, which means the dismantling of our price support mechanism."

The author of *In the Famine Trap* and *GATT to WTO: Seeds of Despair*, Sharma fears India's 550 million farmers will not withstand the pressures of market forces. With them are millions of landless labourers, meaning up to 75 per cent of India's population looks to agriculture for a livelihood. But, says Sharma, industrialization of the sector is putting small farmers out of business.

That and the obligatory open door for foreign exports. The demise of the 'white revolution' illustrates: as food production rose so did that of milk, to 68 million tonnes a year, making India the world's biggest producer and an exporter of skimmed milk powder. For the rural poor it has been a godsend. The income per cow is less than the government subsidy Western farmers are given, but millions of small producers have benefited. They formed cooperatives and of their 80 million members, the majority are women.

The WTO's recent Agreement on Agriculture has brought change. India's barriers have been lifted and imports are coming in. Over a six-month period last year, 16,700 tonnes of highly subsidized foreign milk powder arrived. Says Sharma, "How can Indian producers compete? The subsidy on European imports may be US$ 1,000 a tonne. Our people get none. They will be marginalized. It isn't just the availability of milk that's important. Dairying is a major source of employment and income."

The introduction of poverty reduction strategy papers by the World Bank was an attempt to improve the targeting of new resources to the poor, in the context of the international debt relief initiative. They have, however, been criticized for adding another complex layer of conditionality in accessing development finance.

Climate change-driven disasters cost poorest nations dear

Research presented by the United Nations' Intergovernmental Panel on Climate Change (IPCC) in early 2001 suggests the atmosphere may warm by as much as six degrees Celsius over land areas by 2100, more rapidly than previously expected. If, however, as scientists now expect, 'positive feedback' occurs in the environment due to changes already happening, warming could progress even faster. One scenario for the melting of northern ice fields suggested by the IPCC would lead in the long term to a seven-metre sea-level rise, submerging nearly all the world's major capital cities.

People living in the world's poorest regions are most at risk. By 2080, over 3 billion people across Africa, the Middle East and the Indian subcontinent will suffer an increase in 'water stress'. Agricultural yields in Africa are expected to drop and hunger rise. Both droughts and floods will increase in frequency. And, according to the UK's meteorological office, the most dangerous strains of malaria will pose a risk to 290 million more people as warmer, wetter climates encourage mosquitoes to breed.

The resources available in poorer countries for recovery will be hit hard by the rising economic costs of such disasters. Precise costing is difficult, but one leading British-based development agency estimated that climate-related disasters over the next 20 years could cost developing countries GB£ 6.5 trillion – around ten times total anticipated aid flows. In February 2001, the financial services initiative of UNEP estimated the extra costs from disasters that were attributable to global warming to be US$ 304.2 billion annually.

Andrew Dlugolecki, a director of CGNU, one the world's six largest insurance companies, highlighted recent trends at the UN's climate change conference at The Hague in November 2000. Using projections based on data from reinsurance giant Munich Re and published in the journal *Environmental Finance,* Dlugolecki showed that the costs of climate change could actually overtake the value of total world economic output by around 2065.

Problems with capturing the real costs of disasters mean that even these disturbing projections are probably significant underestimates. In poor countries where many cannot afford insurance, their losses easily go unaccounted, and damage to capital goods cannot, in any case, indicate the value of lost skills, lives and confidence. Less than 10 per cent of private property is insured in the developing world. Work by economist Paul Freeman suggests that the indirect and secondary impacts of disaster "may be twice the size of the direct losses" (see Chapter 8, Boxes 8.1 and 8.2).

As more people begin to feel the impact of climate change and seek help from governments, traditionally vulnerable groups could find their needs further marginalized. In response to the rising tide of disasters, instead of new and additional funds being found, existing resources are being redirected. Funds intended for development are routinely "reallocated to finance relief and reconstruction efforts, jeopardising long-term development goals", according to the World Bank. After Hurricane Mitch, the World Bank redirected US$ 200 million from "on-going projects" to finance emergency reconstruction in the four worst-affected countries.

But, according to Maarten van Aalst and Ian Burton in *Come Hell or High Water – Integrating Climate Change Vulnerability and Adaptation into Bank Work,* "Unfortunately emergency loans for disaster recovery and rehabilitation tend to focus on the restoration of conditions to the pre-disaster state. They thus miss the opportunity to reduce vulnerability to future events, including increased risk from climate change." The same is true for development: from 1992 to 1998, for example, the World Bank spent 25 times more on fossil fuel projects that add to global warming than on environmentally friendly energy sources such as solar and wind.

Coherent international response

How should the international community respond to the perverse distribution of responsibility and harm from adverse climate change? The poorest are left most exposed to the risk of death, injury and loss of livelihood. Yet, they have made only negligible contributions to warming the earth's atmosphere. With just 5 per cent of the world's population, the United States is responsible for around one-quarter of global greenhouse gas emissions. The average US citizen is responsible for 20 times the carbon dioxide emissions of the average Indian citizen, and over 300 times the average Mozambican.

Responses have varied. The decision in March 2001 of the US presidency not to ratify the Kyoto Protocol (the only serious international attempt to tackle greenhouse gas emissions) drew widespread concern from both the European Union and developing nations. Bangladesh's environment minister, when asked what response would be needed to deal with her 20 million compatriots predicted to be left stranded as sea levels rise, said, "I would request developed countries of the world to rethink their immigration policies for the survival of these ecological refugees… America and other big countries, they must accommodate them."

Meanwhile, the Commonwealth Disaster Management Agency has proposed an insurance scheme for disaster-prone countries. The governments of poor countries burdened with foreign debt obligations would pay into an insurance policy, so that if their economy suffered after a natural disaster, the policy would cover their debt service payments. Given the continuing international campaign for debt cancellation, the timing of such a scheme is controversial. The scheme's underlying logic proposes that poor countries should pay further to insure against a problem not of their own making, and in order to continue servicing debts that are hotly contested.

A very different proposal circulating suggests that poor, disaster-hit countries could seek compensation from industrialized countries to pay for reconstruction through legal action. An International Tort Climate Court would provide such a forum. Roughly half of all legal cases in the US are tort claims for compensation and punitive damages where injury or other harm has resulted from reckless, negligent or improper behaviour. Increasingly sophisticated analysis of climate change means that ignorance of the consequences of industrial consumption and pollution can be no defence for inaction.

Legal precedents exist for nations to seek compensation from each other for the results of trans-boundary pollution. There have been successful actions between countries over acid rain, for example. Compensation for climate change would need to be of a much higher order, and would be an acknowledgement of the ecological debt arising from the unequal consumption of finite natural resources and its consequences.

After the Earth Summit in 1992, a new budget line called the Global Environment Facility was set up to fund action in poor countries. But, in common with the so-called 'clean development mechanism' (part of the UN Framework Convention on Climate Change), as a system for channelling resources from rich to poor countries commensurate with the needs created by climate-related disasters, this is clearly inadequate.

In the absence of effective international action, small island states are setting an economic example at the cutting edge of managing disasters. Their typically weak and vulnerable economies provide an indication of which solutions best increase environmental, social and economic resilience. To embrace true sustainability, economic development has to embrace strategies for mitigation, adaptation and recovery. As the post-disaster phase is increasingly also a pre-disaster phase, the focus has fallen on the need for consistent planning that provides an approach continuously working to maximize community resilience (see Box 2.5).

In the case of global warming, this means opting for a low-carbon economy as well as building on economic patterns that maximize social resilience. Leading the way, the prime minister of the small Caribbean island of St. Lucia committed his country at The Hague in November 2000 towards using 100 per cent clean, renewable energy.

The ecology of disaster recovery

Recovery for whom, or of what, is the question that hangs over any effort towards post-disaster reconstruction. What is the end in mind when designing an economic reconstruction plan? Is it targeted towards creating maximum resilience and sustainable livelihoods in the disaster-affected area? Or is its prime aim re-gearing economic infrastructure to meet more abstract economic targets? Being clear about objectives makes it more likely that appropriate strategies will be found.

Post-disaster economic reconstruction will only work if it takes an integrated approach respecting the subtle dynamics of communities' economic, political and cultural life, and how these interact with the natural environment. It is more important to ask people what they need to recover their daily lives, than to rush in foreign contractors to rebuild risks in the familiar shape of major engineering works. Resilient, inclusive and democratic local economies are the best inoculation against the multiple risks wrought by disasters.

Box 2.5 South Pacific islands plan disaster mitigation

Recent work in the South Pacific region to understand the development and recovery implications of increasingly severe climate change has suggested a bridge of planning principles that span pre-disaster preventative action to post-disaster rehabilitation. Studies began by mapping the range of threats posed by 'natural' disasters and then identifying the social and economic strategies that maximized resilience to them.

Sea-level rise and extreme weather events lie at the root of the problems faced by low-lying population centres. Their effects are complex and interrelated. Coastal areas suffer inundation and erosion. Dying coral reefs affect the behaviour of sediment. Freshwater 'lenses' and groundwater sources are also affected. Salt intrusion is a serious problem combined with flooding and changes to run-off patterns.

The impact on agriculture is felt in commercial crop yields, subsistence crops, plant pest populations and soil quality. In aquaculture, the range of species available,

the breeding and productivity of fish are all affected. Port infrastructures are vulnerable as are the beaches that tourism depends on. Forest and wetland ecosystems all stand to be disrupted. Direct impacts on human populations include increased incidence of malaria and dengue fever, heat stress and related conditions, death and injury from extreme events and nutritional problems resulting from disruption to farming and fishing. Stress on sanitation systems is also high. Sewage pollution and freshwater contamination are major threats.

The South Pacific study concluded that reactive strategies following disasters often involved socially disruptive coercive measures, such as relocation, and were generally limited in scope and expensive. Planned, anticipated responses, such as those listed below, on the other hand, proved to be more socially appropriate and economically efficient. The areas studied were highly sensitive to climate change and heavily dependent on their ➡

➡

ecosystems. Effective response strategies therefore require institutional capacity, research and continual monitoring.

Regardless of any coordinating action by governments, it is important to understand that communities and individuals will autonomously make limited efforts at adaptation. But one group's adaptation could disadvantage another group. Many communities will be too poor to adapt. It may be that individual- or community-level adaptation is simply inadequate, that there are too many cultural constraints on action, or that the consequences for future generations are not taken into account. Government, therefore, has a key role to play in providing information, policy coherence for adaptation and financial assistance. Almost every planning decision is affected: the location of industry; tourist developments; housing; transport infrastructure; and farming and fishing development.

The study concluded that the following factors would enhance community ability to recover from 'natural' disasters:

Cultural practices:
- gift giving;
- extended family ties;
- strong local government;
- subsistence agriculture, home gardening;
- forest resources providing disaster foods;
- traditional housing; and
- traditional knowledge and experience.

Economic factors:
- a diverse economy;
- a diverse agricultural base;
- sustainable resource use;
- resource diversity; and
- financial mechanisms to spread losses (e.g., insurance, disaster funds, community trust funds).

Development and institutional factors:
- good transport, communications and sanitation;
- good education and health services;
- disaster preparedness and emergency services; and
- strong community groups, community services and NGOs.

Ecological factors:
- productive and robust ecosystems;
- traditional resource conservation and management practices; and
- resource protection and sustainable resource use.

Conversely, the erosion of such social and economic factors will hamper post-disaster recovery. Crucially, a narrow economic base, over exploitation of natural resources and loss of diversity provide the weakest foundations for recovery.

A recipe for post-disaster economic recovery could include initiatives to:
- **forge sustainable livelihoods** through rebuilding diverse local economies to meet local needs as the foundation for human recovery; maximize contributions to the micro- and small business sector, and minimize environmental impact;
- **create employment,** not just wage labour, to maximize long-term secure work, self-help and self-employment; ensure that the particular employment needs of women are addressed, such as day care for children;
- **set local procurement targets** in disaster response to maximize local economic recovery; use grants and micro-credit schemes to increase support to micro- and small businesses and cooperative enterprises; and ensure reconstruction prioritizes secure local employment as an immediate need;
- **measure the effectiveness of reconstruction** with a 'local multiplier effect' ratio. This would be a new measuring tool to indicate real contributions of aid and investment to the affected area and could help plug the economic leaks. Aid interventions must not undermine incentives for local production or distort markets by undercutting local producers;
- **improve access to resources** for the poorest, such as micro-credit, land, livestock and farm inputs. This will not necessarily be solved by more foreign direct investment which, because of higher-than-usual demands for returns, can drain resources from poor, high-risk economies;

- **rebuild the social economy** through, for example, Time Banks, which could connect those left jobless by disaster to work that badly needs doing to boost recovery. Trading 'time currency' restores trust and liquidity in cash-poor areas;
- **strengthen democracy** to improve recovery planning and efficiency, through: stakeholder councils; citizens' juries; and local micro- and small business alliances for participatory planning from the pre-disaster phase through to relief and reconstruction;
- **focus on community disaster resilience** as the primary economic goal of reconstruction rather than export-oriented production: beware of the economic and environmental vulnerability linked to dependence on a few cash crops; and focusing only on export crops can displace local community-serving activities;
- **create new resource-raising mechanisms:** more grant finance, not tied aid, from rich countries; deeper debt relief; and legal compensation for the effects of climate change are needed to compensate low fossil fuel-consuming countries for the ecological debt of industrialized nations; and
- **plan for climate change:** low-carbon development strategies are needed everywhere to minimize the increasingly hostile greenhouse effect. Risk reduction strategies must be built into disaster recovery plans.

To conclude, lifting people out of poverty is the best way to reduce the number who have to be lifted out of mud, flood waters or drought when disasters strike. Investment in local-level economic recovery is better at creating disaster-resilient communities than investment which depends on dams, dykes and concrete. Sustainable livelihoods may even hold the key to peace in war-torn countries. The poorest can best recover from today's disasters and conflicts on the foundations of strong, inclusive, diverse local economies, rather than trusting to the vague promises of the global economy.

Andrew Simms, head of the Global Economy Programme at the New Economics Foundation, and an advisor and writer on environment, development and globalization issues was principal contributor to this chapter and boxes 2.1, 2.3 and 2.5. Box 2.2 was written by Kies Rietveld, a medical doctor who has worked with ECHO in Afghanistan and WHO in East Timor. John Sparrow, author of Chapter 1, contributed Box 2.4.

Sources and further information

Burton, Ian and van Aalst, Maarten. *Come Hell or High Water – Integrating Climate Change Vulnerability and Adaptation into Bank Work.* Environment Department Papers, Paper No. 72. Washington, DC: World Bank, 1999.

Campbell, John and de Wet, Neil. *Adapting to climate change: Incorporating climate change adaptation into development activities in Pacific island countries – a set of guidelines for policy makers and development planners.* South Pacific Regional Environmental Programme, http://www.sprep.org.ws

Christian Aid. *Global Warming, unnatural disasters and the world's poor.* London: Christian Aid, 2000.

Earthscan. *Poverty in Plenty – a human development report for the UK.* London: Earthscan, 2000.

Environmental Finance. Vol. 1, No. 7, May 2000.

Eriksson, John et al. *The international response to conflict and genocide: Lessons from the Rwanda experience – synthesis report.* Copenhagen, Denmark: Steering Committee of the Joint Evaluation of Emergency Assistance to Rwanda, 1996. http://www.um.dk/danida/evalueringsrapporteur/1997_rwanda

Hadley Centre. *Climate Change: An update of recent research from the Hadley Centre.* Berkshire, UK: The Met Office, November 2000.

Hadley Centre. Climate Change and its Impacts: Stabilisation of CO2 in the atmosphere. Berkshire, UK: The Met Office, 1999.

Jacobs, Jane. *The Nature of Economies.* New York: The Modern Library, 2000.

Kreimer, Alcira and Arnold, Margaret. "World Bank's role in reducing Impacts of Disasters" in *Natural Hazards Review,* February 2000.

Sharma, Devinder. *Selling Out (The Cost of Free Trade for Food Security in India).* The Ecological Foundation/UK Food Group, 2000.

Simms, Andrew. *Who owes who? Climate change, debt equity and survival.* London: Christian Aid, 1999.

United Nations Environment Programme (UNEP). *Trade Liberalisation and the Environment – lessons learned from Bangladesh, China, India, Philippines, Romania and Uganda: A synthesis report.* Geneva: 1999.

Winchester, Peter. "Cyclone Mitigation, Resource Allocation and Post-disaster Reconstruction in South India: Lessons from Two Decades of Research" in *Disasters*, Vol. 24, No. 1, 2000.

World Bank. *Transport Economics and Sector Policy Briefing.* http://www.worldbank.org

World Bank Operations and Evaluations Department. *Post-Conflict Reconstruction, country case study series.* Washington, DC: World Bank, 2000.

Yakub, Nerun N. *Rivers of Life.* London: Panos, 1994.

Web sites

Commonwealth Disaster Management Agency http://www.commonwealthdma.com/
International Labour Organization **http://www.ilo.int**
Munich Re **http://www.munichre.com**
New Economics Foundation **http://www.neweconomics.org**
South Pacific Regional Environmental Programme **http://www.sprep.org.ws**
United Nations Conference on Trade and Development (UNCTAD) **http://www.unctad.org**
United Nations Environment Programme **http://www.unep.org**
United Nations Intergovernmental Panel on Climate Change **http://www.ipcc.org**
World Bank **http://www.worldbank.org**

chapter 3

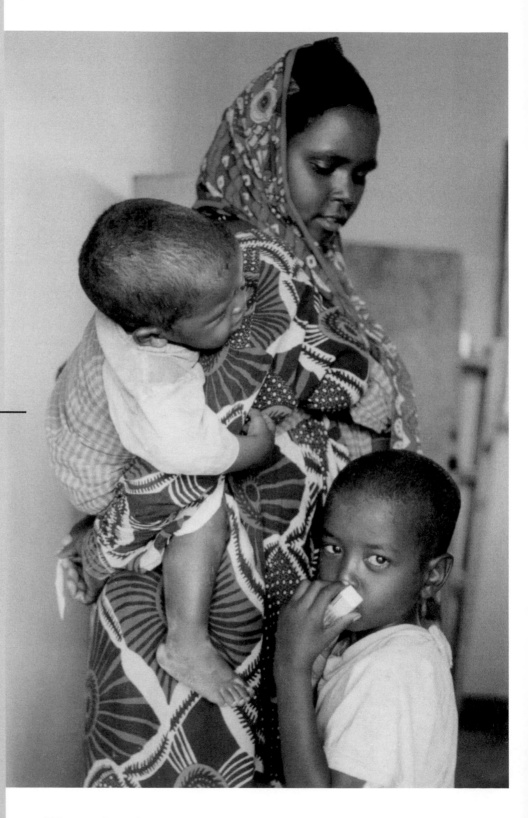

Section One

**Focus on
recovery**

Somalia: programming for sustainable health care

In the current operating environment of weak or failed states, chronic emergencies and media-led donor support, community participation is the key to sustainability in restoring and maintaining health, welfare and education services, and hence the foundation for effective rehabilitation of the service sector. Local communities and institutions bear a major responsibility for rebuilding their own services and infrastructure and therefore should own the overall process of rehabilitation.

Agencies often use the excuses of 'context constraints' and 'lack of resources' to implement quick-fix, project-driven relief programmes with an emphasis on short-term indicators which fail to adapt to the dynamics of local-level recovery. This leads to missed opportunities for harnessing longer-term developmental potential to participate in building a stable and peaceful recovery in conflict-affected communities.

The real challenge for aid agencies today is to develop the institutional capacities to provide assistance to the recovery process which is already under way in communities, in a manner that reinforces the dynamics of the recovery, however tentative they may be, at the local level. In the absence of a strategy to harness local capacities, externally funded service programming will be short-lived or remain chronically dependent on outside resources.

This chapter presents a methodology to guide rehabilitation programming in post-war situations, based on assessing the targeted communities' ability to contribute to, and willingness to participate in, the rehabilitation process.

An overview of conceptual, programming and structural barriers to rehabilitation is followed by a six-step methodology for analysing and planning rehabilitation of social services at the local level. The methodology is currently being field tested through health-sector rehabilitation programming in the Puntland state of Somalia. Success so far suggests that the theoretical framework detailed below is a realistic and practical approach to post-conflict rehabilitation in situations where government capacity is weak or non-existent.

Supporting health-sector rehabilitation in Puntland

The Puntland state of Somalia declared itself autonomous in 1998 following a three-month consultation involving community elders and political leaders. It considers itself to encompass the regions of Mudug, Nugal, Bari, Sool and the eastern part of Sanaag, although it is in dispute with Somaliland over the latter two regions. Puntland has its own government but, unlike Somaliland, considers itself part of Somalia (see Box 3.1).

The health situation across Somalia continues to deteriorate, reflecting the consequences of decades of conflict and the international community's continuing policy vacuum regarding Somalia. The latest survey to date, conducted in 1999 by UNICEF (the United Nations Children's Fund), put maternal mortality at 1,600 per 100,000 births and infant mortality at

Photo opposite page: Community ability and willingness to participate are essential in ensuring sustainable post-conflict rehabilitation.

George Bennet/ International Federation, Somalia 2001

132 per 1,000 live births, an increase on the previously accepted figure of 125. Under-five mortality is an estimated 224 per 1,000 live births – one of the worst in the world. A highly nomadic and dispersed population served by poor or non-existent infrastructure is plagued by major health problems from infectious diseases like acute respiratory infections, diarrhoea, measles and tuberculosis. New cases of polio were registered last year. While the World Health Organization (WHO), UNICEF and the International Federation of Red Cross and Red Crescent Societies organize National Immunization Days, immunization coverage is very low.

In 1993, the Somali Red Crescent Society (SRCS), with the support of the International Federation, set up an integrated health care programme through a network of mother-and-child health/outpatient clinics and health posts. In the absence of a national health service, 32 Red Crescent integrated health clinics and 12 health posts throughout the country continue to serve the needs of 840,000 beneficiaries. Twelve of these clinics are located in Puntland. The Somali Red Crescent remains critically dependent on outside aid from the International Federation for funding to run these clinics, while UNICEF provides some drugs and training support for clinic staff.

Seven years on, the clinics maintain their service on a shoestring budget, delivering basic assistance to vulnerable mothers and children in communities like Balibusle – seven hours' drive from the nearest alternative health facility. The challenge to the Red Crescent today is how to convert an essentially emergency-driven, relief health project, into a sustainable service that meets the needs of communities recovering from conflict and rebuilding their lives.

In April 2000, a joint initiative between the International Federation, the Somali Red Crescent and the World Bank began a health-sector rehabilitation study to draw out lessons learned from Red Crescent health programmes in the north-eastern region of Somalia over the past seven years. By exploring ways in which the National Society can play a catalyst role in the provision of a sustainable service to the population of Puntland, the International Federation is hoping to promote change and improvement in its programming in support of Red Cross and Red Crescent societies which are engaged in social-sector rehabilitation following conflict.

I. Barriers to rehabilitation

Before any kind of support for post-conflict recovery begins, it is critical to analyse the potential barriers to rehabilitation which may block or undermine the recovery process. These can be divided into three broad groups: conceptual; programming; and structural barriers. While a well-conceived rehabilitation methodology can overcome conceptual and programming barriers, structural barriers – such as shattered economic and political structures – are clearly beyond the scope of influence of humanitarian organizations. Nevertheless, these structural factors inform the rehabilitation context and must be clearly analysed and understood in order to develop the appropriate rehabilitation model.

In the early 1990s, academic arguments focused on the debate about rehabilitation linking relief and development. But simplistic temporal notions of a beginning and end to a relief

chapter 3

phase and a convenient transition to rehabilitation and later to development were quickly abandoned. Since the mid-1990s, the concept of *integrating* relief and development activities has increasingly been advocated as the way forward towards rebuilding war-torn societies. But too often in the immediate post-conflict period, when opportunities to undertake rehabilitation activities should be harnessed to consolidate peace, developmental needs are sacrificed to short-term, emergency-focused priorities. Donors and aid organizations alike need to develop the ability to identify and negotiate barriers to recovery and build the capacities necessary to make the transition from relief-based to sustainable service provision.

Conceptual barriers

Defining post-conflict: Problems defining when a country attains 'post-conflict' status may seem academic. But aid agencies' mandates and donors' funding procedures often depend on such definitions – clearly influencing the extent of support for rehabilitation. Donor funding for rehabilitation is sometimes withheld pending assurances of a definite end to the fighting. The London-based Overseas Development Institute (ODI) has set out three conditions defining the process of transition from war to peace: the signing of a formal peace agreement (military transition); a process of political transition by elections, a negotiated or military transfer of power (which may include secession); and the perception among national and international actors that there is an opportunity for peace and recovery.

In many cases, however, war may come to an end, while violent conflict continues for many years, involving former factions, demobilized combatants, bandits or warlords. Civil wars are particularly intractable and may be brought to an end only to break out again within a relatively short interval, as in Afghanistan, Angola and Cambodia. While 'post-war' situations can be clearly defined, 'post-conflict' situations cannot.

Defining rehabilitation: Confusion regarding the aims of post-conflict rehabilitation arises primarily from the broad application of the concept. It is used interchangeably to indicate: *restoration* of the physical infrastructure and essential government functions and services; *institution building* to improve the efficiency and effectiveness of existing institutions; and *structural reform* of political, economic, social and security sectors.

Rehabilitation is both a process and an outcome, based on increasing confidence, at house-hold and community level, in an emerging opportunity for long-term recovery. It involves a wide range of activities that take

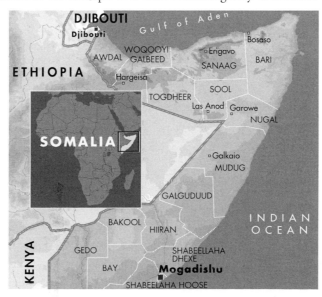

North-eastern Somalia

place in the early stages of recovery. Where recovery is retarded or conflict restarts, these activities may need to be repeated or continued for an indefinite period. The exact circumstances of the context in which recovery is being attempted will dictate the timing, focus and potential impact of these activities.

Timing: During the early 1990s, rehabilitation was generally regarded to occupy a continuum, somewhere between relief and development. Eventually, questioning this artificial thesis gave way to talk of timing and conditions in which rehabilitation can take place. A combination of lessons learned, research and common sense has brought an increasing awareness of the practical reality: rehabilitation doesn't wait for the signing of a peace agreement; the holding of elections; the creation of a transitional authority; or the approval of the donor community. While international assistance is needed for large-scale reconstruction, local-level recovery goes on regardless of policies, interventions or the support of international organizations.

By acknowledging this reality, agencies can get on with the business of detecting such transitional opportunities. By using the local knowledge they have gained during the emergency phase, together with their post-emergency presence and their access to resources, agencies can enable the transition from emergency to rehabilitation programming and provide incentives for sustainable recovery. To do this, indicators must be set up – ideally when planning the emergency intervention – to identify the early signs of local-level recovery (e.g., return of displaced people, local investment, willingness to participate).

Legitimization: In the wake of conflict, the highly politicized context leaves few neutral spaces for intervention and dialogue. Even if aid is intended to be neutral, its provision is often seen as an unambiguously political act, especially in a context where, for example, warring factions explicitly deny food and other basic needs in order to force people to sell their assets or move away from land rich in natural resources. Effective rehabilitation requires agencies to negotiate agreements with host authorities through whom they wish to channel resources. But this can be interpreted as legitimizing those authorities. Whose capacities do agencies choose to strengthen? Where do they restore services and reconstruct facilities? The risk that rehabilitation may strengthen the capacities of belligerents to restart hostilities presents a serious obstacle.

However, rehabilitation models which sideline formal and informal authorities may help undermine peace. As societies emerge from conflict, there are a number of roles that can only be played by political actors, for example, restoring security, regulating informal sectors, framing reconstruction strategies, protecting long-term rebuilding objectives from short-term agendas, and taking responsibility for vulnerable groups. For rehabilitation to be sustainable, a level of legitimacy is required from local authorities. Every situation is different, but experience has shown supporting civil society institutions need not happen at the expense of undermining the role of the state. By distinguishing between political and bureaucratic levels of governance, agencies can build on local institutions to resolve the legitimacy dilemma.

Programming barriers

Relief culture: The most significant barrier for rehabilitation to overcome is the entrenched culture of relief that continues into the post-conflict era. The assumed urgency of emergencies is often used to justify quick fixes. The same way of thinking persists in the aftermath of war, undermining rehabilitation initiatives and straining relationships between donors and recipients, particularly emerging authorities. Employing an emergency mindset, assistance continues to be top-down, paying lip service to concepts of participation and empowerment. Institutional arrangements, financial mechanisms and operational tools of assistance that were put into place under emergency programmes are ill-suited to rehabilitation and longer-term development.

Competence: While many agencies have considerable experience in responding to emergencies, this is not necessarily complemented by equivalent expertise in rehabilitation programming. For example, community participation – the key to sustainable rehabilitation – is widely advocated, but not necessarily well implemented. Moreover, the depth and breadth of the response required to constitute a meaningful response to rehabilitation needs in a region such as Puntland, where there is little international support and limited local capacity, present enormous obstacles. Gearing activities towards a more developmental outcome will require specific, professional expertise and a coordinated approach from agencies and the regional administration to clarify objectives, reach consensus, genuinely enable local communities, build local and institutional capacity, and ensure sustainability.

Knowledge: The coping capacities of communities are neither well researched nor understood, and are often underestimated. Lack of reliable statistics about health, social, demographic, economic and commercial conditions, particularly outside the few major urban centres, presents significant obstacles to planning medium- and long-term rehabilitation programmes. Contradictions abound in Puntland, for example, where estimates of the population vary from 850,000 (United Nations Development Office for Somalia) to 2.5 million (UNICEF and Puntland government figures). Even under normal conditions, accurate population figures would be hard to calculate given that around 60 per cent of the population is nomadic.

Attitude: Agencies can be reluctant at the institutional level to transfer real responsibility and control over resources to local employees, communities and officials. Yet communities should be recognized as the main partners in service rehabilitation projects. Their participation ensures more effective management and more relevant service provision. Rehabilitation should aim to allow communities to own, manage and support the service. A parallel aim should be to build the capacity of the emerging local and central administration to supervise and regulate services, and provide the necessary support to sustain them.

Political will: Agencies often maintain emergency operations for years in forgotten countries where international interventions have gone wrong or whose strategic unimportance ensures that they will remain forgotten. Somalia is particularly instructive: donor countries, whose memories of the United Nations Operation in Somalia's billion-dollar debacle have yet to fade, maintain a careful distance. While the international community has legitimate concerns about the administrations it is called upon to support, procrastination and short-termism will, in the long run, undermine the very processes it is striving to establish. There is an urgent need to develop a coherent, long-term strategy that will provide consistent support to regional and local efforts to provide social services and to establish democratic forms of governance.

Security: Rehabilitation projects not only risk being destroyed by renewed offensives, but the threat to the security of personnel also remains one of the main obstacles to programming. Foreign nationals are often singled out for kidnapping or assassination to deter external assistance or maximize media coverage. However, security constraints should neither detract from the need for nor negate the concept of investing in opportunities to make a transition. Initiating longer-term rehabilitation and recovery programmes builds local people's confidence in their region and may even help improve security.

Structural barriers

Weak states: Post-conflict rehabilitation requires basic institutional frameworks onto which new systems and services can be grafted. In many developing countries affected by conflict, these are either too weak or simply non-existent. The capacity of the newly emerging local and central administrations may have to be built from zero.

Structural vulnerability: In many post-conflict countries, structural vulnerability – in the form of an elite minority's control over power, business, land and education at the expense of the majority – is at the heart of violent opposition and conflict. As a prerequisite to sustainable recovery, major reform programmes may be required to address the structures of inequality that produce and perpetuate vulnerability. Without representative governance systems, accountable politicians and judiciaries, land reform, and access to education and basic health services, recovery will be retarded and stability jeopardized.

Changed post-war reality: Although many of the problems facing post-war societies existed prior to the outbreak of war, the consequences of war can radically alter the political, demographic and economic structure of a country. Intellectual and entrepreneurial sections of society may have migrated. In Rwanda, for example, the 1994 massacre of 800,000 Tutsi and moderate Hutus has had a huge impact on skilled public-sector personnel. More households will be female-headed. And populations may have been prevented from returning home, creating new ethnically homogenous zones. Meanwhile, trading relations and markets are easily lost, either through conflict or sanctions. Industry and infrastructure may be physically damaged or obsolete. Reconstruction may require the creation of new economic foundations.

Inequitable growth: Post-war economies are often structured in favour of powerful political actors. Many have built wartime systems to exploit opportunities through black markets, unregulated trade, seizure of resources, assets and property, and nepotism. In the immediate aftermath of war, pressure (often led by international financial institutions) builds to produce quick results in economic growth, through the privatization of state assets, the reduction of public spending and the removal of subsidies. The result can be a widening gap between an elite group of well-connected individuals and the majority who have no access to any means of trade or production. Rehabilitation programming that provides alternative sources of support for marginalized groups can threaten the 'markets' these elites have cultivated by depriving them of an impoverished and dependent workforce or customer base. Such elites will often undermine long-term rehabilitation assistance, or at a minimum seek to secure some financial gain to compensate for any loss to their own affairs.

Informal sector: The early recovery phase is often marked by the emergence of a plethora of informal, commercial actors who represent the most dynamic force in the drive towards rehabilitation and economic recovery. Rehabilitation programmes should recognize the opportunities presented by this informal sector and seek to accommodate the expertise and investment resources that the returning diaspora offers. However, the informal sector is often totally unregulated and can be hazardous (e.g., poor quality of service, links to criminal activities). It can also present an invisible barrier to effective rehabilitation efforts particularly in health service provision, by giving the impression that the population's health needs are being met when they are not. Apart from the need for policy, standards and regulation to protect the interests of those who can afford these services, donors also need to be convinced that there is a case for humanitarian assistance. Ongoing support of rehabilitation efforts should be based on an accurate assessment of the genuine need for assistance to the most vulnerable people in society.

Unrealistic expectations: International response may raise expectations when new welfare services are delivered at standards unprecedented among target communities. War-affected populations learn to expect more than their government could deliver even without the legacy of violent conflict. Health services in post-war Somaliland, for example, are considerably better today than in 1988 when war broke out. As a result, agencies trying to encourage community support in running or raising funds for social services are frequently met with dependence, apathy and unrealistic demands.

II. Community-led rehabilitation: a methodology

In order to respond to the above challenges to rehabilitation in post-conflict situations, the International Federation and the World Bank have worked with the Somali Red Crescent to develop and pilot a methodology in the Puntland state of Somalia. This strategic approach to effective rehabilitation consists of the following steps:
1. Inception of rehabilitation: are the conditions right?
2. Rehabilitation assessment: context, actor and sector analysis
3. Baseline data: through household surveys
4. In-depth case studies
5. Piloting strategy
6. Designing policy guidelines

Whether the intention is to adapt emergency relief programmes to the changing needs on the ground, or to begin an intervention to support rehabilitation and recovery, agencies need to be trained in effective context analysis to recognize the early dynamics of recovery, seize the opportunity to reinforce community efforts, and consolidate the emerging stability. This analysis provides the basis for mapping the communities to be assisted and undertaking an in-depth study of their inhabitants, their capacities, resources, vulnerabilities and needs. It is then possible to identify an appropriate programming strategy and design relevant components that can be tested and adapted to field realities.

Principle: community ability and willingness to participate

The methodology employed in the Puntland health-sector rehabilitation project is based on the principle that community participation is the key to restoring health services in Puntland today. By acknowledging that communities and local institutions play a leading role in rebuilding and maintaining their own services and infrastructure, the project seeks to place the ownership of rehabilitation programming firmly in the hands of the local community. Service provision in the aftermath of conflict cannot be sustained without participation, which in turn depends on the community's willingness to engage and their ability to contribute.

People's ability to contribute will be determined by their access – either at the individual or collective level – to resources including:
- collective assets such as land, public buildings and water;
- individual resources such as livestock, employment or diaspora remittances;
- traditional social support mechanisms such as clan networks, care for the elderly, etc.; and
- local systems for borrowing against livestock or other fluid assets.

Willingness to participate will be influenced by the:
- existence of a culture of participation in the targeted community;
- need for, or perceived value of, the service being provided;
- extent to which people feel they have been consulted; and
- post-conflict mentality of the people: are they pessimistic or have they seen and seized the chance for peace and recovery?

Taken together these two elements, i.e., the ability to contribute and willingness to participate, constitute the foundation of sustainable service recovery.

The Puntland project proposes a specific methodology to assist agencies in the development of an intervention to provide a service that, based on recognized and acknowledged community willingness to participate, meets clearly identified and agreed needs, accurately assesses the potential for resource mobilization at the local level to contribute to meeting these needs, and integrates effectively with other elements of recovery within the community.

Practice: community-based programming

Standard rehabilitation programming involves international organizations working with government agencies to develop macro-level recovery strategies. While much has been written on the need for participatory approaches, most programmes continue to be based on often externally driven, top-down strategies. There is no easy formula for inclusive planning, and even less for community involvement. It requires time, resources, in-depth analysis and, critically, an acceptance that the solutions international agencies have in mind are not necessarily what the community will need or want. Understanding this requires local-level partnership.

Genuine community involvement in health-sector rehabilitation planning in Puntland would be impossible without the facilitation role played by the Somali Red Crescent. As a key actor in health service delivery for many communities, the society's knowledge, experience and credibility ensures access to and validation of key information. For ten years, non-governmental organizations (NGOs) and humanitarian actors have come to these communities – and gone. Red Crescent staff and volunteers are community members who know their neighbours and whose neighbours know that they cannot move on to the next disaster when the funding runs out.

By focusing on building Red Crescent capacities, the Puntland project has ensured that the skills they acquire today to conduct a household survey on socio-economic conditions in their communities can be used tomorrow to map an outbreak of, for example, meningitis. The household survey questionnaires today are about health facility usage; tomorrow they could be about nutrition, or rubella, or reproductive health. The skills gained by SRCS clinic staff in conducting an in-depth study will be applied to support the opening of a badly needed new clinic in other areas later in the year.

The quality of information obtained when assessments are conducted by local people is significantly higher than that gathered by expatriate programme planners. External bias is less of an obstacle, while suspicions and sensitivities relating to clan, gender, historical divides and cultural traditions are minimized.

Cost recovery or cost sharing?

Health provision, management and maintenance are very capital intensive, and require considerable resources on the part of the enabling authorities. They encompass public regulation, the interaction of private and public sectors, provision of infrastructure and services by the state. Therefore, a health service has traditionally constituted an important part of governance systems.

The way the health service is provided, managed and regulated determines much of the social and economic framework of communities, particularly in cities. However, in the aftermath of war, local authorities' capacities are eroded and their ability to enable such public services to continue and to develop becomes limited, opening opportunities for other non-governmental and private-sector actors to meet the needs. This triggers a process of change in traditional roles and responsibilities.

The overall objective of ensuring that reliable services are provided in the right locations to satisfy local needs becomes the responsibility of a wider circle of actors and stakeholders. Increasingly, cost recovery and user fees are used to claw back costs or in some cases, in what has been called "the corruption of need", to exploit vulnerability.

From the point of view of sustainable recovery, the key issue is neither cost recovery nor cost sharing, but building sound and workable partnerships with the community. Therefore, it is critical that the aim to share the cost should be driven by the need for long-term sustainability and not by a requirement to reduce budgets.

Community contributions do not necessarily have to be in cash only. Innovative approaches should accommodate individual communities' capacities to contribute in-kind, service-related and financial resources. A sliding scale of donor-to-community contributions is best introduced gradually and over a carefully calculated period of time. Donors' contributions can be presented in the form of subsidies to reward achievement and success in relation to pre-set targets. For communities to make contributions to the costs of services, the expectation is that they should be in a position to control quality, in compliance with standards set jointly by the central government and the donor. It would be misleading to assume that any two

chapter 3

communities are identical. Interventions should be informed by specific circumstances avoiding standard solutions.

Step one: inception of rehabilitation

The first stage of any rehabilitation programming is to recognize both the need and the opportunity for it – are the conditions right? (See Box 3.1.) Although a widely-held assumption is that rehabilitation will begin when conflict has stopped, the reality is that people often start rehabilitating their lives and livelihoods before there is a formally acknowledged end to conflict. By looking for signs of *recovery* rather than signs of 'post-conflict', agencies may identify opportunities to support rehabilitation in 'pockets of peace' even though other parts of the country may be engaged in open armed conflict. This has been the approach of several experienced NGOs in Afghanistan over the past two decades of conflict. Likewise with Puntland, while agencies may disagree over whether the region is 'post-conflict' or not, opportunities exist to support rehabilitation for those willing to identify and take them.

Agencies should constantly be on the lookout for activities at national, community and household level which – subtly or blatantly – indicate confidence in recovery and future prospects, for example:

- spontaneous return of displaced populations;
- repairing houses;
- early efforts to repair and reopen schools;
- small-scale investment in construction;
- commercial activity such as buying land;
- restoration of electricity-generating capacity, even at micro-level;
- reestablishment of local communications;
- increased activity in the exchange of foreign currency, however informal;
- changes in spending patterns for diaspora remittances; and
- emerging governmental institutions, structures and strategies.

Recognizing these behavioural changes requires systematic observation on the part of operating agencies. Responding to the need for programming that supports rehabilitation and recovery once it gets under way at the local level requires systematic analysis based on strategies and tools that have been tested and proven at field level. Developments in Puntland since 1998 suggest that the right levels of both need and confidence exist to create excellent conditions for social-sector rehabilitation to succeed.

Step two: rehabilitation assessment

This second step aims to analyse the target context, actors and sector, and to diagnose needs. It can have the following objectives:

- Build consensus in the field on the need for rehabilitation, the usefulness of further comprehensive assessments, and the need for beneficiary communities to remain at the centre of the process. An important aspect is to build trust and reassure stakeholders that their various interests will be protected.
- Articulate a common vision.

- Explore and understand the context, opportunities and constraints within which programmes and any further assessments take place.
- Distil assumptions and lessons from existing relief programme experience and examine how these may inform rehabilitation.
- Identify jointly with local actors the need to propose and validate methodologies with specific time frames.

The expertise of assessment team members should be balanced and tailored to specific needs (e.g., relief, rehabilitation, health, strategic planning, capacity building in a risk environment). Local counterparts with specific expertise should be represented in the team. External members play an important role in bringing a fresh view to the context and increasing confidence at the local level. Their lack of specific contextual knowledge will have to be addressed through good preparation and briefing. Depending on context, this stage could extend from two to six weeks, based on a field visit followed by a detailed analysis of findings. Given the exploratory nature of the assessment, qualitative information-gathering techniques should be used at this stage.

Agreement on a set of principles to guide the conduct of all team members at this early stage has proved useful in terms of building transparency and trust with local counterparts, leaders and communities:

- Recognize that this is not an evaluation, but an overall assessment of the rehabilitation potential.
- Observe the values of action research, which will look for all possible opportunities of building capacities.
- Adopt a flexible approach using an inclusive process, allowing as many stakeholders as possible to participate in setting up the agenda and the elaboration of future steps.
- Build on the experience of local counterparts and their operational partners.
- Take into consideration previous assessments and evaluation reports (identify key documents).
- Focus on achievements and recognizing and rewarding successes.
- Take care not to raise false expectations.
- Respect local traditions and work within recognized structures.
- Recognize the authority of local and central government.

> In return for contributing their energy and resources towards sustaining health clinics, communities will demand a higher quality of service.
>
> George Bennet/ International Federation, Somalia 2001.

Box 3.1 Recognizing signs of recovery

In June 1998, the United Nations declared that it would support regional administrations in Somalia as the building blocks for a future federal state. Two months later, following a three-month consultation involving community elders and political leaders in the north-east of the country, the Puntland state of Somalia was declared. President Abdullahi Yusuf Ahmed, a former Somali army colonel, was elected from a list of four candidates. The new government declared the region as a state within what they hoped would eventually become the Somalia nation made up of a federation of states. Unlike Somaliland, Puntland considers itself part of Somalia.

In a fragmented country with an emerging transitional national government, no effective organs of state, no ongoing dialogue between the different controlling parties and no agreement about the future structure of any emerging political entity, aid coordination and management is a difficult business. Few international organizations maintain a permanent expatriate presence in Somalia, and headquarters are almost exclusively located in Nairobi. Apart from security considerations, communications with the different regions cannot be assured from any one internal location. Decisions about whether and where offices should be established are further complicated by issues of legitimization. The UN decision to support regional administrations has been a key support to maintaining stability and consolidating recovery in Puntland.

Efforts to construct government ministries in Puntland are making progress. There are currently nine:

interior; social affairs (including health and education); finance; livestock and agriculture; trade and industry; religion and justice; commerce, information and culture; water and transport; and fishery and ports.

The government is operating under a preliminary 'charter', which according to President Yusuf defines the primary role of government in the following terms:
- to ensure security and maintain a peaceful environment to encourage investment and development;
- to institute democratic forms of government, including election of leaders;
- to reject pre-civil war scientific socialism and tight state control of the Barre-era government;
- to enact laws and create conditions to promote foreign investment;
- to establish policies that encourage private initiative and free enterprise; that facilitate private-sector ownership and control of major sectors such as banking, electricity and telecommunications; and that minimize the role of state enterprises (although limited support is given to infrastructure development);
- to impose limited taxation, with state budget primarily allocated to law and order and minimal public functions; and
- to encourage the Somali diaspora to return and invest.

Meanwhile, the economy is showing signs of recovery. There is a thriving enterprise culture and informal sector, and several million dollars are sent back to Puntland each month in remittances.

There are three main areas of analysis that should be explored when conducting a rehabilitation assessment:
1. **Context analysis** to establish opportunities for and threats to rehabilitation initiatives; taking into account the conflict, socio-economic situation and institutional factors.
2. **Actors analysis** to establish the strengths and weaknesses of the various actors in undertaking rehabilitation work; taking into account the six prerequisites of any effective action: clarity of mission; competence; acceptance by the community; legitimacy to operate; knowledge; and availability of resources.
3. **Sector analysis** to establish the potentials and limitations of the particular sector being addressed.

Findings from this stage will dictate the rest of the intervention both in terms of further studies needed as well as potentials for rehabilitation. Some of the findings from the rehabilitation assessment in Puntland are outlined in Box 3.2.

Step three: baseline data

One important characteristic of post-conflict contexts is the unreliability or general lack of basic data (census and demographic data, health practices, levels and sources of income, informal sector, etc.). For rehabilitation programmes to be well founded, agencies must research 'baseline data' to validate available information and highlight gaps in knowledge that need to be addressed. In particular, the surveys must establish the community's ability and willingness to participate in rehabilitating social services.

The extent to which community participation and resource mobilization may be successful will depend on the capacities and resources available individually and collectively at household level within the community. Baseline data on socio-economic conditions are therefore needed to provide a benchmark against which all subsequent capacities and vulnerabilities data can be measured. This type of data is usually best gathered through a household survey.

The process should start with a sensitization workshop held in the field. This brings together the staff who will be involved in the survey with community leaders and core researchers. Household surveys should be conducted by local staff from the operating agency (when already on-site), working jointly with community representatives. In addition to generating baseline data, such surveys can provide a number of other benefits from both a research and a capacity-building point of view:

- They validate the findings of the rehabilitation assessment.
- They equip field staff with skills needed to undertake future assessments and data gathering (e.g., to identify the source and pattern of an infectious disease outbreak).
- They strengthen the understanding between staff, communities and their leaders.
- They update programme staff's knowledge of the community, enabling them to identify new opportunities for rehabilitation.

This step was completed in Puntland in September 2000 (see Box 3.3).

Step four: in-depth case studies

The baseline data generated through the household survey will identify various trends and opportunities that are then taken a step further in detailed study of a selected sample community. The aim of the in-depth study is to establish a valid profile of the communities' capacity and willingness to contribute to the running, maintenance, sustainability and ownership of the services to be rehabilitated in a manner that allows the full participation of the community.

Case studies are chosen to represent the different types of community reflected in the baseline survey (e.g., highest/lowest degree of community involvement in projects, level of assets, mobility). In order to engage with the community, an initial identification of local leaders and

Box 3.2 Analysing Puntland's context, actors and health sector

A full **context analysis** will include an examination of both the opportunities and threats which the conflict, the socio-economic situation and government institutions present. In Puntland, for example, while security has been good for the past seven years, a spillover of the conflict from southern Somalia is possible. Meanwhile, the informal sector of the economy is growing swiftly and providing increasing income. In Galcaio, Garowe and Bosaso, scores of building projects are under way; in Galcaio alone, 40 private construction firms are registered. Much of the large-scale investment in Puntland is financed by remittances from overseas Somalis, or by the earnings of Somalis returning after a period overseas. Investment is particularly noticeable in electricity generation, water supply, banking and telecommunications. Private firms such as Galkom provide more than 1,000 of Galcaio's 15,000 inhabitants with international telephone access (local calls are free). A number of private banks provide financial services, maintaining a vital link for Somali diaspora remittances, which amount to as much as US$ 5 to 6 million a month in Puntland. However, the informal sector remains unregulated, something of particular concern to the health sector.

From an institutional point of view, Puntland's charter looks impressive. But the ability of ministries to deliver will depend on the government's ability to raise enough resources to operate effectively. Currently, about three-quarters of the government's income is generated by Bosaso harbour, hard hit by the livestock ban reimposed by the Gulf states in September 2000 in the wake of the Rift Valley fever crisis. Remaining income is raised through airport tax, and the licensing of motor vehicles and businesses such as restaurants. According to the ministry of finance, overall revenue for 2000 was estimated at around 83 billion somali shillings (US$ 8.36 million). Public-sector services, where any exist, are minimal at best, as the fledgling administration struggles with the mammoth task of building a government and nine ministries from scratch without external assistance.

Potential **actors** include government, communities, and international and national organizations. They may not, however, share the same values or even views on what rehabilitation should be about. The starting point for any successful rehabilitation intervention is the recognition of the crucial role played by communities and their representatives in the initiation, identification of needs, design and implementation of programmes. Communities may possess structured social systems through which the process can be managed, or may be represented by civil society groups (e.g., local NGOs, community-based organizations, religious groups). Taking into account communities' capacities and resources as well as their needs is crucial to avert dependency.

Local authorities represented by district governments and municipalities often manage services and in some cases continue to provide some facilities. They are responsible for regulating practice and guarding standards. They often retain valuable information about the local population and public facilities. The role played by local authorities must be acknowledged in order to acquire legitimacy and remove obstacles, as well as to lay the foundation for sustainable health infrastructure. Although national governments may not be in a position to deliver, they are still responsible for setting up overall public-service policies and strategies, including the facilitation of the health sector (except in cases where they simply do not exist). Activities are often coordinated through the designated ministry.

As an intervention is planned, an assessment needs to be made concerning the state of central governance. Who has the authority to facilitate a given service provision? Central government, local government, local leaders? Do national pre-war policies exist and can they be supported? Are there any 'national' rehabilitation plans in the making? How closely will implementing agencies need to work with the government and what kind of relationship will it be: one of equal commitment to improving the service or not? Are there attempts to control outcomes? Are there hidden agenda (for example, against minority groups)? Are there any opportunities for assisting capacity building and institutional development of the various governmental departments through joint planning and partnerships?

The economics of conflict and the various roles played by the informal and private sectors are well documented. The scale of destruction often far exceeds the ability of local authorities or even outside agencies

➡

alone to rebuild, so active participation of the private sector may be critical. And, in the case of Puntland, internally displaced persons (IDPs), mainly from the south, present both opportunities and challenges to the emerging administration. On the one hand, many are industrious, and are taking advantage of Puntland's stability and opportunities for work and trade. In towns like Garowe, Galcaio and Bosaso, they are the driving force behind rehabilitation. On the other hand, many are destitute and vulnerable, and have had to sell their household assets. Their coping capacities have been eroded by a decade of conflict, and they need the administration's help. Given the limited resources and enormous demands on the new government, supporting this caseload will not be an easy task.

As far as the **health sector** goes, Puntland's very poor health indicators, in general, and increases in incidence of malaria, tuberculosis (TB) and polio, in particular, are causes for grave concern. To serve such a disease-burdened and highly mobile population, estimated between 850,000 (UN) and 2.5 million (Puntland government), would require a far greater capacity than exists at present. According to a recent inventory, 63 qualified doctors were registered in Puntland. There are five functioning hospitals, three health centres, 25 mother-and-child health/outpatient departments, and 62 health posts (many of them not functioning). In addition, there exist several hundred private pharmacies, many of them run by unqualified people.

Although Somali Red Crescent Society clinics and other health facilities provide limited primary health care, vaccinations and health education, the main emphasis of the existing health infrastructure, and the preoccupation of health-care providers, is on curative care. Any effort to improve the major health indicators in Puntland will require serious investment in preventive and promotive health activities. One especially damaging habit is addiction to qat, a green-leaf stimulant, which drains an estimated US$ 45,000 from Puntlanders' pockets each day, according to the ministry of finance. This is a conservative estimate, since it does not take into account informal-sector trade. Young men, traumatized by war, unemployed, and with few prospects, seek solace in qat chewing, which often

begins early in the afternoon, and typically continues late into the night. The social and economic consequences are disastrous, affecting people's ability to work, and even to function normally. As the mother of one addict said, "Qat turns night into day and day into night".

The ambitions of Dr Abdirahman Said Mohamoud, director general for health under the ministry of social affairs (MoSA), for improving health in Puntland are tempered by his lack of staff and proper office. WHO is working to help establish his headquarters in Garowe, the administrative capital of Puntland state. The previous health-care system was centralized, free of charge and weak on primary health care. MoSA's major health-care management strategies encompass decentralization, privatization, cost-recovery systems and community participation. None of these was implemented during the previous government and therefore both their introduction and application constitute a major challenge. New levies, taxes and cost-recovery systems have been introduced to support the whole government administration at central, regional and district levels, including some staff salary support at Bosaso hospital. MoSA's health division enjoys minimal financial support (around 2 per cent of national budget).

These circumstances combined with the enterprising initiative of the Somali people have created an atmosphere where private initiatives flourish. This is evidenced by the high number of private pharmacies available in the commercial districts of Galcaio, Garowe and Bosaso for those with sufficient means. UNICEF estimates that up to 80 per cent of Puntland's population has resorted to private consultation, which may prompt donors to question the need for ongoing external aid for health-sector rehabilitation.

However, closer analysis reveals that these private clinics and pharmacies are largely unregulated, often run by unqualified personnel, dispensing sometimes inadequate or incorrect treatment, and charging fees for their services which plunge many patients into debt. Meanwhile, inappropriate use of antibiotics and other drugs may be building up drug resistance to diseases such as TB and malaria. When such poor-quality private health provision is set alongside Somalia's appalling health indicators, urgent support for rehabilitating the health-care system is clearly needed.

structures will then follow. The various actors and dimensions of the in-depth study are shown in Figure 3.1.

In-depth studies employ more qualitative techniques and attempt to pilot new ideas which will lead to the rehabilitation of the service in question. However, ideas should come from the community itself. The most effective way of ensuring this is to employ a community-based action planning technique, with the full involvement of beneficiaries, giving them the chance to:

- create a shared long-term vision for the community's future;
- articulate their willingness and ability to contribute to the management and sustainability of facilities;
- illustrate their coping mechanisms (e.g., patterns of borrowing money);
- identify blockages that can hinder rehabilitation;
- help design short- and medium-term strategies for service rehabilitation; and
- propose suggestions as to how services can be sustained in the future, according to local priorities.

Action planning can be best described through the following features:

Holistic agenda: Although the main aim may be to rehabilitate a particular sector, the action planning process should examine the various problems and opportunities faced by the community in a holistic manner with minimum preconceptions. This allows people to illustrate the interrelationship between the targeted service and other aspects of their lives.

Integrated and multidisciplinary action: Initiate planning as a cross-sectoral process targeting the community rather than the service provided. Relevant agencies should work closely together in a non-hierarchical fashion, while recognizing that one agency may have to take the lead. This is particularly important in the eyes of the community who may not necessarily draw the distinction between different agencies present in their locality, or who are unable to distinguish between their health, education or agricultural needs.

Open community participation: The driving force for successful rehabilitation comes from within the community. Community-based action planning requires a shift in agencies' stance on participation from the mere provision of information on what is being planned or even consultation over the options that are on offer, to a stronger stance on deciding and acting in *partnership* with the community. As planning progresses, it is useful to start thinking in terms of partnerships as different interests willingly come together, formally or informally, to achieve emerging common purposes. The partners do not have to be equal in skills, funds or even confidence; however, they do have to trust each other and share an equal level of commitment. This, of course, takes time and requires greater efforts on behalf of the agencies to demonstrate their longer-term commitment. The process encourages additional options and ideas to emerge and provides opportunities for joint implementation of agreed action. The facilitators should make sure that the event includes all community minorities and vulnerable groups.

Recognition of the responsibility of local authority and leadership: The action-planning event should be planned jointly with local leaders. A clear recognition of their authority will lead to a greater sense of responsibility on their side as well as to a greater willingness to

Box 3.3 Baseline data through household surveys

In September 2000, as part of the Puntland health-sector rehabilitation project, Somali Red Crescent staff from Garowe and Galcaio branches, together with nursing staff and health committee elders from 12 communities where the Red Crescent's clinics are located, conducted a household survey targeting over 6,500 people. The main purpose of the survey was to provide data on socio-economic conditions of the communities serviced by the society's health service and establish their willingness to participate in running and resourcing the clinics.

The survey found that two-thirds of the population served by Red Crescent's clinics are nomadic or rural. Half the households polled stated their main income source as livestock production, while 15 per cent receive some form of remittance from relatives overseas. Livestock is used to meet the cost of purchasing food for 94 per cent of households surveyed, to fund loan repayment (89 per cent), pay for health (87 per cent), purchase clothing (86 per cent), and meet the cost of education (46 per cent). Only 14 per cent claimed to sell livestock to engage in business. This would seem to indicate that for the majority of people, livestock is a fluid asset equivalent to savings in developed countries.

Boreholes for watering camel, goat and sheep herds are often the property of the community, which charges herdsmen for each head of livestock watered, and ensures the upkeep of the facility. In villages like Qarhis, individuals own water reservoirs which capture rain and hold as much 10,000 litres. Water is sold at 10,000 somali shillings (roughly US$ 0.40) per litre to nomads with herds numbering thousands of animals.

All households surveyed were clinic users. Over half also consult traditional healers, 37 per cent seek treatment from private doctors, while 35 per cent procure medicines in pharmacies. Almost three-quarters stated they borrow to meet health needs. The key factor in their use of health facilities remains accessibility, reflecting the reality of life for a highly dispersed and nomadic population.

Over the past seven years, 71 per cent of households surveyed have used hospital services. Of these, two-thirds said their use has fallen during this period, mainly because of declining income. While this may be the reality for households relying on sale of livestock (and therefore seriously affected by the Gulf states livestock ban), it is also linked to the introduction of cost-recovery schemes: 65 per cent of respondents stated they use the hospital less since the introduction of cost recovery. Nearly two-thirds of households using the hospital have had to borrow from family, clan and friends to pay for the treatment. Of those needing hospital services, one household in eight stated they have not used the facility as they could not find money to meet the cost.

Community participation was found to be high. One in five households surveyed has at least one member belonging to committees supporting a community service. One-third of households has at least one member involved in community welfare projects such as maintaining water boreholes or restoring community buildings. Half of those engaged in projects contribute labour, while one-quarter contribute financially. Fifty per cent of those questioned state that inability to access the same service from another source is the reason for their participation. The quality of service was given as the main factor for 41 per cent of households who participate because the facility meets their needs better than existing alternatives. Consultation was another critical issue with one household in four stating that they do not participate because they were not asked.

facilitate the process of rehabilitation. In some cases, the event itself can be used to build leadership.

Independent facilitation: Planning is best facilitated by an independent multidisciplinary team with no direct involvement in the area or vested interests. This helps provide a neutral forum for debate and confidence in the outcome, particularly important in areas where conflict among neighbouring communities lingers on. It also allows the community to air their grievances and disappointments with the previous assistance provided by agencies. And it gives agencies equal ownership of the process.

Intensive work sessions: Community-based action planning should emerge from fast-pace, intensive work sessions, spanning two or three days maximum. The pace and the length of the event are important in order to sustain commitment to the event and capitalize on the emerging ideas. Findings from the event should be processed simultaneously and presented at the end of the event to be approved by the community and the participating agencies before being turned into specific projects. A carefully structured event creates a focus of community attention and provides deadlines for results. A critical mass of activity is generated which is hard to ignore, thus facilitating the participation of a wide range of people.

Realism and relevance: By addressing real and current issues and challenges of rehabilitation, the action-planning process places the community's own concerns on the agenda of agencies and builds confidence between them and the community.

Flexibility: While focusing on the need for some concrete outcomes, community action planning should be planned and run in a flexible way which allows the process to be easily adjusted to suit the needs of each particular community.

An in-depth study and community-based action-planning workshop was carried out in the Puntland village of Qarhis from February to March 2001 (see Box 3.4).

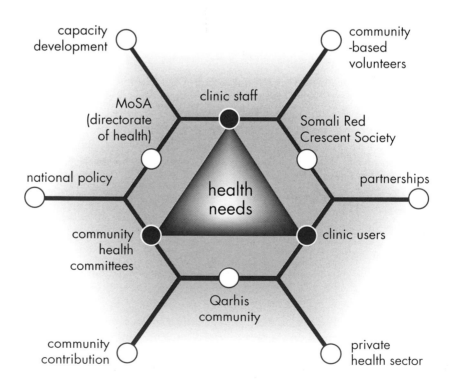

Figure 3.1
The various actors
and dimensions
of the in-depth study.

Step five: piloting strategy

The findings of the action planning event are then turned into specific project objectives with clear outcomes and inputs. When considering inputs it is important to specify:

- What the community is able to provide for itself and who within the community can do so (e.g., land, structures, finance).
- What is needed from the outside in order to kick-start the process (e.g., one-off payment, technical assistance).
- What is required to maintain and sustain the service in the future.

Mechanisms suggested by the community to generate such funds are then articulated into working plans (e.g., attaching a water point to a health project as a means of supporting the health facility by selling the water, the community offering to provide free labour to clean and guard the clinic).

An important aspect of the design of a pilot rehabilitation project is to undertake a risk analysis to determine the likelihood and the impact of various risks on the progress of the project. This analysis will help determine the types of risks that will have to be given priority in terms of mitigation investment.

For piloting to be effective:

- Draw up and share clear plans with community representatives; this helps institute a culture of accountability.
- Discuss plans with local authorities to gain their support.
- Discuss plans with other relief and development agencies working in the area to ensure coordination.
- Establish a joint management committee, comprising community representatives and technical experts (agency staff).
- Keep a continuous record of the programme's progress.
- Ensure the committee provides continuous monitoring of the pilot project.
- Give the pilot project a minimum of 12 months to produce results.
- Evaluate the project and distil lessons jointly with the community and the original facilitation team.

In the Puntland health-sector rehabilitation project, Qarhis village has been selected for a pilot project from April 2001 to March 2002 (see Box 3.4).

Step six: design policy guidelines

For rehabilitation intervention to be effective, findings from the pilot study should be fed into both policy and programme simultaneously. The dangers of not doing so are obvious: root causes of rehabilitation failures will be ignored. When transferring lessons learnt into policy, the various constraints that can often lead to policy failure should be kept in mind:

- poor problem definition;
- ambiguous and inconsistent objectives;
- failure in the implementation process;
- absence of 'bottom-up', community-building/capacity-building strategies;

■ issues of programme ownership;
■ lack of support from affected groups and NGOs; and
■ unstable and uncertain socio-economic situations.

Box 3.4 Qarhis: in-depth study and pilot project

Fostering participation and a sense of ownership by the local community are vital aspects for the success of any pilot project. Consequently the process of selecting a community in which to carry out an in-depth study, prior to piloting a rehabilitation project, began by looking at existing patterns of participation in community services across the 12 Somali Red Crescent clinics in Puntland. The selected community also had to be representative of the average lifestyle as illustrated by the household survey (i.e., 50 per cent nomadic population) and had to reflect the degree of isolation faced by most of the clinics' communities (i.e., two to three hours' walk from the nearest alternative health facility).

A shortlist of four communities was drawn-up, and Qarhis, a village 135 km north-east of Garowe, was selected. The village has 463 houses, the majority of which are stone-built. Its population is around 5,500, half of whom are nomadic. The clinic continues to serve vulnerable members of the population, especially nomads, who walk up to six hours to seek out clinic services because they are provided free of charge. Owing to access problems, however, use of the clinic and vaccination coverage are lowest amongst this most vulnerable group. Vaccination problems are exacerbated by irregular vaccine supply and the absence of a refrigerator to ensure a cold chain.

During the course of the in-depth study, it became clear that the introduction of user fees is *not* the way to increase community participation in the running and resourcing of local health services. Such an approach would spread vulnerability through increased borrowing for health care, resulting in greater indebtedness and entrenched poverty. User fees would also compound poor health by increasing patronage of traditional healers and unqualified 'pharmacists'. The admi-nistrative workload associated with the blanket imposition of user fees would be impractical within current staffing levels, in addition to raising concerns regarding accountability. Given the highly dispersed and nomadic character of the

population, any attempt to means-test patients to determine vulnerability would be difficult, if not impossible.

Nevertheless, Qarhis has a sound socio-economic base, centred on livestock production, lobster fishing and the sale of water to nomads. This diversification of income provides a safety net, at the community level, against the consequences of drought. Clan mechanisms respond well to requests for assistance and support for vulnerable people.

The study found that, taken collectively, the community has the assets, the ability and the willingness to participate in the resourcing and running of local health services. However, in return for their participation, the community indicated their desire to see an improvement in the quality and range of services provided. Observation of staff practice and study of clinic records indicated some instances of inappropriate prescribing, in addition to diagnosis and prescription for absent patients, highlighting the need for training and supervision to improve the quality of clinic services. Likewise, the current 'one-size-fits-all' approach to clinic resupply is inadequate, and does not consider seasonal and geographical variances in clinic needs.

The clinic's lack of basic laboratory facilities means that patients needing lab tests must spend considerable time and money on journeys to and from Garowe hospital, in addition to test, consultation and medication charges on arrival. Providing primary health-care laboratory tests through the Red Crescent clinic would ensure tests are done, save patients time and money, whilst enhancing the value of existing clinic services. Lab tests are charged for at the Garowe hospital, and elsewhere in Puntland, and the community has indicated a willingness to pay for these services, if they were made available at Qarhis.

The in-depth study found that the sustainability of Qarhis clinic is a function of genuine participation in, and a sense of ownership of, the facility by the ➡

community, as well as the continued commitment of the directorate of health at the ministry of social affairs (MoSA). To maintain such ownership, the clinic must address both the needs and, to a certain extent, the aspirations of the community, and align its services with emerging governmental policies.

During the course of the week's research, a meeting was held between community leaders and senior members of the research team, at which the idea of joint participation in a community health fund (sandouq) was first proposed. Over the next two days, community leaders were left to think of the possible format for their contribution, while the research team met with representatives of MoSA and UNICEF to consider possible models for joint community, Red Crescent and MoSA cooperation. Meanwhile, community leaders consulted with the wider network of 17 sub-clans to build consensus for whatever was agreed during the ensuing action-planning day.

On 8 March 2001, a joint action-planning meeting was held at the school in Qarhis. This was attended by all members of the research team, community leaders, representatives of youth and women's organizations, village and health committee members, a representative from UNICEF and the director general of the department of health in MoSA. After much deliberation, community leaders indicated their wholehearted cooperation with the plan outlined, and committed themselves to a sandouq contribution of 15 per cent of the annual clinic budget.

In an important gesture symbolizing government cooperation with the plan, the director general pinned a one-dollar bill to a picture of a collection box drawn on the blackboard at the front of the room, to represent MoSA's commitment to cover 5 per cent of the budget. Picking up on the spirit of the meeting, other private individuals came forward to pin varying sums of money to the picture of the sandouq. Altogether six contributions were made representing the central government, local government, UNICEF, Red Crescent and the community.

Key components of the action plan were presented at a final meeting with the community the following day. The plan's overall aim is to pilot a new strategy for sustaining primary health care in Qarhis, based on a community-

assets approach to participation in the resourcing and management of the clinic. Objectives are to:

- increase the level of community participation in the running and resourcing of health service provision;
- upgrade the level and coverage of services provided;
- strengthen partnerships;
- align health service provision with emerging national and regional health policies;
- situate health service provision within the existing and emerging private health service sector; and
- promote community-based SRCS volunteer action.

The Somali Red Crescent agreed to improve on the existing clinic by establishing a cold chain for vaccines and adding a laboratory service, to be charged for. The mother-and-child health/outpatient services will continue to be provided free of charge. It was explained that the laboratory service and cold chain would require additional space and the community agreed to contribute locally available materials, water and labour. Additional work was planned to upgrade the environment around the clinic, through, for example, tree-planting.

The pilot project is based on the establishment of a community health fund or sandouq and all charges collected from patients using the new laboratory services will be paid into the sandouq. The value of the fund matches the overall cost of the clinic. In addition to their cash contribution, the community will undertake other voluntary work, including committee membership and construction work.

For a one-year pilot period (April 2001 to March 2002), contributions to the sandouq will be split among the three main partners. MoSA will contribute 5 per cent of the overall budget; the community 15 per cent; and Red Crescent and partners (World Bank, International Federation, UNICEF, WHO) 80 per cent. All partners agreed to make six months' contribution in advance.

A six-member management board was established to manage funds and ensure transparency and accountability. The community agreed to provide three members (including the chairperson); Red Crescent, two members; and MoSA, one member. If the sandouq is left with a surplus at the end of the first year, it can be carried forward for the next year or invested in additional services for the clinic as the management board sees fit.

Local ownership for sustainable recovery

Investing in rehabilitation can be a means of investing in peace, no matter how far away peace may seem. The long-term recovery of war-torn societies is dependent on increasing people's confidence in their future both at household and community levels. This is best achieved through initiating community-based rehabilitation programmes.

Timing is crucial. Rehabilitation efforts should start as soon as possible in order to minimize relief. Agencies should be looking for indicators of people starting their own processes of recovery. If programmes need to be delayed for circumstances that are more suitable than already exist, then maybe the programmes themselves are faulty. Difficult working circumstances should be seized upon as an opportunity to maintain high professional standards rather than resorting to quick fixes.

Rehabilitation interventions should take into consideration the various conceptual, programming and structural barriers that exist in the operating environment, while keeping future development firmly in sight. Programmes will only be as good as the analysis of context, actors, sectors and communities. Good analysis should prepare agencies to take one of the following decisions: gear up relief operations into rehabilitation; look for rehabilitation and development partners; or hand over the programme to local partners.

For such programmes to be sustainable, agencies need to place communities at the centre of the design and implementation processes. By working with local structures, at both community and institutional levels, agencies can create opportunities that outweigh the contextual difficulties that may exist.

Sustainable recovery is dependent on the development of local institutions. Investing in building the capacity of local institutions can overcome their perceived inefficiency. Post-conflict local institutions can only be as good as the investment made in them, whether this relates to finance, information, participation, attitude or development training. Fostering participation and a sense of ownership by the local community are vital aspects for the sustainability of rehabilitation initiatives. This in turn depends on the community's willingness to engage and their ability to contribute in cash or kind. However, in return for their participation communities usually demand improved quality and transparency.

Community-based action planning is an effective method for creating a shared long-term vision for rehabilitation and articulating the community's willingness and ability to participate. When joint action plans are reached, commitment by donors and implementers is vital. Partner local institutions and community representatives should, where appropriate, be encouraged to adopt a constructively critical approach in their demands for high standards. Funding should not be used to force local institutions into changing their agenda or compromising standards.

Major contributors to this chapter and boxes were Sultan Barakat, director of the Post-war Reconstruction and Development Unit of the University of York, UK, and Sean Deely, senior officer in post-disaster recovery at the International Federation in Geneva, members of the World Bank/International Federation Somalia Health-Sector Rehabilitation Project research team.

Sources and further information

Barakat, Sultan et al. *Urban Rehabilitation in Kabul, Bridging between Communities and Institutions.* York: University of York, 1995.

Hamdi, Nabeel. *Housing without Houses, Participation, flexibility, enablement.* London: Intermediate Technology Publications, 1995.

Leonhardt, Manuela. *Conflict Impact Assessment of EU Development Co-operation with ACP Countries: A Review of Literature and Practice.* International Alert and Saferworld, 2000.

Visman, Emman. *Co-operation with Politically Fragile Countries: Lessons from EU support to Somalia.* ECDPM Working Paper No. 66, Brussels, 1998.

Wates, Nick. *Action Planning: How to use planning weekends and urban design action teams to improve your environment.* London: The Prince of Wales's Institute of Architecture, 1996.

Wilcox, David. *Community Participation and Empowerment: Putting Theory into Practice.* Joseph Rowntree Foundation, 1994.

Web sites

International Federation **http://www.ifrc.org**
Post-war Reconstruction and Development Unit, University of York
    http://www.york.ac.uk/depts/poli/prdu/
UNICEF **http://www.unicef.org**
World Bank **http://www.worldbank.org**
World Health Organization **http://www.who.int**

Section One

Focus on recovery

Trapped in the gap – post-landslide Venezuela

Jenny Mujica is terrified of letting her three children out of her sight. They could easily plunge to their death from the fifth floor of the cement shell where they live – it has no external walls or stair railings. The Mujicas and another hundred families have been squatting in four unfinished apartment blocks by the airport, facing the Caribbean, since December 1999, when massive landslides on Venezuela's northern coast destroyed their homes.

In Vargas state alone, the landslides wiped out 5,500 homes and apartments, damaged another 25,000, and wrecked roads, hospitals, and water, sanitation and communications infrastructure. Between 80,000-100,000 people were affected. Up to 30,000 died.

Eight months after the disaster, 7,500 homeless families (over 33,000 people) still lived in makeshift shelters and squatted buildings in Vargas or in military barracks in other states. They have fallen into a gap. In jargon, it is the gap between relief and rehabilitation. In real life, it means their living conditions are appalling; their prospects for the future, uncertain. Emergency food aid has ended, yet these people have no jobs, no home, no plans and few options. One solution would be resettlement in other states – the government's preferred option. Some 5,000 families have taken it. But many who stayed in Vargas don't want to leave, however wrecked it is. They want a local solution. It is not forthcoming.

Aid flows in quickly in disasters. After the standard three-month emergency period, it dries up. Meanwhile, experts and technocrats devise long-term recovery plans that take years to materialize: infrastructure repair; low-cost housing; job recovery; reviving the local economy. But who takes care of the in-between? To provide humane solutions for disaster-affected people does not require huge funding or high technology. It does, however, require the political will to put people at the centre of disaster recovery as well as the commitment to ensure that temporary solutions do not become permanent.

Venezuela's worst disaster for a century has left many questions unanswered. Could the disaster's effects have been mitigated? What is the right balance between 'hardware' and 'software' solutions? Most pressing of all: how can the gap between immediate relief and longer-term recovery be managed? In the absence of resources or guidance, many Venezuelans are living in limbo or returning home to, literally, 'reconstruct the risk'.

La Niña triggers torrential rain

At dawn on 16 December 1999, water gushed into Jenny Mujica's brick home on a hill overlooking the port of La Guaira. In minutes it was at waist-level. She put the two toddlers on top of the fridge and held the baby up with arms stretched over her head. Grabbing an axe, her uncle smashed a hole in a wall to let the water out. As houses crumbled around them, the family fled uphill. They climbed down a day later amidst mud, boulders and wrecked homes.

Photo opposite page: In December 1999, torrential rain led to Venezuela's worst floods and mudslides for a century. Economic damage was estimated at US$ 1.9 billion.

International Federation, Venezuela 1999

Along a 52-kilometre-long strip, whole neighbourhoods had been washed away into the Caribbean or buried by walls of water, mud and boulders 15-20 metres high. Unusual rainfall triggered it. Due to the global weather phenomenon of La Niña, the high-pressure front, which usually sits over Venezuela late each year, moved north. As a result, fronts with low, water-filled clouds moved across Venezuela's northern coast. When they met the 2,700-metre-high Avila mountain range that lies between Vargas state and the capital, Caracas, the heavens opened.

In December's first fortnight, it rained eight times harder than normal. Some villages reported mudslides. Floods cut others off. From 15-16 December, two years of rain fell in just two days. Only one rainfall monitoring station was working in the area, at Maiquetia. In just one hour on 16 December, it recorded an extraordinary 72 millimetres of rain.

Maiquetia is at sea level. High on the water-saturated Avila, rainfall is on average double. Mudslides washed away topsoil and vegetation. Rainfall increased pore and hydrostatic pressure, opening cracks in the ground. Rockslides followed, with truck-size boulders and huge trees crashing down towards the Caribbean at speeds of more than 60 km an hour.

Floods and mudslides hit eight states, but Vargas suffered 80 per cent of the damage and 99 per cent of the death toll. Most of those killed were black Venezuelans, prompting one senior aid official to term it a "race disaster". In Caracas, mudslides and floods damaged highways and informal settlements on slopes, killing 59, destroying 1,842 homes and damaging a further 2,261, according to Venezuela's Civil Defence.

In the eastern part of Miranda state, El Guapo reservoir burst, releasing a wall of water 18 metres high. The wave carved a mile-wide path of destruction on its way to the ocean, flooding 30,000 hectares and demolishing 790 homes, 60 per cent of the crops, the mains water system and a key bridge. Just 50 deaths were reported, thanks largely to the governor, Enrique Mendoza, who warned people of the imminent disaster. When the dam burst, the governor flew in a helicopter ahead of the flood waters, shouting at residents through a megaphone to flee.

The United Nations' Economic Commission for Latin America and the Caribbean (ECLAC/CEPAL) estimated economic damage at US$ 1.9 billion. Of this, 30 per cent was in infrastructure – especially in water and sanitation, transport and communications – and 41 per cent in housing and education.

Disaster's unnatural root causes

Floods and landslides are not new along this coastline. Explorer Alexander von Humboldt described one such disaster which took place in 1798. In 1951, a similar rainstorm hit roughly the same area as in 1999. It was less populated then, so fewer lives were lost, but physical destruction was huge. The accounts sound eerily similar to 1999: rivers reclaim old beds that had been built on; flood waves carrying trees; and boulders wreck homes. But the memory soon faded.

Unlike other recent disasters in Latin America (for example, Hurricane Mitch), environmental degradation and mismanagement cannot be blamed for the intensity of the mudslides and flash floods in Vargas state, argues Andrew Maskrey, senior advisor for United Nations Development Programme's (UNDP) disaster recovery and reduction programme. The Avila mountain range is a protected area, free from the extensive deforestation and inappropriate land use which often intensify hydro-meteorological hazards elsewhere.

However, Venezuela's tropical weather ruthlessly exploits human failings. Slopes that were stable 30-40 years ago have become unstable over time. While the hazard was an extreme natural event, the extent of its impact was a product of the unplanned way Vargas has developed over the years.

Vargas had poverty, health and urban problems before the landslides. Heavily urbanized, the state is a narrow strip of land, squeezed between the Caribbean and the Avila mountains. It has 37 rivers and 42 canyons. On an area of 1,448 square km, Vargas had Venezuela's highest population density: over 200 inhabitants per square km, about ten times the national average.

The port, airport, fishing and tourism attracted job-seekers from all over Venezuela. The most recent national census (1990) projected 310,000 residents for 2000, and it most likely fell short. Pre-disaster official statistics show that 54 per cent of families were poor. In this fast developing region, people, rich and poor alike, built with little or no control. Squatter shanties sprang up on slippery slopes and near ravines. Upmarket high-rises and summer villas crowded onto flood plains and close to riverbanks. When a fast highway linked Caracas to the coast, Vargas became the capital's weekend playground. In 1998, Vargas acquired statehood. Its new administration was barely in place when disaster struck.

Mixed response as military move in

As the magnitude of the disaster sank in, a wave of shock swept the nation. Many individual Venezuelans, businesses and churches responded spontaneously and generously. Families sheltered homeless members and loaned money. But by the afternoon of 16 December 1999, witnesses also spoke of people coming down from the hills, like ants, crawling into broken buildings and carrying off looted goods.

The next day, Venezuelan President Hugo Chavez, a former army colonel, put the military in charge of the emergency. His government dispatched paratroopers to control the looting – by now widespread in Vargas. Military helicopters and frigates evacuated 70,000 people. Another 110,000 left by their own means. Evacuees flooded into the airport, schools and sports centres in Vargas and Caracas. From there, they moved in with relatives or into government shelters.

As more and more people were evacuated, sporadic looting continued – especially in deserted upmarket neighbourhoods. Neighbours were even reported to have looted each others' homes. One local commentator observes that looting in Venezuela is common when the opportunity arises – a kind of "impromptu redistribution of wealth".

By 13 January, 74,000 people were in civilian shelters and 55,534 in seven military bases around the country. To make room for them, the army had sent 15,000 conscripts home.

Those who favour evacuation say it was carried out quickly and efficiently by the army. But those who argue it is preferable for people to remain in their homes, whenever possible, say evacuation was unnecessary in many cases and led to looting, family separation, cultural tensions and delayed recovery. According to Joel Hirst of the non-governmental organization (NGO) World Vision, "The military organized good evacuation and registration of affected people. But when longer-term solutions were slow in coming, as with all emergencies, the military did not know how to deal with the ongoing needs of the people."

Worse still, while many soldiers acted with courage and selflessness, some committed human rights abuses, according to local human rights watchdogs. Among these, the *Defensoria del Pueblo* (ombudsman office) lists summary executions, forced disappearances, torture, rape, beatings and illegal arrests.

During the evacuation, 120 children went missing. Some fled alone when their parents died or got lost. Others were airlifted by the military without family members. They were registered at reception centres and then vanished. In the rush, some were given, without proper documentation, to foster families or orphanages. A poster with the children's faces is splashed across Venezuela. Thirteen were found – some on the streets – through a strong nationwide media campaign in September 2000.

Aid dependency delays recovery

Aid staff from NGOs and Red Cross teams arrived from all over the world and worked overtime, literally day and night, at the reception centres, shelters and barracks – driven by adrenaline and commitment. Food aid and hygiene kits were rapidly distributed. Water and sanitation were immediate priorities.

Ordinary Venezuelans responded generously to the emergency, sending truckfuls of bottled water, clothes and toys. The governor of Vargas supplied shelters with towels and bedding. Warehouses overflowed with international food aid.

Yet, argues Father Janssens, president of the NGO Sinergia, "To give and give alone encourages passivity; dependent people do not take control of their lives." Reconstruction requires the active involvement of those affected, but six months of aid created dependency among the homeless, argues Janssens. At one point, they were demanding pay to sweep the shelters. Some had jobs but didn't bother going back to them.

Because of its oil wealth, the Venezuelan government has always been paternalistic, argues Joel Hirst. "Their response in the disaster was no exception," he says. "Money was handed out for 'loans', food was given out and houses were offered with no intention of receiving payment. This has been a problem for NGOs, which are treated by the *damnificados* [the disaster-affected] in much the same way as they treat the government – simply more agencies giving money away. This has led to difficulties in executing transition projects."

"People had to be 'detoxed' from humanitarian aid," says the Spanish Red Cross's Patxi Gastaminza. Many agencies required that, to receive food aid, people should get organized into committees and help themselves. Venezuelans who stayed at home after the disaster and coped alone often proved more proactive in reconstructing their lives than those returning from shelters sustained by aid (see Box 4.1).

It was a slow process to overcome dependency on humanitarian and state aid. Politicking also affected the recovery process. "The flurry of electoral promises eroded gains in community organization," says Enfants du Monde's Sandrine Rivet. When people were promised they would be out of the shelters in three months, their interest in chores and meetings slumped. But many of them would still be languishing in shelters a year after the disaster.

Box 4.1 People-centred disaster recovery pays off

Members of the water and sanitation (watsan) team at the International Federation's delegation in Venezuela have first-hand experience of the destruction wrought by the catastrophic landslides of December 1999. One lost her father and her home. Others lost relatives. Some Red Cross staff from Vargas state had to move temporarily into the capital, Caracas. For those not evacuated, the lack of sanitation and potable water proved a major health hazard. The landslides destroyed 70 per cent of Vargas's sewerage system and badly damaged the state's water supply. Watsan became a priority in the Red Cross relief operation.

The International Federation set up an operations room for all NGOs involved in watsan at the Vargas headquarters of the local water utility, Hidroven. Previously, they had met at the Hilton hotel in Caracas. Following emergency distributions of water, the next step was to increase regular availability of potable water, in line with Sphere standards. Their approach was emphatically people-centred.

"People are part of the problem and of the solution," says Julio Rodriguez, the International Federation's watsan coordinator for Vargas. "The key is to get communities organized. We succeeded about 80 per cent and that made our job easier." For example, neighbours organized and supervised the schedules for drawing water from emergency tanks. Some were trained to operate and maintain equipment. In the badly-hit resort of Caraballeda, the community, with Red Cross help, restored and now runs a temporary gravity-fed aqueduct.

Returnees complicate the task by constantly altering beneficiary numbers. Often, returnees don't see the need to help. "They keep their old habits but we need to change our ways. It is our only hope," says Lubieska de Gutierrez, of the Neighbours Association of Corapalitos, in Vargas. Residents who stayed in Corapalitos after the disaster endured 90 days without power and 41 days without potable water. They had to work together. Volunteers from the association removed debris, collected rubbish, supervised water distributions by tanker, and attended Red Cross and Civil Defence workshops. Returnees have yet to develop this spirit of cooperation.

By October 2000, Red Cross teams were providing 200,000 litres of fresh water daily in Vargas, Miranda and Falcón states. They rebuilt aqueducts and latrines, set up a water purifying plant, restored water systems damaged by broken dams and distributed water purifying pills and 20,000 jerrycans. This reflects a two-year-old policy shift within the Red Cross in Latin America, based on the experience that potable water and sanitation are post-disaster priorities.

But hardware is only half the answer. Putting people at the centre of disaster recovery has proved crucial. As well as physical measures, Red Cross teams provided psychosocial support and a family tracing service. They organized dozens of community health and sanitation workshops and distributed health education pamphlets to 10,000 families in the three hardest-hit states. Educational material specially developed for Venezuela has been given to 2,000 schoolchildren in Vargas. More materials are being designed. And the Red Cross aim to develop youth cleaning brigades. "People need to participate," says Tim Forster, an International Federation watsan delegate, "not to be lectured."

Electioneering interferes with aid

"The worst disaster is the one that happens at election times," says Commander Angel Rangel, head of the Civil Defence. The landslides hit on the day of a constitutional referendum. Some say the government was negligent in warning residents of the impending disaster because it was busy with the crucial vote.

The new constitution mandated re-election of all political officials in May 2000, later postponed to 30 July. In the lead-up to elections, emergency aid became a political commodity, and disaster-affected people, pawns in the campaign.

A personal and political feud between the governor of Vargas, Alfredo Laya, and President Hugo Chavez hampered relief and recovery efforts. "Personal and professional jealousy between Laya and the president delayed aid," admits Antonio Rodriguez San Juan, Vargas's new governor.

The alliance of Governor Laya's small leftist party with the president's 23-party coalition had turned sour before the landslides. The first clash occurred when Chavez put the army in charge of the emergency. Laya complained that civil society and his authority were sidelined. While Laya campaigned on the back of his relief efforts, Chavez responded by withholding central government's emergency funds from the stricken state.

After four months of consuming his own state's reserves, the Vargas governor had to trim or cancel relief programmes. One casualty was the popular cash-for-work clean-up brigades where homeless people could earn 35,000 bolivares (US$51) a week. Subsequently, however, Laya was investigated for misappropriating over US$ 500,000 before leaving office.

Aid organizations were caught in the political crossfire. All NGOs interviewed said that working in Vargas was problematic. Directives on priorities and rebuilding were confusing, while administrative delays were frequent at all levels. And there were many levels: the president, the military, state bureaucracies, the planning authority, the governor, the mayors, corporate philanthropic foundations, donors and residents.

"The sad reality is that we wanted to work in Vargas and we couldn't," says Nattacha Jauregui, the local coordinator for World Vision. "NGOs should be above the politics but we aren't."

In contrast, in neighbouring Miranda state, the governor welcomed NGOs. Perhaps because, coming from one of the traditional parties that oppose Chavez, and in his second term as governor, he did not expect much help from central government. Moreover, rural Miranda has many years' experience of community associations and development work. Local NGOs like CESAP, an umbrella group of 32 Catholic groups, have set up community groups.

European interests in Miranda, where El Guapo dam will eventually be rebuilt at a cost of US$ 30 million, also played a part. As did the need to show quick results to donors before the next emergency elsewhere. As a result, many NGOs flocked to Miranda. The needs were larger and more complex in Vargas, but red tape and politicking made working there much harder, hampering rehabilitation.

Chavez' coalition won Vargas in the July 2000 elections. A week after the vote, Vargas's new governor was visiting shelters and promising 3,000 new homes by the end of the year. Soon aid started flowing again. More trucks and bulldozers appeared on the streets. Mobile health clinics visited shelters and squatted buildings, like Jenny Mujica's. "This is the first time we've seen them here," she said, eight months after the disaster.

Techno focus fails to tackle human misery

On 15 December 1999, President Chavez, appearing on television, quoted national hero Simon Bolivar, "If nature opposes our will, we shall fight her and make her obey us." That night, the Avila mountains exploded.

The quote, emblazoned on the headquarters of the Civil Defence in Caracas, dates from Bolivar's attempt to cross the Andes in the mid-19th century. Its spirit still seeps through today's response to the disaster: the emergency as a military logistical exercise; floods and landslides as a technical problem; human and social issues treated in a techno-centric way.

Venezuela's plans for long-term transformation of the stricken states are no exception. In January 2000, the government appointed a team of experts, led by the minister for science and technology, to design a master plan for Vargas. The vision of *Autoridad Unica de Vargas*, later restructured as CorpoVargas, is to rebuild the coastal strip as Caracas's weekend playground. But its slick computer graphics of pleasant apartments and palm-clad seaside promenades clash with the stark reality on the ground.

Venezuela: states affected by the December 1999 disaster.

While the government has taken measures to relocate those families left homeless or at risk from disaster to other states, some argue that the poorest people who remain in Vargas are not represented in the state's reconstruction. "Noticeably absent from these plans are solutions for the slum-dwellers whose barrios cover the hills," says World Vision's Joel Hirst. "They are simply left out." Hirst says that if reconstruction of Vargas as a resort is successful, it will generate jobs, but adds, "These decisions are being made from Caracas and not taking into account the inhabitants of the state. The people are seen as a secondary concern, placed beside the need to rehabilitate Vargas as a resort town."

Are there channels for regular interaction of planners with local residents? Looks of incomprehension greet this question at the oil industry's glamorous research institute in Caracas where CorpoVargas is headquartered. "Oh, there is an office at the airport where people can go," says a spokeswoman vaguely. And why is CorpoVargas in Caracas? One of several undamaged hotels in Vargas could be its headquarters and the trickle down would boost the local economy.

Disaster-affected people themselves seem low on the recovery agenda. Even the United Nations' (UN) damage assessment study, published by CEPAL in March 2000, uses circumlocutions. Among the report's 24 recommendations (which include a botanical registry, soil map, impact on marine life, beach erosion, seismic micro-zoning, and carbon-14 dating to estimate periodicity of landslides), only one deals with people. It recommends action "to reduce anthropic actions on river beds and ravines and their effects on slope instability".

According to UN sources, after heated discussions, CEPAL deleted references to affected people from the final version of the study because government officials resented its mild criticism of their resettlement policy. The removed text had warned that Afro-Venezuelans – a large part of Vargas's population – have strong family ties and that their social fabric and cultural identity should be respected in any resettlement scheme.

Large-scale engineering works following the disaster were impressive. Hundreds of machines toiling around-the-clock took eight months to remove 6 million of the estimated 15 million tonnes of debris in Vargas, opened roads, excavated river channels and reinforced mountain dykes. But, says UNICEF officer Carlos Luis Rivero, "The government gives priority to road rehabilitation and less to social issues." In June 2000, Rivero coordinated a survey among 1,184 families in 37 makeshift shelters and among 11,550 families living in the three worst-hit neighbourhoods of Vargas.

In the latter, 61 per cent of families lived in houses with structural or minor damage. Over half lacked potable water and adequate disposal of solid and human waste. Among one-third of families, three to eight people were sharing a room.

Conditions were worse in the crowded warehouses and dilapidated factories used as shelters. Some had one toilet for 120 individuals. Others only got partitions for privacy six months after the disaster. Women in these warehouses had to carry sticks and pipes to protect themselves from the advances of *malandros* living in the same shelters.

UNICEF reports that the majority of people surveyed were living in extreme poverty, with 50 per cent unemployment and high rates of teenage pregnancy (one in ten in shelters). Enfants du Monde links poor conditions and accumulated uncertainty over the future with rising rates of rape, domestic violence, child prostitution and drug abuse in shelters. Says UNICEF, "Six months after the tragedy, living conditions in Vargas are still highly precarious."

Relocation needs rethinking

By August 2000, conditions in shelters and squats remained appalling: overcrowded, with poor hygiene and sanitation, and often plain dangerous, as in the case of Jenny Mujica. Abandoning people to such squalor is not, of course, government policy. But, as Miguel Rosales Ruiz, director of EFIP (a local NGO working with shelter communities) points out, "not solving problems in shelters is a way of putting pressure on people to leave the state". To decongest Vargas, the government favours relocation to less populated states. Their approach to resettlement is essentially to tell people, "It is bad here and it will be better there, so move."

"The government wanted to take advantage of the disaster as an opportunity to transfer people from the densely populated coast in order to accelerate the development of sparsely populated, rural areas in the south. This was based on a pre-existing plan for territorial development," says

Box 4.2 Resettlement update – February 2001

In February 2001, *Fondo Unico Social* (FUS), the Venezuelan government institution that deals with *damnificados* (the disaster-affected), said that no shelters are left in Vargas state. There are only *auto albergues* (self-shelters) where people rent a room or house, and 'solidarity refuges', where people are guests with family or friends. A complex of new homes for *damnificados* is being built in Vargas. By January 2001, 120 units had been finished and handed over to their new owners, and 500 more will be finished soon. More are planned, but no dates are given.

Homes built and handed over in states other than Vargas include 12,575 units for poor people and 480 units for middle-class people. Finally, says FUS, the relationship between affected people and the government has improved, thanks to the *Dignidad 2000* scheme, which convinced people in Vargas to move to other states.

Commenting on FUS's update, EFIP, a Venezuelan NGO very active among the *damnificados*, says that, while President Chavez fulfilled his promise of emptying the shelters by 16 December 2000, this came with hidden costs for those resettled. In some cases, says EFIP, *damnificados* were shown photos of model homes and accepted to relocate. But they were then given half-finished houses, without toilets or sinks, because of the government's haste to meet the relocation deadline. The first groups relocated more or less willingly, but the last families were pressured badly, says EFIP.

New settlements are often far from towns, work opportunities, schools and health clinics. Of those relocated, around 80 per cent lack jobs and still depend on food aid from FUS, which is gradually being phased out. Although the resettled were promised school places, about 40 per cent of their children do not attend school for lack of places or money for transport. Says Miguel Rosales, EFIP's coordinator, "The needs of youth, and of all people, are not taken into account by the authorities." He says local people resent the newcomers and accuse them of bringing with them drugs and prostitution.

UNDP's Andrew Maskrey. "From a technical standpoint, if this could be achieved it could potentially reduce future vulnerability to disaster on the coast."

But people are more than just demographic statistics, who can be moved at will from one region to another, argues Maskrey. The people of Vargas have a sophisticated urban culture, social networks and way of life configured around the service industries of the coastal strip. Adds Maskrey, "Imagine what would happen if you tried to take a group of city taxi drivers and set them up as hill farmers!"

As of August 2000, some 5,000 families were resettled and the government grandly promised 22,000 new houses across the country by the end of the year. In October, President Chavez pledged that not one family would remain in shelters or barracks by 16 December, one year after the landslides. He kept his promise, but at a price. According to one NGO, some families were pressured to move and about 80 per cent of those resettled lack jobs, leaving them reliant on government food hand-outs (see Box 4.2).

The resettled get a 70-square-metre home, equipped for free with a fridge, TV, fan, furniture, mattresses, linen and a one-month supply of groceries. In one year they start paying for the house – if they can earn an income. But unhappy settlers have staged demonstrations protesting at a lack of jobs in their remote locations. The houses look neat on aerial photos. The Red Cross, however, found new houses in Zulia state without sewerage and with salty tap water, which causes diarrhoea. The president of the National Housing Council blames corrupt builders from the previous government for such problems.

A survey by *Fondo Unico Social* (FUS), the state body responsible for the homeless, showed that, in the aftermath of the disaster, 80 per cent of disaster-affected people did not want to stay in Vargas. With time, the mood changed. An unknown number of the 5,000 or more resettled families are trickling back to Vargas – to their damaged homes in Carmen de Uria, for example (see Box 4.3). Adults return while children remain in the new settlements with a spouse or relatives.

The very fact that authorities considered relocation shows they are trying to deal with the problems of overcrowding and disaster risk. And safe building land in Vargas is in such short supply that resettlement may be the only option. But NGOs are concerned that relocation has not been carried out sensitively enough. World Vision's Joel Hirst says, "The people who live in Vargas's slums are considered inferior. Therefore they can be

The coastal state of Vargas was worst hit by mudslides and floods: the state suffered 80 per cent of the damage and 99 per cent of the death toll.
International Federation, Venezuela 1999

Box 4.3 Reconstructing risk in Carmen de Uria

"Carmen de Uria will never die" is spray-painted across the village. The graffiti jostles for space with the black letters "XXDC" (signifying 'to be demolished') daubed on every building by the Civil Defence.

Once a charming village of some 700 houses, today Carmen de Uria, in Venezuela's Vargas state, looks like a postcard from Angola or Chechnya – a shattered core with just a handful of houses still standing.

On 16 December 1999, the swollen Uria stream broke out of a man-made channel along the western hillside and regained its former bed across the town centre. A 15-metre-high wall of water and mud carrying huge boulders and trees swept through the town. The church, two-thirds of the houses and perhaps 800 people were washed away. Where pastel-coloured houses with bougainvillea once stood, now the Uria flows along an eight-metre-deep gorge.

The authorities ruled out rebuilding the village, wedged in a narrow canyon (400 metres at its widest), between steep, unstable slopes prone to mudslides in the rainy season. It is dangerous and it would be too costly to make it safe. "Carmen de Uria is a trap," says geologist Rodolfo Sanzio.

To reinforce the slopes or to rebuild the town on a *meseta* (a flat terrace of land) high on the eastern hillside is expensive for the government but not, perhaps, for a tourist developer. Residents suspect a beach-and-mountain hotel is planned and they are angry. Stubbornly, 150 families will not budge.

"To persuade them requires a lot of social work and a new home," says Josefina Baldo, president of the National Housing Council.

Meetings with authorities have been few and tense. "We want to be part of decision-making, not sidelined," says Julio Diaz, a builder, resident for 37 years, and chairman of the neighbours' association.

Since Carmen de Uria is on 'death row', services have not been restored. "It's gradual intimidation to leave," says Diaz. Residents improvise. Plastic tubes bring clean water from a mountain source. A generator provides energy. Neighbours sweep streets and bury rubbish. Two volunteer teachers tutor 60 children.

Many residents who fled to other states are trickling back, to their homes if not too ruined, otherwise as caretakers or squatters.

Mariela Rodriguez, 36, her unemployed husband and their nine children spent three months at a military barracks in another state. Fed up, they returned to a wrecked, mosquito-infested home hanging precariously on a slope. The Uria flows below. Across the narrow road, all the houses were destroyed. The cash-for-cleaning brigades ended in June 2000 and free food aid finished in July. Now the Rodriguez family fish and pick bananas. Neighbours and relatives help.

Edgar Mejias, a waiter, is shovelling dry mud 1.5 metres high that filled up his house. "I clean, repair and wait," he says. Eight months after the disaster, Carmen de Uria awaits its fate while its people are rebuilding the risk.

The pain of people here is deep and moving, and probably without a solution to their liking. But in the absence of any dialogue with the authorities, villagers remain defiant. "I was born here and I will die here," says one piece of graffiti. It could become true too soon.

sent somewhere that people sending them would never live. They were treated like cattle instead of like real Venezuelan citizens."

Employment gap

Why are people returning to their disaster-prone old homes? Unemployment in the areas where they were relocated is the main reason. Earning an income is clearly one of the best, and most obvious, ways to recover from disaster.

"In international responses to disasters… job recovery is neglected by governments, donors and people, and it is a mistake," says Alfredo Lazarte Hoyle, senior officer in charge of socio-economic reintegration of crisis-affected groups at the recovery and reconstruction department of the International Labour Organization (ILO).

Lazarte Hoyle says that informal settlements and crime often increase after a disaster. In the developing world, most disaster-affected people have little or no savings, social security, safety net or formal jobs. "What can they do?" he asks.

Local economic recovery is often seen as dependent on macroeconomic recovery – which can take years. This is why the ILO proposed a more quick-footed job-recovery plan for Vargas and Miranda states. It recommended local procurement of building materials, a labour-intensive approach to rebuilding, and extending small-scale tourism to Miranda state, based on partnerships between the public and private sector. "Self-building schemes and recovery of both family and local economy are so small-scale that they cannot be catered for by the public sector alone through large agencies and state control," says Lazarte Hoyle.

However, over a year after the disaster, no donor had stepped forward to fund the ILO's proposed contribution to local economic recovery. Nor did the government seem interested in job creation in Vargas. The opportunity for applying the resources that flow after a disaster to reactivate the local economy and recover jobs had been lost.

Damnificados voice demands

Employment in Vargas is just one of many demands of the homeless, who believe they are entitled to a local solution. "To rebuild Vargas should not entail kicking us out," says Jodely Palacios, coordinator of one of 37 shelters in Vargas.

Box 4.4 Ideas to fill the gap

Disaster experts, NGOs and residents of Vargas came up with these suggestions which the government and humanitarian agencies could consider as measures to fill the gap:

- Rent an undamaged private golf club and build a camp of prefabricated houses, with clean water and sanitation, so that people could live in decent conditions while waiting for relocation or new land-use regulations to take effect.
- Give financial incentives to businesses to reopen small factories in Vargas.
- Bringing work closer to shelters would avoid transport problems.
- Recreate the social context in shelters as soon as possible: schools; jobs; work brigades.
- Organize women for day-care and unemployed graduates for tutoring schoolchildren in shelters.
- Reserve for locals a quota of jobs with companies clearing debris and rebuilding infrastructure.

- Organize specialized work brigades to employ people's existing skills more productively.
- Keep neighbours in the same shelters. Maintain the social fabric in shelters and build upon it
- Use 'waiting time' productively: skills training; education; community organization.
- Provide psychosocial support, preferably in groups.
- Use boats or rent out bicycles for transport along the coastline while the road is poor. Due to bad roads, public transport fares tripled.
- Reopen the seaside highway quickly to encourage weekend tourism and revitalize the economy.
- Before implementing any projects, listen to affected people, help them articulate their needs and visions, and inform them quickly of any decisions which may affect them.
- While implementing any projects, coordination and a shared vision between all actors is essential.

After three meetings to exchange experiences, shelter committees in Vargas merged in May 2000 into the Association of *Damnificados*, comprising 1,076 families. In September, all the *damnificados* held a national meeting to coordinate their demands. They identified short-term needs, such as improving life in shelters, and long-term needs, such as new homes and jobs, and then discussed possible solutions.

Short-term proposals include specialized cash-for-work brigades, instead of having a dozen people to sweep one block or carry rocks, regardless of their skills. Another idea is for unemployed graduates to tutor children. Due to slow rehabilitation, schools are overcrowded. Shifts are only two hours, lowering academic results and posing childcare problems. Jenny Mujica, for example, could not join the work brigades because of reduced school hours and lack of crèches (see Box 4.4).

For housing in Vargas, members found ten plots, either state-owned or available to buy or expropriate. Instead of the rows and rows of matchbox houses in empty treeless spaces, which government resettlement schemes have created in other states, the association proposed building small clusters of houses through self-help. This would involve training families in construction skills so they are involved in building their own homes. In self-help schemes, says EFIP's Miguel Rosales, "People start to own their homes and visualize a community."

To draw attention to their plight, the association blocked roads in Vargas and marched into Caracas. Since June 2000, weekly meetings between authorities and the association have taken place. "They [the *damnificados*] have learned to negotiate and that they have the right to discuss their problems with authorities on an equal footing," says Rosales.

One problem was the low level of government staff at meetings, at least before the elections. "We only see the clowns, never the circus' owners," says Shelter 23's Jodely Palacios. At least the homeless in Vargas have turned the technocratic monologue into a dialogue. They now have a voice – but will it be heard?

Reconstructing the risk

Many of the disaster-affected, however, have become fed up with life in makeshift shelters or in remote states where they have been relocated. They cannot wait any longer in limbo, while the authorities debate policies and design long-term master plans. In the absence of clear land-use regulations and guidance from municipal authorities, they have returned to the scene of the disaster to rebuild their old homes. They are, literally, reconstructing the risk.

"In March I saw people repainting homes by the ravines," says Virginia Jimenez, a geographer working on a risk map for Vargas with World Bank funds. "A minimum delimitation of risk areas is needed quickly because we are rebuilding vulnerability." But who's there to stop rebuilding the risk? "The ministries, the mayors, the builders, and the people, and everybody must help in not reconstructing it," she argues.

Recurrent storms and landslides underscore the need for urgent action. In November 2000, torrential rains once again lashed the Venezuelan coast, leaving at least 3,000 people homeless, damaging agricultural land and destroying communications. In just one neighbourhood of

Vargas, 40 families left homeless by the 1999 disaster were living in a temporary shelter which was itself swept away by the November mudslides.

The Venezuelan government is aware of the risk, as shown by its resettlement policy. Every time a storm destroys homes, President Chavez and Commander Rangel visit the stricken areas or feature in the media, urging people to evacuate. But this is easier said than done. "They move us up and down like we're elevators," retorted 80-year-old Giorgina Morjan to a reporter of the Associated Press.

Move to other states where there are no jobs or networks of friends and family? Stay in a military camp, dependent on aid handouts? Perch on the fifth floor of a half-finished apartment block? Or return 'home' and rebuild what's left of what was before, in the path of future disaster? Not an inspiring range of choices – no wonder thousands of Venezuelans feel trapped or manhandled.

The gap in which disaster-affected people find themselves has many dimensions. It stretches between immediate relief and longer-term recovery; between the destitute and the authorities or agencies tasked to deal with them; between technical hardware approaches to recovery and softer people-sensitive solutions; between the moment disaster strikes and the time when those stuck in shelters have a secure home and job once more.

The Venezuelan government saw disaster response as a military-style logistical exercise. They see rehabilitation as repairing infrastructure. And recovery as a macro-level problem that requires technical solutions implemented by bureaucratic machineries. But such a 'hardware'-only approach means that the people hardest hit by the disaster are often not consulted when recovery plans are laid.

Meanwhile, donor-driven funding schedules, typically requiring relief funds to be spent within three months, put pressure on NGOs to pursue short-term projects not necessarily in line with what was most needed. "The inflexibility of the emergency time frame does not take into account the magnitude of the disaster, the urban disorder and political problems in Vargas," says Professor Mario Fagiolo, of the Italian NGO *Movimiento de Laicos para America Latina* (Lay Movement for Latin America).

Both governments and international agencies need to rethink their post-disaster responses, argues UNDP's Andrew Maskrey, "There is a gap: the relief stops, but reconstruction is too often understood solely as the national-level, formal-sector planning exercise. Often six months to a year or more go by between the disaster and the implementation of reconstruction plans and projects, funded by the international development banks. People don't and can't wait that long. At the local level people begin rebuilding their lives and livelihoods days, sometimes hours after disaster strikes. They aren't interested in relief then – they're interested in recovering. That is when people need technical assistance and orientation to use disaster as an opportunity to reduce their future vulnerability and risk."

But, adds Maskrey, "That opportunity is lost because no one is working with them at that time, except to offer relief. Without that assistance, while the national-level planning and programming process drags on, people are already reconstructing the risk of the next disaster."

This failure to put people at the centre of disaster recovery is aggravated by the financial gap in international aid. For donors and charities, emergency aid has glamour, media impact and quick, tangible results – and therefore attracts funds rapidly. Further downstream, long-term recovery projects bring measurable development and, possibly, contracts for businesses from donor nations. And large-scale reconstruction attracts large-scale loans from the international financial institutions.

But transitional aid – the aid needed to help people like Jenny Mujica back on her feet – has less media appeal, more complications and thus attracts less funding. Some NGOs in Venezuela, for example, reported problems in securing funds for hard-to-quantify projects such as organizing people in shelters to lobby for improved living conditions.

The idea that people like Jenny Mujica or Jodely Palacios should live in limbo, dependent on government-delivered aid and internationally-brokered reconstruction projects is flawed. The period of recovery, which starts just hours or days after the disaster, provides an unrivalled opportunity not merely to rehabilitate what was there before, but to improve on it. Delay simply squanders that opportunity.

Maskrey identifies the two key disaster recovery challenges as:
- accelerating local-level reconstruction, in parallel with national-level planning, in order to close the 'gap'; and
- injecting risk reduction into all aspects of the recovery process.

Yet the types of post-disaster damage assessment which international agencies engage in are not sufficiently orientated towards risk reduction. "The whole logic of calculating down to the last dollar everything that was destroyed is based on a logic of justifying an international loan to rebuild what was there before," argues Maskrey. "That logic needs to be questioned. I would prefer a focus on reducing future risks, rather than on reconstruction per se, and that requires a very different approach to impact assessment."

Reducing and spreading risk

Risk reduction has many components, of which improved physical infrastructure to try and prevent future disasters is just a part. More emphasis needs to be placed on 'software' measures, such as sharing information with those at risk on how to mitigate and prepare for the effects of disaster. "Actions to date are based on risk mapping and widening of channels for greater flows, but people need to learn how to react in emergencies," argues Venezuelan geologist Rodolfo Sanzio (see Box 4.5).

"The magnitude of the disaster was not foreseen by the national authorities… There wasn't a preparedness plan in place in the affected areas," says Maskrey. Strengthening local capacities for disaster risk management is a crucial part of the recovery process, he argues. "If highly vulnerable communities had had local contingency and risk reduction plans, complemented by appropriate early warning capabilities, then much of the loss of life that occurred in December 1999 in Venezuela could have been avoided," he wrote, a month after the disaster.

Box 4.5 Communities learn to map risk and response

Venezuela's disastrous storms of December 1999 laid bare the lamentable lack of preparedness for a country that sits astride four seismic faults and suffers innumerable tropical rainstorms and cyclones. "Neither the government, nor state agencies, nor citizens have a culture of prevention," says Commander Angel Rangel, head of the Civil Defence (CD).

Venezuela's main problems are its "lack of detailed risk and vulnerability assessments...of reliable early warning and alert systems; ineffective communications strategy and arrangements to trigger quick and effective response to natural disasters," says a World Bank project document.

To boost local people's capacity for self-protection and help them discover both their risks and resources, the Civil Defence has embarked on something entirely new to Venezuela – community risk education. The hardest-hit state of Vargas has been divided into 40 zones. In each zone, CD teams meet with community leaders. "First we listen to them," says CD engineer Luz Gamarra. Locals know a lot about where, how and why disasters happen.

Together with CD staff, community leaders walk around the neighbourhood, identifying risky houses, evacuation routes, shelters, helicopter-landing sites, alternative water and power supplies, pharmacies and food shops, homes of nurses and paramedics. Then residents plot this information on detailed local maps (provided by the Civil Defence) which remain at the nearest school. Community leaders share this information with neighbours. Many are eager to learn.

Some, especially the elderly, show resistance, fearing it brings bad luck to talk of future disasters. Others fear eviction. "We first make it clear we are not here to evict anybody"" says CD engineer Crisanto Silva.

"The best preparation is to be organized. This is new for us," says Marisela Blanco, a civil servant and community leader in Macuto, an area badly hit by the landslides. The Civil Defence's approach is low-cost and low-tech. Locals learn to measure rain with a simple *pluviometro* (rain gauge) made of a two-litre plastic bottle with a funnel and a measurement cup. Danger levels must be reported to the Civil Defence by telephone or radio. A vertical pole sunk into rivers and channels measures rising waters. Danger levels set off an alarm.

As residents of Caraballeda found out last June, a floating log can set off the siren. Soon a crowd had assembled at the church, complete with suitcases, identity papers, blankets and bags of food. Amid laughter and relieved anxiety, Blanco explained it was a false alarm. "It shows we've learned the lesson," she says.

The CD teams return periodically to do refresher training. They also receive and channel complaints – about, for example, rubbish collection or drainage – to relevant authorities. "Governments only throw money at prevention for a short time after a disaster," complains Silva. But following the catastrophe, the Civil Defence received US$ 80 million from the government to buy equipment, pay new staff, and set up disaster preparedness programmes nationwide – as much as their budgets over the last 37 years combined.

The problem is that physical reconstruction is big business, and many players – from governments, to local authorities, to commercial contractors, to cash-strapped humanitarian organizations – are attracted by the resources available and want a slice of the action. Software measures like local disaster risk management look good on paper, but don't attract big investments and therefore remain in the realm of theory.

"In Venezuela," adds Manuel Santana of USAID's Office of Foreign Disaster Assistance disaster mitigation team, "disaster mitigation is driven very much by fads. After an earthquake, everybody wants earthquake mitigation strategies. Yet after a short time this fades until a mudslide and then everybody wants mudslide mitigation. We need to have a sustainable and integral process of mitigation that is followed through in governmental and civil sectors."

Spreading risk through insurance is one solution for mitigating the effects of disasters. Yet even though the 1999 disaster hit many middle-class apartment owners in Vargas very hard, few were able to 'transfer' the costs of recovery onto insurance companies. CEPAL reports that only 12 per cent of cars and less than 1 per cent of homes in Venezuela were insured against natural disasters. Even the UNDP expert on disaster prevention and the president of the Vargas Red Cross had not insured their apartments in Vargas.

"Premiums are steep and we lack a culture of insurance in Venezuela," says UNDP's Enrique Gajardo. Adds David Meneses, president of the Vargas branch of the Venezuelan Red Cross, "We believe that Daddy God is always on our side. We are not well prepared for disasters."

Ongoing disaster

Venezuela's ongoing, invisible disaster is this lack of disaster preparedness and risk-aware regulations. Disasters expose and magnify existing structural problems, such as the lack of land-use planning and building controls. And, as Krishna Vatsa and Frederick Krimgold point out in a recently published World Bank document, "Governments cannot… shift their primary responsibilities. They are required to make certain long-term investments for hazard mitigation and habitat improvement… Governments also have the primary mitigation responsibility of enforcing land use regulations and building codes, and carry out a mandatory planning role."

Land-use planning in Venezuela is presently either non-existent or disregarded. "Corruption and permissiveness among politicians are responsible for this free building," says Commander Rangel. "Mayors and governors should control it even if it costs them votes." Adds Virginia Jimenez: "Evicting people does not win votes but government cannot be an accomplice of this process [of unplanned building]."

The state is the largest landowner. But successive populist governments have turned a blind eye to infractions, according to Nancy de Cabrera, an urban planner with CorpoVargas, "Nothing illegal is ever fined or demolished in Venezuela," she says. Vargas lacks a land and building register. Only four cities have a municipal urban development plan. Under political or financial pressure, city councillors may resist or change zoning and land use.

Civil Defence estimates that 4 million people (over 17 per cent of Venezuela's population) live in risk-prone areas, 1 million of them in Caracas. In every rainy season, mudslides claim dozens of lives, livelihoods and homes. Between 1984-1999, just one municipality in Caracas recorded 674 floods and landslides, affecting 11,265 families. In August 1993, tropical storm Bret destroyed 196 houses, damaged another 885 and killed 84 people in Caracas alone.

Ongoing problems, according to the Civil Defence, include:
- homes which are built on unstable terrain;
- disregard for zoning or building codes;
- lack of public services or systematic maintenance of drainage network;
- drainage channels which carry raw sewage and rubbish thrown by residents; and
- risk-taking among people who settle on riverbanks and canyons.

Sorting out this chaos is a long-term, complex task, which will probably prove unpopular. As poverty rises in Venezuela, so has rural-urban migration. This flow is hard to reverse. People object to leaving cities with more job opportunities and neighbourhoods where they have social, cultural and economic ties.

Re-zoning Vargas and enforcing land-use planning will reduce risk but it was unlikely before the elections. "The government did not want to pay that political cost in Vargas," says the Spanish Red Cross's Patxi Gastaminza. Lack of clear zoning directives has hampered Red Cross rehabilitation projects and reconstruction in general. With the elections behind, it is hoped that CorpoVargas will issue zoning directives.

Dilemmas for international agencies

With such macro issues as land-use planning, poverty, economic diversity and political will to deal with, there is no limit to the extent that vulnerability could be reduced. How far should humanitarian agencies go in dealing with these issues – issues which are ultimately the host government's responsibility?

Venezuela is not one of the world's poorest countries – per capita gross national product was US$ 3,690 in 1999. Poverty, however, has spread during the 1990s – 52 per cent of all households were considered below the national poverty line in 1999, against 34 per cent in 1990. This runs counter to prevailing poverty reduction trends in Latin America. Yet Venezuela's revenues were boosted in 2000 by record prices for oil, which accounts for 80 per cent of exports and half of government income. During the same week that the UN/CEPAL report estimated total damage from the 1999 disaster at US$ 1.9 billion, Venezuela's state-owned oil company announced a US$ 2.1 billion profit. So one could argue that the government is perfectly capable of resourcing its own reconstruction and recovery projects, without external assistance.

That is, in part, what it did. When the World Bank offered to reallocate US$ 150 million of development assistance for emergency purposes, Venezuela turned it down – apart from US$ 1.5 million for risk mapping. Yet Caracas also denied Vargas's governor the money to respond to the disaster because of political differences. And pursued techno-centric relocation and reconstruction schemes which failed to put people at the centre of the recovery process.

What role can humanitarian agencies play, faced with a catastrophe in a country with rising oil revenues and rising poverty, run by a powerful centralized administration? Many organizations found themselves forced by politics to ignore the greater needs in Vargas and seek opportunities elsewhere. But should agencies give in so easily to the 'tarmac bias', seeking out aid-friendly environments where projects and donor money come quicker? Or do humanitarians not have a moral duty to expose the political and economic failings which turn the natural hazard into *un*/natural disaster? World Vision's Joel Hirst points out that "it is very difficult for an international NGO, entering a country and just learning its laws and intricacies, to stand up against the host government".

Yet, at least humanitarian organizations have a responsibility to advocate for people-sensitive disaster recovery – and to make their aid conditional on such priorities. To act as the counterweight of humanity in the scales of post-disaster reconstruction which are so often tipped towards technological, hardware solutions. In a disaster of such scale and complexity, a gap between relief and recovery is to be expected – planning and financing major reconstruction takes time. But the gap should not be ignored – people have a right to transitional solutions with decent conditions.

If the disaster-affected were given a better idea of how long they may have to remain in shelters, they could form plans – demand and make improvements in temporary infrastructure, invest in some kind of community life. If re-zoning high-risk areas means residents will be evicted, they should know before they start reconstructing the risk in the belief that everything will be as before. Humanitarian organizations could enable and encourage the disaster-affected to voice these concerns to relevant authorities. Speaking with one voice, with the backing of disaster-affected people, NGOs and aid agencies can build bridges between formal and informal structures; between the macro and the micro level; between Jenny Mujica and CorpoVargas.

Finally, whatever else humanitarian organizations do, they must inject risk reduction measures into every post-disaster intervention – "from moment one," says Maskrey. "Most relief people right up to this day don't even think about this. They think about logistics… and that's as far as it goes." By simultaneously pursuing action at the community level and advocacy at the political level, aid agencies can help put people – and risk reduction – at the centre of disaster recovery.

Mercedes Sayagues, a freelance writer based in Uruguay, was principal contributor to this chapter and boxes.

Sources and further information

Colmenares, Magdalena. *Notas para Mision de Cepal y Banco Mundial.* Caracas: 2000.
UNICEF Venezuela. *Situación de la Niñez en el Estado de Vargas, seis meses despues.* Caracas: UNICEF Venezuela, 2000.
United Nations Development Programme/UN Office for the Coordination of Humanitarian Affairs/Corporación Andina de Fomento. *Efectos de las lluvias caidas en Venezuela en diciembre de 1999.* Caracas: CDB Publicaciones, 2000.

Web sites

Centro Regional de Información sobre Desastres en America Latina http://www.crid.or.cr
El Nacional http://www.elnacional.com
Huracan.net (web site with information about hurricanes) http://www.huracan.net
Inter American Development Programme, Sustainable Development Department http://www.iadb.org/sds
Servicio de Enlace con las ONG Internacionales **http://www.enlaceong.org.ve:84**
World Bank **http://www.worldbank.org/data/countrydata/aag/ven_aag.pdf**

Section One

**Focus on
recovery**

Post-flood recovery in Viet Nam

It is 2 November 1999 and a festive crowd is jostling in the centre of Hue, former imperial capital of Viet Nam, and jewel in the tourist crown of the centre of the country. Some young people are even trying out a few dance steps in the already ankle-deep water. After all, it is the rainy season, and water means a good rice harvest. But a few hundred yards away, on the banks of the Huong (or Perfume) River, panicking inhabitants are fleeing their homes: the river is on the point of bursting its banks. A few hours later, the streets have become rivers, five metres deep in some places. The force of the current is such that the 60,000 residents will be stranded for three days, cut off from the outside world. Telephones no longer work; the traditional warning system didn't work either.

Decade's development washed away

Tropical storm Eve hit the central provinces of Viet Nam on 20 October with tragic consequences. In just six days (from 1-6 November) the skies dumped the equivalent of two years of rain. The flood of the century had begun: there had been nothing like it since 1886. All the rivers of the region burst their banks, the rate of water rise at times defying imagination: the Perfume River rose a metre an hour.

A month later, just when the rainy season should have dried up, a second tropical storm unleashed fresh torrential rains, hitting five provinces for the second time in one month. In the worst-affected areas, ten years of development were wiped out. According to official Vietnamese figures, the two floods resulted in 793 people dead or missing and made 55,000 homeless; hundreds of thousands more had their homes seriously damaged and lost their livelihoods. In all, 1.7 million people were directly affected out of the 8 million or so inhabitants of the central provinces.

Economic activity suffered a direct hit – especially agriculture, which employs 70 per cent of the labour force. The central region is among Viet Nam's poorest, and depends for its income on rice paddies and fishing. When flood waters receded, more than 60,000 hectares of paddy had been rendered unworkable by salt water or sand, countless farm animals had drowned, and hundreds of fishing boats lay shattered. Food stocks set aside from the September-October harvest had been destroyed.

Infrastructure was no less seriously affected: bridges, roads, dykes, railways, telephone lines, electrical cables, schools and clinics succumbed to the waters. In all, the Vietnamese government assessed damage at US$ 290 million – not counting the overall impact on economic activity, estimated at US$ 488 million for November alone. Nature showed no mercy on the destitute: it continued raining and the months of December and January were the coldest on record.

Double disaster dragged many into deep depression: "In some villages, people's faces were expressionless, they were simply prostrate and psychologically incapable of returning to the

Photo opposite page: Vietnamese Red Cross workers preparing the foundations for the central frame of a 'little mountain' house. By August 2000, the Vietnamese Red Cross had built 7,400 'stronger houses', designed to withstand high winds and floods.

International Federation, Viet Nam 2000

fray. I had never seen the like in Viet Nam," testifies Karine Treherne, working for the International Federation of Red Cross and Red Crescent Societies (International Federation) in Hue.

Almost a year later, in August 2000, another tropical storm lashed the region with yet more torrential rains. To the south, the Mekong delta was submerged beneath the worst floods for four decades – inundating 800,000 homes in Viet Nam alone and prompting major international appeals for aid. Recurrent natural disasters are sweeping away development gains, while emergency aid risks doing little more than setting up the vulnerable to get knocked down by the next flood or typhoon. How can relief dollars make a more lasting impact? How can development interventions become more disaster-savvy? How can the opportunity provided by disaster be seized, not simply to rehabilitate what was before, but to improve the chances of the Vietnamese to avoid or at least mitigate the devastating effects of future floods? For one thing is certain: the next floods are just around the corner.

Geography and demography drive disaster

The whole of Viet Nam lives with the threat of water. Too much water generally speaking – but sometimes not enough. Losses, even in 'normal' times, are colossal: flooding destroys on average 300,000 tonnes of food every year.

Hue is "one of the most extreme cases you can find as far as natural disasters are concerned," according to geographer Marc Goichot, who is writing a doctoral thesis on the region. He notes that "the frequency and the scale of high-water levels affecting Hue seem to have been on the increase for the past few decades". Recent research suggests that the El Niño/La Niña phenomenon is contributing to more recurrent typhoons and floods in Viet Nam (see Box 5.1).

While typhoons strike mainly coastal regions of the north and centre of Viet Nam between four and six times a year, they can be predicted and populations warned in advance, using radio and television. Similarly, the much slower, but equally life-threatening, rises in the level of the Mekong delta to the south can be announced up to ten days ahead, if regional cooperation along the Mekong River can be assured.

But the central provinces face a graver problem: flash floods, like those that tropical storm Eve unleashed in late 1999. The narrowness of this coastal strip (70 km from the mountains to the sea in some areas), combined with very steep mountain slopes, makes floods occur with lightning speed. Torrential rains burst river banks in barely five or six hours, leaving very little time to predict – let alone to announce – imminent floods.

Demographic pressure – Viet Nam's population of 78 million has doubled since 1975 – exacerbates the rain's effects. Firstly, by increasing the number of people at risk: given that three-quarters of the country is mountainous, the majority of the population crowds into exposed coastal areas, where rice can grow. Which means that 70 per cent of the Vietnamese live under the permanent threat of flooding. The disproportionate significance of agriculture in the national economy increases their vulnerability.

Box 5.1 La Niña fuels Viet Nam's tropical storms

During 2000, water once again exacted its tribute from Viet Nam: more than 5 million people were affected by a succession of severe weather events. Late August brought flooding – exceptionally early – to the central provinces, and with it dozens of dead and injured. On 10 September, tropical storm Wukong struck the north-central province of Ha Tinh, directly affecting 100,000, and destroying 3,000 houses and much of the rice harvest. This was despite the early warning system, which worked perfectly and greatly limited the damage. Another storm caused destructive flash floods in several of the mountainous central provinces, seriously affecting coffee and rice smallholdings.

But the Mekong delta in the south suffered worst. From July onwards, an ocean of water covered vast areas not only of Viet Nam, but also in Laos and Cambodia. The flood waters crept slowly to a high point of five metres on 23 September 2000 (the highest for 40 years) and subsided just as slowly, leaving tens of thousands of families stranded for months on the dykes. It was not until the end of the year that the Mekong regained its original level. As the months passed, 411 died in Viet Nam alone, including 291 children; 800,000 houses were flooded and damage was estimated at US$ 236 million. To meet the country's huge humanitarian needs, the International Federation launched an appeal for US$ 3.2 million, while the United Nations inter-agency appeal called for US$ 9.4 million to tackle both emergency and rehabilitation needs in the delta.

Is climate change increasing the number and severity of disasters in Viet Nam? Climatologists do not yet have a conclusive answer. But all agree that given the same amount of rainfall, the impact on a country now more densely populated and more built up is increasingly disastrous. Experts believe much more can be done to limit nature's negative effects. More accurate, easily understandable and usable climate forecasts for the wet May-October season and dry November-April season could enable agricultural adaptations (e.g., selecting alternative crops, or managing water reserves differently), depending on whether heavy rain or drought were forecast.

Meanwhile, El Niño and La Niña have "a definite influence on the climate of Viet Nam", asserts a recent study by the Asian Disaster Preparedness Center (ADPC) in Bangkok, relating to the period 1970-1999. Until this report was drafted in October 2000, there had scarcely been any systematic research to establish links between El Niño and the incidence of tropical storms, rainfall or variations in temperature in given regions of the country. The study reaches the following conclusions: although El Niño and La Niña have only a marginal effect on the north, they have a "discernible impact" on the centre of the country (i.e., between latitudes 10.6° and 20° N). In the south, typhoons – which are fairly infrequent during El Niño periods – can be exceptionally destructive. Catastrophic Typhoon Linda in November 1997 coincided with an El Niño event. In central provinces, typhoons occur less frequently during El Niño phases. But there is also less rainfall, hence more drought. La Niña, however, encourages more tropical storms, sometimes in quick succession, causing torrential downpours followed by flooding. Which is what happened in 1964, 1970, 1971, 1996 and, of course, in 1999.

The authors of the study conclude that there is a gap to be bridged between long-term forecasts relating to El Niño/La Niña and their use in Viet Nam. It is therefore a matter of urgency for the hydro-meteorological service to include this aspect in their own forecasts, and for these forecasts to be downscaled to the local level and translated to a format that meets the needs of each region and sector. This requires a much greater interaction on a continuous basis between forecasting institutions, a range of intermediary organizations (such as the agro-meteorology department) and end-users (such as agricultural extension organizations). Systems for this exist in countries like Australia and are beginning to develop in Indonesia and the Philippines. But, argues ADPC, while forecasts remain too general (covering El Niño/La Niña rather than local climate conditions and their impacts) and while forecasting systems fail to work hand in hand with those who use their outputs, they will have limited application in disaster reduction.

Secondly, people are modifying the environment in numerous ways that make it more vulnerable to flooding; deforestation, for example. Wood for heating purposes still meets 80 per cent of domestic fuel needs. Timber is also widely used in the building of traditional

Box 5.2 Coastal erosion threatens thousands

Twenty metres from the beach at Thuan An, a twisted mass of concrete blocks and metal rods poke out above the sea – remains of a house rebuilt after the 1999 disaster. The owners, whose original house had been destroyed, thought its new location was far enough from the waves. But a few months later, the sea caught up. Eelko Brouwer, head of the International Federation's office in Hue, points out a spot to the right, where boats are bobbing about: "That's where the floods opened a new breach."

We are in the province of Thua Thien-Hue in central Viet Nam, on the shores of a lagoon which the locals will proudly tell you is the second largest in Asia. Around its shores live 300,000 people, many earning their living from large prawn farms. Previously, two passages allowed fresh water to flow into the sea. But in November 1999, the violence of the Perfume River's flood waters punched a third passage. "Luckily for us, this let a huge amount of water flow into the sea," says Tran Xuan Phat, president of the provincial Red Cross branch; "without this, there would have been a lot more deaths." Initially providential, the new breach has nevertheless had negative effects. The disappearance of the road there cuts 80,000 people off from the mainland, forcing them to use boats to get around. And the sea water entering via the new breach threatens the fragile ecological balance of the lagoon and its prawns. The network of currents has also changed and the shoreline is eroding.

In 1999, 19 people drowned in the lagoon. Since then, 50 families have been relocated a few kilometres away. Further along, more inhabitants are planning to abandon their homes soon, as the sea devours two metres of shoreline a day. Sinking sands have been dubbed "man traps" after a crevice opened suddenly, swallowing a small boy. One morning, a 20-metre-deep abyss appeared where once a forest of 50,000 marine pines had protected the village from waves and sandstorms.

The infrastructure intended to combat the damaging effects of flood waters has proved counteractive. Brouwer points out the concrete breakwater blocks protruding in a line offshore from Thuan An: "They are in practice a buffer preventing sediment from coming in." But as sand is no longer being deposited, the shore is continously eroding. According to geographer Marc Goichot, these breakwaters, built in 1997 to protect the road, are partly responsible for the weakening of the shoreline and for the breaching of the third passage. Guichot adds, however, that the opening was inevitable: "When there is major flooding, the quantity of water accumulated in the lagoon is too great to flow through two passages." But by building dykes which are too strong, the problem is merely pushed further along: rising waters will sooner or later find a new route to the sea, threatening more lives and homes.

In early 2000, Dutch and French donors suggested closing off the third passage with sand. This "fuse" solution would protect the lagoon under normal weather conditions, while providing a point of least resistance for flood waters to reach the sea in the event of future disasters. The project also recommended building a bridge somewhere less risky to reunite isolated communities with the mainland. But there were two stumbling blocks: technology and money. Only a Dutch company could provide a boat capable of pumping such large quantities of sea sand. And the Netherlands was offering to cover just 35 per cent of the costs, the remainder being Viet Nam's responsibility.

The proposal was politely rejected by the provincial authorities, who preferred to build their own rigid dyke, employing local contractors – even though they knew the Dutch project was technically superior. The authorities also had to act quickly, before the next rainy season. The dyke was completed by autumn 2000, using voluntary local and military labour and local materials. It cost half the Franco-Dutch project's proposed budget.

houses. Deforestation continues at a rate of approximately 200,000 hectares a year – enough to eradicate what is left of Viet Nam's forests within 50 years.

Marc Goichot identifies a whole series of "human activities" which have "aggravated the flooding" in Hue. These include not only deforestation and mining gravel from the rivers, but the physical walls of the city which, with the bridges, railway line and trunk road, create a barrier across the valley and prevent high water levels from draining away freely. The rapid growth of the city of Hue over the last ten years, "has put up a corresponding number of obstacles in the path of water run-off", writes the geographer. He concludes: "Public works which help the city of Hue to develop, in the long term work against Hue." The debate over the most appropriate forms of infrastructure was heightened following the devastation of Hue's coastal lagoon by the December 1999 floods (see Box 5.2).

So, while experts are not yet sure if more rain is falling on Viet Nam, human factors are clearly compounding the effects of floods and planting many more people and assets in the path of disaster.

Breaking out of the vicious spiral

In this context of accelerating vulnerability, tens of thousands of Vietnamese cannot recover from one disaster before the next hits. Recurrent floods are wiping out the benefits of relief and development aid. Humanitarian organizations are faced with a dilemma: how to respond both swiftly, to save lives, and sustainably, so that interventions have a lasting effect?

One area illuminates this relief/development dilemma: that of private family housing. "We realized that each time there were floods, the same families were once again made homeless," explains Ian Wilderspin, of the International Federation in Hanoi. Often it was the poorest whose homes, being exposed and badly built, were entirely destroyed, together with all they contained. Families are sucked into a downward spiral with no end in sight, says Wilderspin.

Viet Nam's traditional architecture was perfectly suited to typhoons and flooding: the houses had no foundations, but their extremely heavy roofs, in particular, made them very strong. However, here as elsewhere, traditional materials (especially wood) have given way to corrugated iron sheeting, cement and bricks, without any subsequent adaptation of building techniques. Even if they have brick walls (locally, but wrongly, perceived as 'strong'), buildings without foundations or strong bracing are swept away by storms like strands of straw. And this is unfortunately what is in store, when the next floods strike, for the houses rebuilt by Vietnamese using concrete pillars, bricks and tiles provided by the authorities or non-governmental organizations (NGOs), without the necessary training in more suitable building techniques.

In the aftermath of the November 1998 floods, which destroyed over 11,000 houses, the International Federation and the Vietnamese Red Cross (VNRC) decided, in the words of Wilderspin, "to go one step further than simply rehabilitating" houses which, for most of the victims, represent their greatest financial loss. Two teams of architects, in Hue and Hanoi, developed two models of 'stronger houses' displaying the following key features enabling them to face up to high winds and flooding:

- good foundations;
- strong bracing;
- a fixed frame; and
- good connections between the frame and the roof (see Figure 5.1).

While surface area is relatively small (12-18 square metres), the designs provide a strong, two-storey central core which will hold firm in the event of disaster. The household's most valuable belongings and food reserves can be stored on a gallery floor above the level of flooding. The Red Cross theoretically provides only the central frame; beneficiaries must build the walls, and any side extensions, out of light materials such as rice straw. But even this meagre contribution can prove beyond the means of the poorest, and here local solidarity swings into action. In several areas, local authorities and Red Cross branches finance two of the four walls.

When the next disaster strikes, even if the walls and extensions are swept away, the family will still have what is most valuable to them: the structure of the house and the belongings they have stored high up. Hence the new design can achieve three results simultaneously:
- save lives (roofs as refuge);
- save the family's greatest material possession (the house itself); and
- save livelihoods (the first floor as a storage area for seed and agricultural tools).

Almost one house in four destroyed in 1998 was rebuilt using this model, by local skilled workers organized by Red Cross volunteers, who themselves received on-the-spot training.

The villagers were quick to dub these new houses 'little mountains'. They proved themselves worthy of the name: only one out of 2,450 succumbed to the 1999 floods. Their metal roofs, recognizable at a distance, became a very sought-after refuge from the floods. A second series of houses built after December 1999 also fulfilled their promise during the high waters of 2000. In all, by the end of August 2000, the programme had built 7,400 'stronger houses' for a total of US$ 3.7 million. This works out at US$ 500 per unit – cheaper, for example, than the US$ 850 unit price of the Philippine government's 1988-1993 wooden house programme.

Beneficiaries are selected on the grounds of vulnerability: the handicapped, the elderly and single female-headed households, who have lost everything and are particularly powerless to recover. They are chosen using official 'poverty lists' and following consultations between the village community, the local authorities and the VNRC. An external evaluation carried out in May 2000 by the Asian Disaster Preparedness Center (ADPC) – an independent research organization based in Bangkok – estimated that the selection of beneficiaries was 85-90 per cent successful.

But why prioritize relatively expensive houses rather than, for example, helping farmers relaunch their agricultural activities? For the Vietnamese, the reply seems self-evident. "The way we look at things, you will find deeply entrenched the notion that without a safe haven, it is impossible to start up a successful life again," summarizes Nguyen Thanh Ky, director of the VNRC's international department. Remarkably, the Red Cross stronger housing programme was the first large-scale attempt to provide Vietnamese with flood-resistant homes. Following past disasters, the government had only rebuilt public infrastructure – while disaster-affected families had received new building materials but no construction training.

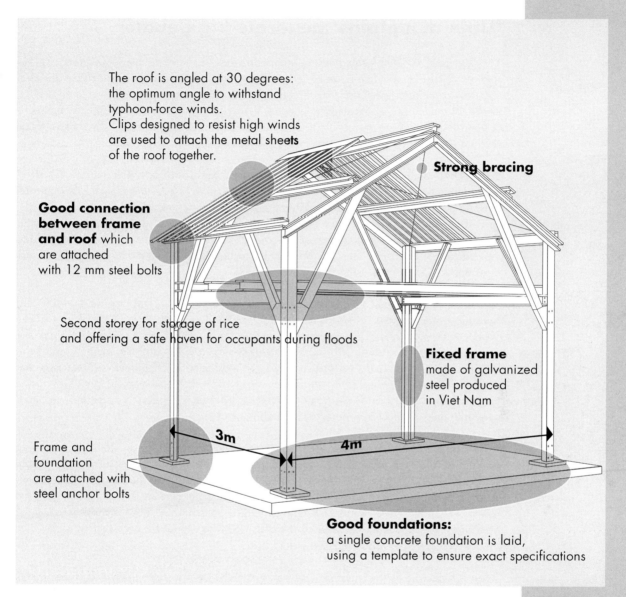

The roof is angled at 30 degrees: the optimum angle to withstand typhoon-force winds.
Clips designed to resist high winds are used to attach the metal sheets of the roof together.

Strong bracing

Good connection between frame and roof which are attached with 12 mm steel bolts

Second storey for storage of rice and offering a safe haven for occupants during floods

Fixed frame made of galvanized steel produced in Viet Nam

3m

4m

Frame and foundation are attached with steel anchor bolts

Good foundations: a single concrete foundation is laid, using a template to ensure exact specifications

Figure 5.1: The Hue model of the 'stronger houses' developed by the Vietnamese Red Cross to withstand high winds and floods. The Red Cross provides the central frame and beneficiaries build the walls and any side extensions.

There is little doubt that the houses are seen as successful. By the beneficiaries, of course. Like the elderly man we saw in Quang Binh province – extremely poor, and responsible for his two grandchildren – he possessed nothing before the floods except his flimsy hut which had been carried away. In August 2000, he was grinning toothlessly from ear to ear as he showed us the roof of his new house: "Never in my life did I dream of building such a strong house!" By the Vietnamese public in general, amongst whom the houses have given the image of the Red Cross a major boost. And by the donors, delighted at emergency aid which proves durable and "not money which pours down the drain at the next flood", as one ambassador puts it.

'Little mountains' generate big debate

The success of the Red Cross housing programme has generated as many questions as it has answers. Most commentators agree that the post-disaster environment provides an ideal opportunity to inject some risk reduction into the recovery process. And few would argue that, ideally, all the millions of Vietnamese living in disaster-prone provinces should inhabit typhoon- or flood-resistant houses. But whose responsibility is it to make this happen? Who should decide on the right design, materials and price? Who should build them? Who should pay?

The ADPC evaluated the Red Cross programme and concluded that while very good technically, it would do better to embrace the differences in provincial, social and cultural housing norms, in local materials and in methods of construction. ADPC stressed that, in the heat of the emergency, locals were not involved in the elaboration of the project. As a result, neither the beneficiaries nor the rest of the community understand the structural features that make these houses strong. They are therefore incapable of replicating the model for themselves or of building extensions using the same principles.

ADPC's criticism is based on the premise that the primary responsibility for building and funding stronger houses rests with householders themselves, however poor they may be. The World Bank seems of a similar opinion. Ronald S. Parker, in his article *Single family housing: the window of opportunity for mitigation following natural disaster*, published by the World Bank in June 2000, argues that: "Reconstructing safer housing with techniques and materials that are beyond local skill levels, and costs that greatly exceed what is traditionally spent for housing in the victim country, ensures that improvements will not be replicated as families expand a core unit and construct new units for expanding families."

If project success is defined by how easily a poor villager can replicate the design of a stronger house, then the Red Cross 'little mountains' may not be considered successful. Firstly, because of the design features, which were not explained to beneficiaries at the time of construction. Secondly, because of the materials chosen: while the galvanized steel of the frame and the concrete foundations are produced nationally, these materials are not available at village or even district level. Thirdly, because of the cost: US$ 500 is a lot for a villager whose average income is likely to be US$ 80-120 a year.

But is it realistic to expect a near-destitute villager – who has just seen all his or her assets, means of livelihood and, quite possibly, loved ones swept away by a devastating flood – to be in a position to rebuild any kind of house, let alone a disaster-proof one? Without any collateral, such a villager couldn't borrow money to rebuild anyway. It may be more realistic – and more compassionate – to identify the most vulnerable in each community and provide them with a new home, thereby breaking the downward spiral of disaster into which they would otherwise be drawn. A US$ 500 house could be home to perhaps seven people – an investment of US$ 70 per potential life saved. Thousands of at-risk families in Viet Nam need houses like this. Even if this investment is beyond the means of humanitarian organizations, it should not be too much for the Vietnamese government and international financial institutions to take on.

Peter Walker, head of the International Federation's regional delegation for south-east Asia, admits that "the issue of replicability is a tricky one. But almost by definition the 'little

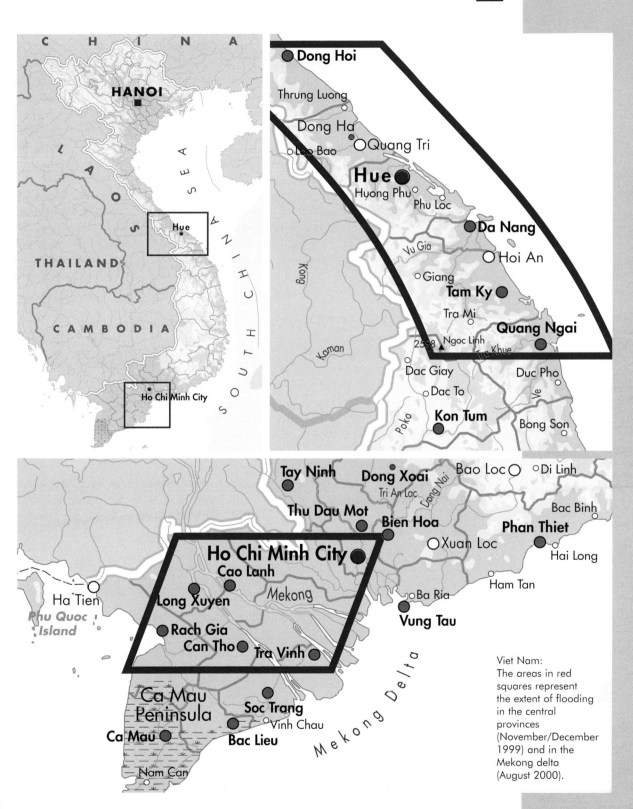

Viet Nam:
The areas in red squares represent the extent of flooding in the central provinces (November/December 1999) and in the Mekong delta (August 2000).

mountain' is not replicable by individual households using their own resources. If stronger houses were cheap and affordable, then they would have been built already!" Given this situation, argues Walker, "the logic then is twofold. Firstly, to use [relief] funds to make a real difference to those families who benefit directly from the houses. Secondly, to demonstrate what is possible with a few simple changes in, for instance, the types of loan banks give in Viet Nam, or the ways local authorities fund disaster preparedness. The houses are affordable if you change the economics from family to local community economics, within an agreed national disaster preparedness strategy."

Looked at this way, the burden of replicating stronger houses falls not on individual householders, but on their local, state and national authorities. And the role of humanitarian organizations is to show, by example, what is possible, to spark debate about disaster mitigation measures and to help mobilize the resources necessary for authorities to meet the challenge. In this context, the developmental mantra of "local solutions for local problems" – in which the destitute householder has to pick up the tab for his new house – looks suspiciously like an excuse by donors and host governments alike to disengage from any commitment to break the cycle of disaster.

Of course, those communities, authorities or companies engaged in constructing disaster-resistant houses must still find the design culturally acceptable, affordable and comprehensible. Ronald Parker emphasizes that, "for private single-family housing, durable solutions involve using locally available materials, culturally appropriate styles, and traditional building techniques. Any deviation in this respect is highly counter-developmental... post-disaster reconstruction is no time to experiment with new materials, radical designs, or elaborate techniques beyond the skills of local masons and carpenters. Such things allow the window of educational opportunity to close without leaving behind sustainable improvement."

Yet traditional building techniques in Viet Nam involved building heavy-roofed, disaster-resistant houses out of solid tropical hardwoods – no longer a valid developmental approach, given the rate at which Viet Nam's forests are being denuded. But does that mean concrete foundations, steel frames and corrugated iron roofs are too radical, elaborate or culturally inappropriate? The best judges of that, surely, are not foreigners, but the Vietnamese themselves. Which is why the Red Cross sponsored a housing competition during 2000 to give indigenous organizations, companies and officials the chance to express their own ideas and preferences.

The housing competition attracted 15 major companies in Viet Nam to enter in the categories of (a) mass-produced relief house; (b) individual house; (c) development programme house; and (d) most innovative design. The jury for the competition comprised experts from people's committees (local government), the ministries of construction and finance, the prime minister's office, engineers, Red Cross officials, international NGOs and relief planners. The competition final was organized as part of a national seminar hosted by the VNRC. Six finalists were chosen to build on a site which has become a permanent display, with families living in the finalists' houses.

The jury decided that for mass production, quality assurance, speed and simplicity – not to mention financial 'leakage' – the combination of steel frames and concrete foundations could not be beaten when it comes to emergency production of relief housing. For development programmes where on-site supervision by trained engineers could be assured, then a method of using locally produced, high-quality concrete blocks was the winner. This solution also won the prize for most innovative design. No company used bamboo or wood as these are perceived by Vietnamese as too weak, too expensive, not durable enough (in the case of bamboo), or in too short supply (in the case of hardwood) for any large-scale programme.

Spreading the message by example

"Reconstruction projects promoting mitigation need to send the message during the first months after disaster that safer housing is within everyone's reach," argues the World Bank's Ronald Parker. The head of the International Federation's Viet Nam delegation, John Geoghegan, argues that "by building such a large number of houses, the message of the need for stronger housing is getting through – by simple presence in so many places. The model may not be replicable by the most vulnerable, but the realization that a stronger house is important is there. And pressure is growing from academics, local government, the local population and the media in Viet Nam for national authorities to provide this kind of housing to people."

The Vietnamese government has responded by investing its own money in building 4,000 houses in Hue, based on the Red Cross model. It has also added first floors to schools in the central region so they can be used for storage and refuge. Foreign NGOs have followed the lead of the 'little mountains', too. In total, by mid-2001, the Red Cross and the government between them will have built over 20,000 flood-resistant houses in 16 provinces. Geoghegan believes the 'little mountains' have reignited the debate. "All of a sudden, it has become sexy to talk about houses," he says, adding, "There has been a public debate carried out in the media concerning design of safer housing in the Mekong – would it have happened three years ago?"

The success of the 'little mountains' could be seen just in terms of saving lives and breaking the cycle of disaster for those lucky enough to be selected. But the Red Cross programme also seized the opportunity that disaster presents – the media coverage, the international money, the attention of the government and local people – and initiated a debate on how best to respond to future disasters in a way both life-saving and sustainable. The stronger houses not only made relief dollars last longer, they arrived in time for the next flood and proved they could save lives and livelihoods. As a communications tool, they sent a powerful message that families and belongings need not be swept away every year. The challenge now is to hang on to that message, but adapt its practical realization to local conditions. That means working with government, communities and villagers to replicate the structural principles of stronger house design in a sustainable, affordable way (see Box 5.3).

Sustainable change comes from within

While the Red Cross believes the Vietnamese government and its creditors should take up the challenge of providing stronger housing, some believe that a more locally-based approach is needed. Engineer Nguyen Huu Huy, who is familiar with the Red Cross programme, argues that: "No funder will be able to cover the entire region with these houses. But teach people how to go about them, and they'll get going." He believes that 'how to go about them' means explaining that there is no need to make exact replicas of the Red Cross house to achieve the requisite strength, provided one respects the basic construction features.

Box 5.3 Principles for sustainable post-disaster family housing

According to a World Bank report, published in June 2000, "over 20 years, natural catastrophes worldwide are responsible for nearly 1 billion people losing their homes. On average, estimating average family size at five, this comes to 10 million homeless a year." The following principles define the best approach to improving the disaster resistance of family housing for a given target community – especially where the aim is to enable local people to replicate houses using their own resources:

- **Context analysis:** Identify the particular vulnerabilities of the local built environment and determine how to reduce them in ways that lead to durable solutions.
- **Cost:** Both economic acceptability at the local level and economic feasibility at the national level are required.
- **Appropriate objective:** For example, in an area regularly struck by typhoons and floods, stronger houses are clearly an appropriate objective. But the community must be convinced: their perception of risk has to exist or be enhanced.
- **Fitness for purpose:** Do the houses actually resist the effects of the next catastrophe? Proving the efficiency of the design is crucial in convincing the community to adopt new building techniques – "seeing is believing".
- **Social acceptability:** This requires excellent prior knowledge of the target community, so that the building design corresponds to local taste and traditions. As much locally available material as possible must be used. The aspirations of the community have to be taken into account.
- **Replication:** Designs using locally available materials, culturally appropriate styles, and traditional building techniques will prove easier for poorer families to replicate.
- **Communication:** During the first months after disaster, send the message that safer housing is within everyone's reach. Then reinforce with classes, model buildings, and posters. Find the most effective modes of disseminating information and knowledge.

- **Clarity of technical message:** Explain what the fundamental building principles are. It is not necessary for a house to look exactly like the model, as long as it respects the basic rules. Most mitigation projects promote too many changes to traditional styles – too complicated a message becomes incommunicable. Research should focus on what are the three most important modifications that can be made.
- **Cultural and educational issues** relating to training modes. Before trying to teach, find out how people learn. How do new practices enter local society – by radio, TV, posters, theatre, meetings "under the baobab tree" in the village? Is a physical demonstration of how to build necessary? How are women or village elders involved?
- **Effective leadership** is essential for training to work. Leadership not only from NGOs but within the local community. Identify existing leaders and/or existing organizations, and work through them rather than creating new ones. Find the "gatekeepers of the community" – those people whom everyone wishes to imitate. If they accept the need to change their building techniques, the rest of the community will follow.
- **Timing:** The window of educational opportunity is narrow – don't let it close without leaving behind sustainable improvement and mitigation messages. One resource which should not be wasted is the attention of local people.
- **Responsibility:** Consider what is the optimal distribution of responsibility for reconstruction between individual, community, regional and national levels. It is the individual homeowner who makes the critical decisions during reconstruction.
- **Involve the beneficiaries at all stages** to ensure that the above principles become practice.

Sources: *International Federation, Aga Khan Trust for Culture, World Bank*

Who then is responsible for such wide-scale training of local skilled workers, a task which far outstrips the capacities of the Red Cross? The government, replies Yasemin Aysan, acting chief of disaster reduction and recovery for the United Nations Development Programme (UNDP) in Geneva. For no NGO is sufficiently large to train an entire country, even if the role of NGOs at community level remains irreplaceable.

The Vietnamese government did issue building directives taking account of natural disasters in the mid-1990s. But without providing the means – training, preferential loans – to ensure the directives were applied to individual homes. When we visited the ministry of construction in Hanoi, a civil servant pulled a builders' manual out of his drawer – but he has no access to the funds needed to launch a genuine training campaign. Once again, it is not just a question of money, but of political will at the highest levels.

One initiative aimed at village level is that of the Franco-Canadian NGO, Development Workshop (DW). DW does not build housing but teaches communities to construct with natural disasters in mind. Their first attempt in Viet Nam in the late 1980s, in partnership with UNDP, had no long-term impact – the authorities were more interested in acquiring equipment than skills. But ten years on, "the thinking has changed", according to John Norton, president of DW France. In 1999, DW began working in partnership with local authorities and communities in the coastal districts of Thua Thien-Hue.

DW's two-tier approach encompasses village animation activities in parallel with practical demonstrations. Plays, concerts, school competitions, poster campaigns and local media all send one message: typhoon and flood damage must be prevented by strengthening (or better still, rebuilding) your existing house now. While expensive, it will cost a lot less than seeing your home destroyed by the next disaster, explains DW. "Having the population talk about the whole issue of prevention is central," says Norton. Integral to animation activities are demonstrations of how to build stronger homes, using ten key principles (similar to those used by the Red Cross). During 2000, DW has strengthened several dozen homes and built one 'demonstration house', working closely with the families involved – who provided labour and some of the materials – and with local builders, organizations and authorities.

Marooned in flood waters: in 1999, Viet Nam's central provinces suffered the worst floods for a century. A year later, it was the turn of the Mekong delta, inundated by the heaviest flooding in 40 years.

Viet Thanh/ International Federation, Viet Nam 2000

Only local materials, such as tiled roofs, are used and specific cultural preferences are taken into account. Regular seminars help Vietnamese participants redefine for themselves their priorities and plan future phases of work. A process as deep-seated as changing building habits "has to be driven by the population, otherwise it is doomed to failure", maintains Norton.

Problems, however, remain. A completely new, stronger building costs 10-15 per cent more than a poorly designed house. But strengthening existing homes costs up to 45 per cent more. The poorest can't afford it – particularly as their houses are often so badly built they would have to start from scratch. So DW is studying ways of targeting credit to the most vulnerable.

First destruction then debt

Anh Thu is 36 years old. The flood left her, her parents and her four children without a roof and submerged her little bit of rice paddy in the commune of Phu An, near Hue. The Red Cross provided her with a new house and the government loaned her 1 million dong (US$ 72). When we met her in August 2000, she knew she would be unable to repay this money at term, in November: "But I daren't ask for an extension. So I'll borrow from friends to pay back the loan. The only thing is, I'll have to pay them 30,000 dong interest every month. That's the same as the authorities ask for in a year."

This woman typifies the rural flood victims of central Viet Nam: their homes washed away or badly damaged; their rice harvest and new seedlings flooded; their ducks and chickens, buffaloes and pigs, drowned; their coastal prawn farms damaged by salt water; their tools lost. Recovery before the next serious floods may be unlikely, when, as Carrie Turk of the World Bank in Hanoi points out, "Farmers will tell you that it can take them three to five years to recover from the loss of a single cow." In these circumstances, rural communities have no choice but to rely on external aid.

Hanoi made a major effort in the wake of the 1999 floods, as did provincial and local authorities: state loans to individuals totalled approximately US$ 36 million. Typically, loans were between 1-1.5 million dong (US$ 72-107), repayable within one year at a low rate of interest (around 3 per cent). But it's not enough: Anh Thu's experience is typical of the chronic shortage of affordable credit in rural Viet Nam, a shortage particularly severe following a natural disaster. Both because a large number of people suddenly need loans, and because their needs are particularly great, since many of them have lost everything. And their capacity to offer any collateral is reduced to zero.

Banks remain remote from farmers. Geographically, since they are located in towns and cities, requiring farmers to make journeys costly in terms of both time and money. And remote for bureaucratic reasons: in order to borrow, one has to fill out all sorts of forms and provide collateral, which often proves impossible. Popular organizations, such as the Vietnamese Women's Union, which provides loans at community level on the model of Bangladesh's Grameen Bank, are undoubtedly successful. But the union, which is the main partner of most credit schemes involving international NGOs, meets only a fraction of the need. And even the union demands collateral, so the destitute cannot get credit and remain trapped in a downward spiral.

More significant than the lack of micro-finance is the lack of any savings structures readily accessible at village level. "NGOs are more successful when they set up savings schemes than when they offer loans," notes Turk. For even relatively poor farmers could set aside small sums every month, which could cushion them against hard times. It is estimated that 50-70 per cent of credit needs are met by 'informal' sources – neighbours, family members or village moneylenders who apply high rates of interest (3-10 per cent per month), leading to widespread indebtedness.

This lack of funding both masks and underlies a more serious and deeply rooted structural problem: the lack of economic diversification in rural areas, where farmers depend almost entirely on traditional agriculture. Nguyen Ty Nien, director of the department of dyke management and flood control (DDMFC), is well aware of this: "In the long term, only improved standards of living will really enable the inhabitants of the centre to protect themselves against flooding." But this is no easy matter, and lack of money is not the only culprit.

Researchers have shown that very few farmers invest the money they borrow in ways which create new economic activity. Most use their loans to enlarge their home, to repay their debts, or simply to survive between two harvests. So loans must go hand in hand with major inputs of technical and economic expertise to provide rural inhabitants with the skills they need to diversify into, for example, food processing or other 'multiplier' activities.

Software vs hardware

Accustomed to centuries of water damage, Viet Nam has developed remarkable civil and political institutions to try and prevent disaster. Major structural works intended to hold back flood waters – notably 5,000 km of river dykes and 3,000 km of sea dykes – are supervised by the DDMFC, a specific department of the ministry of agriculture. When disasters occur, the central committee for flood and storm control (CCFSC) – whose director is also that of the DDMFC – facilitates coordination between different ministries and agencies. Both organisations have their own representatives at all the country's administrative levels, right down to the village. Every citizen is supposed to devote ten days' labour per year to maintaining public infrastructure. Experts have estimated that, as a result, the number of victims in 1999 was relatively low given the violence of the floods and the fact that, in November, they took communities by surprise.

But slabs of concrete and stronger houses alone will not save lives. On a national level, a disproportionate emphasis has been placed on structural 'hardware' measures (particularly dykes and reservoirs) at the expense of non-structural 'software' measures, such as disaster preparedness (DP), education/training, early warning systems, flood-plain management, communications, insurance, revolving funds, economic diversification and so on. The assumption that floods must be kept away from people, as opposed to keeping people away from floods needs to be challenged. Educating those at risk in how to prepare for and respond to disasters, for example, is essential (see Box 5.4). The International Federation has received

Box 5.4 Education saves lives

Strange as it may seem, educating schoolchildren about natural disasters was for many years the odd man out of the Vietnamese school curriculum. Even though experience has shown that in this field, information alone is grossly inadequate and only in-depth education of the population saves lives on a large scale. It is not enough to know that a typhoon or tropical storm is on its way; it is also vital to understand which preventive measures should be taken and which reflex actions will save lives and property.

In 1999, a disaster preparedness manual was drafted jointly by the International Federation, the Vietnamese Red Cross and UNDP, with European Union funding. First tested in three of Viet Nam's 60 provinces, it was distributed to children aged 9-12 years, together with a teacher's guide and a useful little gadget: a plastic bag in which parents were invited to preserve their most precious documents in the event of flooding. The book was crammed with illustrations and subjects covered ranged from the dangers of domestic fires to flash floods.

"The manual was well received, but we took into account the comments of the children and their teachers and we started again from scratch," relates Ian Wilderspin, the International Federation's disaster preparedness delegate in Hanoi. This time, funding came from the American Red Cross. The new version, clearer and with colour pictures (as requested by the children), was distributed during the 2000-2001 academic year in seven central provinces. The target audience is some 2,000 teachers and 95,000 children in their fifth year of primary school. "This will enable us to reach – counting the families – half a million people in the central provinces," underlines John Geoghegan, head of the International Federation's Hanoi delegation.

Although it is vital to train children, education goes far beyond this. The Vietnamese Red Cross is aware of the need for greater training of its own personnel – be they volunteers or paid staff. A relatively comprehensive manual is now available to them and this finally enables shortcomings due to language difficulties to be overcome: "There is very little in Vietnamese," notes Wilderspin. Regular training cycles are now being introduced, with the assistance of the International Federation. And Wilderspin is very hopeful that this training can gradually spread beyond the immediate circles of the Red Cross and of children. "Red Cross trainees are now providing very practical guidelines to the commune authorities about the things to do or not to do in case of disaster," he argues. "We need to shift towards community-level preparedness."

US$ 3 million over two years to pay for DP training of local staff, provide rescue equipment and promote preparedness within the region's most disaster-prone districts.

Communication of information at all levels is another critical software measure which saves lives and assets. While those with computers can access huge quantities of relevant information online (see Box 5.5), communications at the local level are less efficient. An official Vietnamese document sets out the early warning system of the meteorological department in Quang Tri province (flooded in November 1999) as follows: "Three seasonal posts during the four months of flood risk: use the residents' telephones." In other words, the upstream observation posts did not have their own means of communication in 1999, and relied on the few telephones amongst the inhabitants. Yet these telephone lines were the first to be cut by rising waters. As for Quang Binh province, the village authorities told us they had had to use loudspeakers to warn inhabitants of imminent flooding. Without sirens, those working in the mountains received no warning and some perished. On a broader level, many observers argue that, since Viet Nam's entire river network is linked to that of China, any genuinely efficient early warning system must involve transborder collaboration.

Box 5.5 Online information – bridging the media gap

Anyone with access to a computer and needing the latest news on natural disasters in Viet Nam has only to log on to http://www.undp.org.vn/dmu between May and December. Here you can find the day's weather forecast – warning of storms, typhoons or the Mekong River in spate – relevant safety measures, detailed assessments of the season's disasters, how much humanitarian organizations are appealing for, and so on. There is a database of disasters which have struck since 1996, with a whole arsenal of maps, graphics and comparative tables. Plus an excellent series of background briefs on climate, its effects on the economy and society, and the complex political and social structures introduced to combat disasters.

The Disaster Management Unit (DMU) was set up in 1994 by the Vietnamese government and UNDP to "support the natural disaster mitigation efforts of Viet Nam". The concept: bringing together "over 1,000 years of Vietnamese flood protection culture with 21st century western technology". By 1996, the DMU's Internet site – in English, and subsequently in Vietnamese – became its showcase. "We translate and make available to anyone the information which lands on the prime minister's desk on a daily basis," claims Marshall Silver, the site's creator. He enjoys quoting experts who reckon his brainchild to be "the best of its kind in Asia".

But its success was far from a foregone conclusion: in 1993, when Silver, an engineer specializing in combating floods, first set foot in Viet Nam, data on disasters were top secret. Little by little, however, the authorities came to realize that far from "discrediting the country", spreading news of this kind can only help the victims. According to Silver, the turning point was Typhoon Linda, which took the south of the country by surprise in 1997, killing 3,000 people. The surge of international solidarity which followed overcame any lingering doubts amongst the Vietnamese.

In contrast to more journalistic media, which rush in when disaster strikes, only to scurry away a few days later to another 'hot spot', the DMU's site provides continuity in data provision. Such continuous communication not only raises disaster awareness among government ministries and donors, but also encourages preparedness and mitigation measures in the 'downtime' between disasters.

To ensure the message is getting through, news is faxed daily to embassies in Hanoi and to humanitarian organizations. The result: a large number of locally-based diplomats who can expand with surprising ease on the concepts of 'disaster preparedness' or 'disaster mitigation' and who are Viet Nam's best advocates with their respective governments.

Viet Nam's pyramidal administrative structure has in the past hampered the rapid sharing of information in the disaster zone. No serious decision could be taken at provincial level without informing Hanoi. Following the Typhoon Linda catastrophe in December 1997, the prime minister created a direct link between his office and the CCFSC (which comprises members from different ministries), enhancing the lateral flow of information to key people. And, with the powerful Vietnamese army now under the coordination of the DDMFC during disasters, this means government response to floods has greatly improved since 1997, according to John Geoghegan.

Finally, Viet Nam, like so many other poor countries, has no system of insurance against natural disasters. In the absence of such insurance, according to Tran Nguyen Anh Thu, sustainable development programme officer with UNDP in Hanoi, "The country should have a separate budget line for disasters. For the time being, there is only a social fund aimed at a very wide group in need of aid." Such a budget line, or a revolving fund, could also fill the financial gap in the post-disaster reconstruction phase, when international generosity, which is often very great during the emergency phase, tends to dry up.

Disaster shocks donors and government into mitigation

The 1999 floods in central Viet Nam acted like an electric shock, underlines Marshall Silver, UNDP consultant in Hanoi: "Before that, neither I nor other international experts saw the chronic link between natural disasters, poverty and unsustainable development."

Yet the lagoon in Thua Thien-Hue province *had* been identified years earlier as an area at great risk: 300,000 people eke out a marginal existence on a shoreline highly vulnerable to typhoons, storms and flash floods. But no one wanted to foot the bill to do anything about it. In 1995, France had offered to fund an early warning system in the lagoon, but it was in the form of a loan, which Hanoi had refused. Then, in November-December 1999, the floods of the century struck Thua Thien-Hue, ravaging the lagoon, killing hundreds and wiping out a decade of development in just days. A few months later, donors (including ECHO and the International Federation) were financing a complete, integrated early warning system, with sensors both in the lagoon and upstream of the rivers, along with radios and a training package.

Agencies are now changing the way they do development too, as reflected in the Central Provinces Initiative (CPI) which emerged just weeks after the 1999 floods, spearheaded by the Dutch Embassy in Hanoi, the ministry for agriculture and rural development and UNDP. CPI's objective is to inject the 'disaster dimension' into any development project, be it new or ongoing, and to be prepared as far as possible for future disasters. This culminated nine months later in a memorandum of understanding, committing the Vietnamese government and the international community of donors to a 'strategic partnership'.

Silver sums up: "It went without saying that you don't do anything without an environmental impact assessment. Well, we won't do anything from now on without a disaster mitigation assessment. Otherwise, everybody is just wasting their money." The World Bank adds that "spending as little as an additional 10 per cent on mitigation can stop recurrent losses".

Actions speak louder than words: by late July 2000, US$ 40 million in the form of aid and loans had been promised (and for the most part, paid). This money was intended for emergency repairs to infrastructure, but also for strengthening disaster mitigation, through early warning and information systems, flood maps to facilitate future zoning, and training in disaster preparedness at community level.

Nor was the government slow to follow: new directives were published relating to disaster preparedness. These included adding a first floor to primary schools and other public buildings, setting aside food stocks, providing rescue equipment. Longer term, Viet Nam's national institute for urban and rural planning is working on relocating parts of the central region's population most at risk – ideally as close as possible to their original homes. An inter-ministerial coordination mechanism is slowly being set up, through twice yearly seminars which coincide with the release of seasonal forecasts in April and November.

Seizing opportunities

Despite the electrifying effect the 1999 floods had on disaster-prone Viet Nam, things don't change that fast. When fresh floods inundated Thua Thien-Hue in late August 2000 (exceptionally early in the season), the promised early warning system had still not been introduced. And yet, never had the sense of urgency to 'do better next time' been greater than in the aftermath of the 1999 floods.

Memories fade quickly. But there is a brief period following disasters when people are willing to change their habits – and that should go for international agencies as much as local communities. This window of opportunity must be seized to go beyond the mere rehabilitation of what was there before – towards rebuilding in a better way, taking full account of the disaster dimension.

In countries like Viet Nam, which are in a state of constant recovery between disasters, emergency humanitarian aid is intrinsically linked to development. But this poses a series of dilemmas, which are perfectly illustrated by housing. In the aftermath of a disaster, survivors need help to get a roof over their heads fast. But humanitarian organizations alone cannot re-house millions of exposed inhabitants. So agencies are faced with a choice: pursue the long, slow path of developmental change, or the quicker, unsustainable path of relief housing. The developmental approach may yield long-term fruit, but not in time for next year's flood. The relief approach may save lives, but risks setting unreplicable standards.

The answer must lie in a combination of the two. For those left destitute by disaster – those who cannot afford to build a new home of any kind, who have lost all their assets and cannot even raise a loan – a new, stronger house may be the quickest, most cost-effective way to break the spiral of disaster which threatens to swallow them. A lecture on how to build a flood-proof house is not enough. While humanitarian organizations like the Red Cross can initiate this process, the principal responsibility for protecting people from disaster must rest with their own government and the major lenders who support them. This is a debate which relief agencies can, and must, spark following every disaster.

For the less destitute, however, providing off-the-shelf kits doesn't teach communities how to change their own ways of building, which may be the most viable long-term solution in the absence of government intervention. So both approaches – that of quickly providing life- and livelihood-saving homes, and that of transmitting improved construction skills over the long term – are indispensable. And inextricably linked. Ensuring smooth integration of one with the other, however, remains a challenge – one which the International Federation's housing competition may provide a model for meeting.

Another challenge relates to donors. While building disaster-resistant houses is relatively quick, visible, easy to measure – and therefore attractive to donors – changing indigenous building techniques demands long-term commitment and funding. Training, educating, and convincing people – whether communities or governments – is by definition labour-intensive, media-unfriendly and potentially less attractive to donors. The Central Provinces Initiative, however, may signal a shift of donor approach towards a more continuous commitment to reducing disaster risk in Viet Nam.

Finally, no externally imposed solutions, whether as part of relief or development intervention, will work long term unless beneficiaries and authorities can express their points of view – through, for example, a housing competition. Only via closer collaboration between all stakeholders will the most appropriate solutions emerge and the tide of recurrent disasters be stemmed. Foreign agencies could do more to cultivate relationships with Viet Nam's central state services; to work with, rather than to circumvent, a bureaucracy which has demonstrated that it is capable of change. Failing which, there is a danger of resorting to local projects which may be excellent in themselves, but run the risk of remaining bonsai gardens blooming in the desert.

Iolande Jaquemet, an independent writer based in Geneva, was principal contributor to this chapter and boxes.

Sources and further information

Asian Disaster Preparedness Center (ADPC). *Report on ENSO Climate Forecast Applications Projects, 1970-1999.* Draft. Bangkok: ADPC, October 2000.

Aysan, Yasemin and Davis, Ian (eds.). *Disasters and the Small Dwelling. Perspectives for the UN IDNDR.* London: James and James Science Publishers Limited, 1992.

Aysan, Yasemin. *A Study of the State of the Art in Earthquake Mitigation Projects: Training Local Builders and the Public in Rural Areas.* Report for the Aga Khan Trust for Culture, November 1990.

Aysan, Yasemin and Davis, Ian. *Rehabilitation and Reconstruction. Module prepared for the Disaster Management Training Programme, UNDP/DHA.* First edition, 1993.

Benson, Charlotte. *The Economic Impact of Natural Disasters in Vietnam.* London: Overseas Development Institute, 1997.

Central Provinces Initiative (CPI). *Central Provinces Initiative to Mitigate Natural Disasters in Central Vietnam. Summary Report.* Hanoi: September 2000.

Dudley, Eric and Haaland, Ane. *Communicating Building for Safety.* London: Intermediate Technology Publications, 1993.

Goichot, Marc. *Intégration de nouveaux principes d'aménagement du territoire dans la province de Thua Thien-Hue : adapter le développement à la réalité de l'inondation est devenu une priorité.* Hue: January 2000.

Hollister, David T. *Vietnam Red Cross and the International Federation of Red Cross and Red Crescent Societies. Disaster Resistant House Rehabilitation Programme. Mid-Term Evaluation and Recommendations.* Bangkok: July 2000.

International Federation of Red Cross and Red Crescent. *World Disasters Report.* Oxford: Oxford University Press, 1997 and 1998.

International Federation of Red Cross and Red Crescent. *World Disasters Report.* Geneva: International Federation, 1999 and 2000.

Norton, J. and Chantry, G. "Promoting principles for better typhoon resistance in buildings – a case study in Vietnam" in *Natural Disasters: protecting vulnerable communities*. London: Thomas Telford, 1993.

Parker, Ronald S. "Single family housing: the window of opportunity for mitigation following natural disaster" in *Managing Disaster Risk in Emerging Economies*. Washington, DC: World Bank, June 2000.

The Economist Intelligence Unit. *Country Profile: Vietnam*. London: The Economist Intelligence Unit Limited, 1998 and 1999.

Tukker, Henk. *Income Generation Activities for Vulnerable Groups in Vietnam*. Hanoi: International Federation of Red Cross and Red Crescent Societies, Viet Nam delegation, December 1999.

Wickramanayake, Ebel. "Flood Mitigation Problems in Vietnam", in *Disasters*, Vol. 18, No. 1, March 1994.

World Bank. *Vietnam Environmental Program and Policy Priorities for a Socialist Economy in Transition*. Hanoi: World Bank, 1995.

World Bank. *Vietnam – Attacking Poverty. Vietnam Development Report 2000*. Hanoi: World Bank, December 1999.

Web sites

Asian Disaster Preparedness Center **http://www.adpc.ait.ac.th/general/links.html**
Central Provinces Initiative **http://www.undp.org.vn/cpi**
Disaster Management Unit **http://www.undp.org.vn/dmu**
United Nations Office for the Coordination of Humanitarian Affairs (UNOCHA)
    http://www.reliefweb.int/w/rwb.nsf/s/

chapter 6

Section One

Focus on recovery

Food crisis in Tajikistan: an unnatural disaster?

In 2000, Tajikistan experienced its worst drought in 74 years. Domestic cereal production fell 47 per cent on the previous year, and over 1 million people faced hunger and malnutrition requiring immediate humanitarian response. For the past eight years, food aid has been provided to the country, but recent appeals have been very poorly funded. Recovery of food security depends on more than relief alone. Root causes need to be addressed – but how far can humanitarian agencies go before the political and financial stakes get too high?

This chapter examines dilemmas posed for effective humanitarian action when an apparent 'natural disaster' masks and obscures deeper, structural causes which are at the root of suffering. Only full analysis of the political, economic and social context of the crisis can set proper parameters for humanitarian action and ensure coherent disaster responses that do not make things worse in the long term even as they ease suffering in the short term.

Better analysis could provide the basis for a recovery strategy encompassing a range of sectors and levels of engagement, from the most neutral (such as food aid at the household level), to the most political, such as electoral reform at the national level. Mapping the root causes of food insecurity will enable a range of local, national and international actors to cooperate in a recovery strategy in which they can select the form and level of intervention most appropriate for their mandate.

The chapter will examine some root causes of food insecurity in Tajikistan – 'barriers to recovery' – then suggest lessons that agencies committed to supporting recovery can draw, and conclude by presenting a mapping tool to promote a more strategic approach to recovery.

I. Barriers to recovery of food security

During 2000, the worst drought in Tajikistan for three generations prompted emergency international appeals to address acute food insecurity for 1.2 million people, one-fifth of the population. However, contextual analysis clearly indicates that the 2000 drought, severe as it may have been, has merely amplified endemic food insecurity that already existed both in Tajikistan and regionally (see Box 6.1). This food insecurity is generated primarily by structural factors arising from post-Soviet transition and the legacy of civil war. Specific factors include problems with clarity of available information on food provision, water management, land use, access to land and drug trafficking.

Post-Soviet and post-conflict legacy

Until 1991, Tajikistan was one of five Soviet central Asian republics. Each republic was economically co-dependent, and specialized in just a few commodities. Because of Tajikistan's abundant water supply, Moscow ordained aluminium smelting, cotton cultivation and hydro-electricity as principal economic activities and, in return, provided food. Following independence in 1991, and the withdrawal of former Soviet support, Tajikistan – a landlocked country, isolated from world markets – faced the tough challenge of transition to a free market economy.

Photo opposite page: Since independence in 1991, Tajikistan's irrigation system has seen water volumes plummet by 50 per cent.

Roger Bracke/ International Federation, Tajikistan 2000

Box 6.1 Drought overlaid on structural problems: a regional crisis?

Tajikistan's severe lack of rainfall has been mirrored across other central and south Asian states during 2000-2001. And, as in Tajikistan, the relationship between food insecurity and deeper structural problems is starkly revealed.

In Afghanistan, the UN warned that at least 1 million Afghans face starvation because of devastating drought compounding the effects of two decades of civil war. In India, reports indicate tens of millions are at risk across six states from a drought as much man-made as natural, because of ongoing problems with water management. In Pakistan, the impact of drought has been exacerbated because local communities, now dependent on pumps and irrigation systems, have forgotten traditional methods of water conservation.

To the north, in Mongolia, warnings of severe food shortages have been triggered by winter blizzards striking after summer drought. The present crisis follows several years in which structural changes in the Mongolian economy have triggered a precipitous fall in domestic food production. State farms, previously heavily subsidized, are being dismantled and privatized; 70 state farms have so far been turned into 300 farm companies. Production has declined progressively, as newly private companies have been unable to access necessary loans to buy machinery and inputs. This, coupled with a lack of managerial skill, has meant that yields and areas under cultivation have both declined considerably.

Drought is severe in northern and western Uzbekistan and Turkmenistan, downstream from Tajikistan, where irrigation supplies become more depleted. In both countries, estimated cotton and food production is down on previous years. Unsustainable cropping patterns and the collapse of irrigation systems have exacerbated the drought's impact. Though aggregate grain production in Uzbekistan for 2000 is estimated down by just 6 per cent, it plummeted by 54 per cent in the Autonomous Republic of Karakalpakstan.

Meanwhile, in August 2000, Radio Free Europe reported that some central Asian countries are diverting irrigation water before it even reaches Kazakhstan (by far the most massive of the five new central Asian republics). Central Asia's two major rivers, the Amu-Darya and the Syr-Darya, originate in Kyrgyzstan and Tajikistan and meander through Uzbekistan, Turkmenistan and Kazakhstan on their way towards the Aral Sea.

A Soviet-era system of reservoirs on these two rivers was designed to provide a steady flow of water to all five Soviet central Asian republics. However, since transition, it now serves five sovereign nations, each with their own priorities. In 1999, for the first time, Kyrgyzstan used its water for political leverage, demanding that it be recompensed regionally for its maintenance of the Syr-Darya reservoirs. When Kazakhstan did not provide the coal it had demanded, Kyrgyzstan closed off the reservoirs. The leverage worked.

In 2000, Uzbekistan followed suit, cutting off water supplies to Kazakhstan over alleged non-payment of debts. This time, Kazakhstan responded in kind, cutting phone lines that run through its territory. In a complicated move, it then asked Tajikistan to release more water to Uzbekistan so that the latter, in turn, could release more to Kazakhstan. Surprisingly, given its own 'drought', Tajikistan obliged, but there is as yet no sign of the extra water being passed on from Uzbekistan to Kazakhstan. Tajikistan's deputy minister of water resources, Vohid Shefiev, was reported by Radio Free Europe as saying, "Although we ourselves are experiencing a shortage of water, we decided to supply Uzbekistan with water and we expect that our neighbour will help us with electricity in the winter."

In short, the newly independent central Asian states have inherited a hugely sensitive interlinking of water resource dependencies. Regionally, the impact of drought has been to expose this sensitivity to political and economic power plays, risking not just humanitarian suffering but increased regional rivalry and instability.

Political turmoil following independence led to armed conflict in 1992 and, in the bloody civil war that followed, an estimated 50,000 to 100,000 lives were lost. The conflict caused around US$ 6 billion of damage to industrial, agricultural, communications and transport infrastructure. The destruction wrought by the civil war, the ending of direct Soviet subvention (previously accounting for 40 per cent of Tajikistan's budget) and its import-export network, a massive brain drain of professionals employed in strategic industrial enterprises, and an exodus of local and national administrators have all contributed to economic collapse.

While all five central Asian states experienced a sharp deterioration in economic performance in the years following independence, Tajikistan was worst affected with real gross domestic product (GDP) falling by 60 per cent from 1992 to 1996. The country emerged from conflict in 1997 to begin rebuilding its economy on the eve of the Russian financial crisis, which seriously weakened a significant export market and destroyed any prospects for a peace dividend of increased foreign investment. Cotton and aluminium production continue to be the main sources of hard currency, but output has halved in the past decade.

While the peace agreement has improved stability, the downward spiral for ordinary people has continued. Despite an estimated gross national product (GNP) per capita of US$ 2,901 in 1999, two-thirds of the population subsists on less than a dollar a day. Yet, at independence, Tajikistan ranked as a middle-income nation. Government expenditure on health and education has fallen to 1 per cent and 2.1 per cent of GDP respectively – lower now than for any other central Asian republic. At the war's end, an estimated 16 per cent of households were critically food-insecure. More recently, chronic malnutrition rates greater than 40 per cent have been reported by the World Food Programme (WFP) and a recent nutrition assessment by Action Against Hunger reported acute malnutrition rates of up to 12 per cent in children in the south of the country.

Despite formal peace since 1997, instability continues to threaten the country's prospects for recovery. Regional threats to stability include the Ferghana valley, a meeting point between Kyrgyzstan, Tajikistan and Uzbekistan, which is particularly vulnerable to conflict because of its strategic location and mixed ethnic population. The valley is a prime source of water and food for all three countries.

To make the twin transition from conflict to recovery, and from Soviet state to modern market economy, Tajikistan must ensure peace and stability, consolidate democracy, rebuild institutions and infrastructure, establish new trade links to integrate its economy with the rest of the world, combat drug trafficking and corruption, address inequitable privatization and deliver on land reform. In this light it would be wrong, even dangerous, to view the food insecurity crisis of 2000-2001 as purely a drought-driven 'natural disaster'. It is an emergency with complex political and economic root causes, requiring a recovery strategy able to tackle those causes.

Clarity of available information on food provision

Overall food availability within Tajikistan remains unclear and, to some extent, relief is being planned in an information vacuum. However, Tajikistan's food balance sheet reveals an ongoing structural deficit, aggravated by drought but pre-existing it. No long-term strategy to address this deficit has been elaborated by either the government or the international community.

Assuming a 6.22 million population and average yearly consumption of 146 kilograms of cereals per person, together with necessary seed saving (74,000 tonnes) and inevitable losses (41,000 tonnes), Tajikistan's total annual cereal need can be estimated at 1,023,000 tonnes. In a normal, non-drought year, this food balance sheet is made up in four ways: domestic cereal production; commercial food imports; kitchen garden production; and food aid.

Since 1997, national cereal output has declined continuously, but 2000's drop has been the largest: a 47 per cent fall over 1999. In a normal year, domestic production meets 45 to 50 per cent of national need. WFP's final estimates for the 2000 harvest, however, were just 256,000 tonnes, or around 25 per cent of total needs. The president of Tajikistan issued famine warnings in mid-2000. However, the ministry of agriculture said in November 2000 that producers systematically under-report harvests to avoid taxation and that the harvest would be higher than predicted, underlining the absence of clarity around food availability.

Even in a good year, Tajikistan commercially imports cereals from Kazakhstan and the Russian Federation. The deputy minister of agriculture says that information on the economics of food importation "is not publicized". WFP estimates food imports have totalled about 300,000 tonnes annually since 1994-1995, rising to 400,000 tonnes in 1999 (or 40 per cent of total need). The Economist Intelligence Unit's (EIU) country report for 2000 says that Qalla, the state grain company (newly 'privatized' as a joint stock company under the control of the former minister for grain production) imported 208,000 tonnes in the first half of 2000, with a further 250,000 tonnes planned for later in the year – totalling 458,000 tonnes for the whole of last year.

By any reckoning, such a massive yearly import of food is big business: at a conservative estimate of US$ 150 per tonne, 458,000 tonnes generate an annual turnover of almost US$ 70 million. Transport, storage, distribution and sale represent a major revenue source for a network of businesses. While the liberalization of grain imports has helped to develop a dynamic private sector, the absence of a long-term strategy to increase grain production and decrease dependence on external sources means such large-scale imports drain hard currency reserves, undermine local incentives for recovery and draw accusations of elite profiteering and corruption.

Some 93 per cent of the rural population has access to kitchen gardens (plots under 0.5 hectares attached to family houses) which produce vegetables and other foods. It is very difficult to quantify the role of these gardens in meeting the population's food requirements, because such production remains invisible in national-level statistics. However, it is believed to be in the region of 5 to 10 per cent of total food needs.

Food aid aims to make up the shortfall left by domestic production and imports. WFP provided 116,623 tonnes of food aid in Tajikistan between 1993 and 1999. Over the nine months of most severe need from September 2000 to June 2001, WFP aimed to bring about 126,000 tonnes of food into Tajikistan at a cost of US$ 67.2 million. But all agencies responding in Tajikistan are combating donor lethargy: by February 2001, only 30,000 tonnes of confirmed pledges for food had been made to WFP.

Water management

To add to the confusion of the food-availability picture, Tajikistan, a land in 'drought', is extremely water rich, suggesting that water management has as much impact as poor rainfall on food insecurity. Melting snow from Tajikistan's mountains supplies the irrigation network with up to 52 million cubic metres of water per year, enough to supply all five central Asian republics. So, although snowfall for 2000 was somewhat down, input to the irrigation system is not the problem: decaying delivery systems and massive leakage is. According to the World Bank's June 2000 poverty assessment, "The irrigation and drainage systems have seriously deteriorated since the break-up of the Soviet Union. As a result, irrigation volumes have been reduced by as much as 50 per cent." The Bank says this means about "200,000-300,000 arable hectares, or 20-30 per cent of the total production area, may now be out of use".

Only 7 per cent (960,000 hectares) of all land is arable. Of this, over one-half (555,000 hectares) is classified by the government as 'irrigated', served by the vast, intricate, but decaying Soviet-era network of pipes, canals, ditches, aqueducts and pumps criss-crossing the country. In 2000's 'drought' year, functionally irrigated agricultural land reported reasonable crop yields. But as much as half of the land officially deemed 'irrigated', in effect, lacks functioning irrigation. The remaining 405,000 hectares of arable land are designated as 'rain-fed'. Of this, 110,000 hectares are not currently in use, leaving 295,000 hectares under crops, at least in theory. It is here that the lowest rainfall in 74 years has had its impact, decimating yields.

However, while 2000's cereal production plunged 47 per cent from 1999's total, cotton production actually climbed by 6 per cent. Reasons why cotton yields increased during a 'drought' year include the higher-than-usual temperatures, in which cotton thrives, but also the prioritization of irrigation resources for cotton over cereals.

Intensive, collectivized cotton production began during the Soviet era when Moscow imposed a cotton monoculture on Tajikistan, Turkmenistan and Uzbekistan. Cotton covers 250,000 hectares, accounting for most of the arable land that remains functionally irrigated. Hence,

Tajikistan: only 7 per cent of this mountainous land is arable.

most of the land under cereals, which was once irrigated, is no longer so in practice. Officially, the ministry of agriculture denies a trade-off between cotton and cereal production in terms of use of functionally irrigated land. However, the EIU's country report, dated January 2001, notes, "It is likely that water had been reserved for the cotton and not the grain crop, since the former brings the country much-needed export revenue."

As the Soviet-era irrigation and drainage systems fall further into disrepair, so the pressure for quick economic results leads to choices which provide little direct benefit for the most vulnerable people. The need for a long-term strategy to support the rehabilitation of irrigation infrastructure on grain-producing land is starkly apparent.

Land use

"Cotton is given absolute priority at all levels of government," according to the World Bank's poverty assessment, which adds that the production and delivery of cotton dominates the agricultural economy. Cotton accounted for 17.6 per cent of exports in 1998 and is one of the country's three main hard-currency earners. There is no export market in grain, and Tajikistan, lacking domestic financing from non-bank sources and with little access to international capital markets, has had little choice but to meet macroeconomic stabilization targets by maximizing earnings from cotton. So far, however, this strategy has not benefited the majority of Tajikistan's poorest. As in other post-conflict transitions, the pressure for quick economic results is aggravating vulnerability.

In the absence of a convincing strategy to restore irrigation to grain-producing land, there is concern that the prioritization of water resources for cotton over food may be in the interests of new profit-making elites into whose hands cotton ginning mills and farms have been privatized. According to the EIU, "The government will have to ensure that rent-seeking activities are minimised – there have been concerns in the past over insufficient transparency in a privatisation process that has not been adequately explained to the local population, and has resulted in local interest groups controlling most of the newly privatised enterprises."

Meanwhile, the ordinary peasant frequently has little choice but to provide labour on state cotton farms for nominal wages and is unable either to grow food or to purchase the imported variety. According to the World Bank's poverty assessment, prices paid to cotton producers are "extremely low", while "non-payment of wages and wage arrears have had a major impact on poverty". Despite significant progress in price and trade liberalization in agriculture, the lack of development of the market infrastructure has meant that, in practice, farmers have little say in the sale of their goods.

Cotton production could provide smallholders with a valuable income. However, notes the Bank, "Although by law farmers are free to sell their cotton harvest to whomever they choose, not all of them are actually able to do so in practice. Many farmers in the southern districts, for example, have not received payment for their cotton for two to three years. Moreover, the prevailing policy of determining cotton prices in contracts without determining input prices leaves most farmers at the mercy of local officials and subsequently in debt." The Bank concludes, "The cotton sub-sector, as currently managed, prevents the development of the agricultural economy."

Access to land

Tajikistan's high mountain ranges make food production difficult. Only 7 per cent of land is arable, yet 70 per cent of the 6.2 million population lives in rural areas. Their livelihoods depend on the recovery of an agricultural sector which accounts for 20 per cent of official GDP, 30 per cent of export revenues, and up to 40 per cent of government revenues, mainly from taxation of cotton.

As in other central Asian republics, all land in Tajikistan remains the property of the state. However a series of decrees and other resolutions throughout the 1990s has attempted to accelerate the pace of land reform. In principle, there are at present some 359 state farms (*sovkhoze*) still functioning, ranging in size to a maximum of 2,000 hectares. Collective farms (*kolkhoze*) range up to about 1,000 hectares and number 251. Formed on land that has been carved from these state and collective farms, some 14,000 private peasant associations now exist, varying in size up to 1,000 hectares. An additional 13 inter-rayon associations, 86 joint stock companies and 109 cooperatives also operate with varying sizes and dispensations. In principle, all of these rely on forms of land-leasing, some renewable, some not. In theory, leases may not be sold on or traded.

Two other forms of land arrangement also exist. First, 'presidential decree land' is a relatively recent phenomenon granting land to peasant families. Some 75,000 hectares have been set aside for allocation across the country, allotted in units of 0.5 hectares per family. They may not be sold or built on, and are intended for food production only. Secondly are the kitchen gardens referred to earlier. Ranging in size between 0.1 and 0.6 hectares, ownership of these plots is effectively uncontested. However, they are far too small to provide adequate food for the average family and may, in any case, be shared between a number of families making up a household.

According to the World Bank, "When asked about survival strategies, participants rank their household plot and livestock at the top of their lists, ahead of migration, trade, humanitarian assistance, wages and pensions." This leads the Bank to conclude that "improved access to land needs to be considered a priority in a poverty reduction strategy". The International Monetary Fund (IMF) adds that ongoing land reform is the key to reducing poverty and addressing food insecurity "if carried out equitably and efficiently".

However, efficiency of land reform demands that the process be decentralized to the level of district authorities (*hukumat*), which may compromise the fairness of the process. As the World Bank's poverty assessment notes, "If the chairman of the *hukumat* is prone to abuse of position, it is the poor who tend to suffer the most due to their inability to pay bribes or peddle influence... it is reported that some farmers have to resort to bribery and influence peddling to obtain land use rights, water, fertiliser and other inputs. Commissions in charge of allocating land and converting collective farms into *dehkan* (private) farms sometimes do not consult with local farmers, preferring instead to use the allocation and conversion process to grant land use rights to the more powerful and wealthy members of the community in exchange for favours."

Most worryingly for aid agencies working in rehabilitation, allocations frequently alter year on year. With little security of tenure, peasants, who may have spent years making land productive, suddenly have it repossessed by local elites, who then move them on to poor-quality holdings. These problems were highlighted in February 1999's presidential decree, which stated that, "Some community leaders are allocating unsuitable land, with defective irrigation and drainage systems, to citizens, in violation of the President's decree."

Meanwhile, presidential land is intended to be gifted directly from the state to the peasant, and taxed at a flat rate of US$ 3.50 per 0.1 hectare annually. However, the collective and state farms from which that land is taken often levy 'rents' well in excess of the legally determined rate, in the form of a sharecropping 30 per cent tax on harvests. Peasant farmers receiving land may also be obliged to work on collective or state farms, ensuring a cotton harvest which is no longer even in their indirect economic interest.

Drug trafficking

According to a report of the United Nations (UN) secretary-general, dated August 2000, "A significant and increasing proportion of Afghan opium, morphine and heroin is being smuggled through central Asia, mainly through the 1,700-kilometre border between Afghanistan and Tajikistan... Although some drugs are absorbed locally along the routes, the final destination of the bulk of the narcotics is Europe and, to some extent, the United States." While authorities seized a total of 8 tonnes of narcotics in 2000, the Centre for Preventive Action says that about 60 tonnes of dry opium per year are smuggled through Tajikistan from the Afghan province of Badakhshan alone. According to the UN's Integrated Regional Information Network, an estimated 30 to 50 per cent of the entire economic activity of Tajikistan is linked to drugs with Afghanistan.

Tajikistan – a water-rich land – suffered from the worst drought in 74 years in 2000. Grain yields dropped 47 per cent while cotton thrived.

Roger Bracke/ International Federation, Tajikistan 2000

In June 1999, the government of Tajikistan established a state anti-narcotics agency with UN support. The reality is, however, that many people have few alternative sources of income. According to the UN's country coordinator, there are food-processing factories in Tajikistan that could be viable if they were rehabilitated. But in the absence of investment incentives and a conducive marketing atmosphere, drug trafficking will remain a more viable alternative. Efforts to bolster law and order in the country are likely to be resisted by those for whom drug trafficking is a source of wealth.

The growing problem of drug trafficking underlines the need for rehabilitation of local industries, significant levels of development aid, foreign direct investment, market opportunities and incentives for job creation, within a national framework supported by government initiatives in such areas as land reform and employment legislation.

II. Lessons for coherent aid response

In the light of the foregoing analysis, this section sets out to examine how humanitarian agencies should respond to disasters whose roots lie in structural causes. An ongoing, structural food deficit exists in Tajikistan and no clear strategy is in place to reduce it. How do humanitarian agencies respond to widespread acute malnutrition in a country with so many interrelated causes of food insecurity?

To decide whether they have a role to play in addressing structural causes of vulnerability, agencies must first analyse these causes and identify specific solutions. Only by clear and detailed analysis will agencies be able to decide what they can and cannot do to address these causes. What does their mandate allow? What resources are available? Whom do they need to work with? At what level should the intervention be targeted – household, district, national? What are the limits of their responsibility? What impact can they expect to have?

In the case of Tajikistan, structural causes of food insecurity include: lack of clear information on food availability; water management; land use; access to land; and drug trafficking. Some lessons and solutions are suggested below.

- **Lack of clear information on food availability** leads to confusion as to the real needs for relief and rehabilitation assistance and is hampering the elaboration of a national strategy to address food insecurity. It is attributed to under- and over-reporting of crop estimates to avoid taxation or attract incentives to support continued production. Solutions to this obstacle lie in the development of an effective, accurate reporting system, based on incentives that reward, not sanction, accuracy. Responsibility for the implementation of such a system lies clearly with Tajikistan's ministry of agriculture, which may be supported by the UN Food and Agriculture Organization (FAO), the World Bank or the Asian Development Bank (ADB).
- **Poor water management** is exacerbating structural food insecurity in two ways: collapsed irrigation and drainage systems affect half of all formerly irrigated land; and irrigation water is prioritized for cotton production to the relative exclusion of grain. The World Bank has made a series of specific recommendations to address these problems:
  - i. irrigation rehabilitation should be pursued on the basis of economic viability;
  - ii. rain-fed, livestock and non-agricultural technologies should be investigated and introduced for areas where irrigation is not economically viable;
  - iii. user charges for irrigation water should be applied and extended; and
  - iv. institutional reform of irrigation management systems should be carried out at the community, district and regional levels.

  The reform framework for a poverty alleviation strategy to produce agricultural growth has already been initiated by the government of Tajikistan. This framework specifically targets the restoration of a sustainable irrigation and drainage system. Support is being provided by the World Bank, the IMF, ADB and the United Nations Development Programme (UNDP).

- **Land use** as a structural cause of food insecurity relates less to the question of whether cotton or grain is grown than to who benefits from what is grown. Cotton can be successfully grown on a small scale and has the potential to be a remunerative cash crop for farmers. However, vested interests ensure the Soviet-style centralized system restricts the number of contracts for producers, thus depriving small farmers of the opportunity to engage in limited cash cropping that would significantly increase their returns. In its June 2000 poverty assessment, the World Bank recommends that the ministry of agriculture develop new institutional arrangements to permit the practice of small-scale cotton production.

- **Access to land** is widely acknowledged as an essential factor in food insecurity. A key improvement would be the provision of wider and deeper land access and use for family-based farming. According to the World Bank, this would require a number of reforms at central level, including:
  i.   the presidential land reform programme should be extended and an equitable and inclusive distribution of access to land should be ensured for rural households;
  ii. there should be transparent legal protection of land access and use rights for individual shareholders of privatized land;
  iii. comprehensive information should be provided to shareholders on individual land rights and on choices of farm management systems; and
  iv. participatory consultation approaches should be undertaken for land stakeholder decision-making.

- **Drug trafficking** presents structural obstacles to food security in two ways. Firstly, narcotics trafficking works against the government's efforts to improve governance and undermines the overall reform process. Secondly, trafficking diverts badly needed domestic and external investment funding from the food manufacturing industry, undermining market development and recovery. As noted above, efforts are under way to address these obstacles. The UN Office for Drug Control and Crime Prevention (UNDCCP) is providing assistance to Tajikistan's authorities to strengthen drug control efforts through reinforced border control and the establishment of a new national drug control agency.

The above range of solutions to structural food insecurity in Tajikistan is being supported by a series of loans and grants from the World Bank, the IMF, UNDP and the ADB. The World Bank has allocated US$ 93.4 million to provide technical cooperation over three years and US$ 100,000 in the form of grants. The IMF is providing US$ 9 million in balance-of-payments support, while US$ 20 million from the ADB is aimed at rehabilitation activities. UNDP is implementing rehabilitation projects worth US$ 10 million, and working with multilateral institutions to support long-term recovery. Cooperation is ensured in a number of ways, including: the consultative group for Tajikistan; the public investment programme; and the living standards survey.

An analysis of the crisis in Tajikistan reveals a complex environment in which a difficult recovery process must address the frequently conflicting interests of a wide range of stakeholders. Major reform programmes are already under way to address the structures that hinder progress in development or produce and perpetuate vulnerability. Responsibility for the success of these programmes lies with the government of Tajikistan and its various ministries. The Bretton Woods institutions and other regional financial organizations, together with a range of other intergovernmental organizations have been mandated to support the government in elaborating and implementing recovery and reform strategies. These strategies include the establishment of representative governance and judicial systems, electoral and land reform, economic recovery, and the restoration of accessible education and basic health services.

How can humanitarian agencies engage?

Should humanitarian agencies engage in these programming areas? Their aim is to alleviate suffering. But limiting humanitarian aid to addressing immediate needs, without considering underlying causes, would mean that aid could never alleviate long-term suffering. In such cases, aid which supports the status quo may be perceived as perpetuating the cycle of vulnerability. On the other hand, interventions designed to address structural issues relating to reform, justice and rights require engagement in political processes that may undermine the neutral stance of humanitarian organizations.

The *Code of Conduct for the International Red Cross and Red Crescent Movement and non-governmental organizations (NGOs) in Disaster Response,* to which almost 200 organizations have subscribed, makes it clear that relief has a duty not just to meet basic needs but also "to reduce future vulnerabilities to disaster".

When addressing Tajikistan's emergency needs last year, the International Federation of Red Cross and Red Crescent Societies aimed to reduce future vulnerabilities. Responding to a request from the Red Crescent Society of Tajikistan, and following emergency warnings of impending famine issued by the government of Tajikistan, FAO and WFP in mid-2000, the International Federation deployed a field assessment and coordination team (FACT) in August. The FACT's mission was to conduct an assessment of the needs triggered by the severe drought, and to propose an emergency plan of action in response to those needs. Following a two-week assessment, the FACT designed a plan to address the following objectives:

- improve food availability for 31,250 households in drought-affected rain-fed areas across the country;
- ensure target groups will have seeds to plant for next year's harvest;
- improve or expand the water system for the target population through repairs and cleaning of water channels within food-for-work activities;
- strengthen the community health sector through health education initiatives and initiating public awareness programmes on the use of safe drinking water;
- increase the quality of drinking water through chlorination of 100 shallow wells;
- give access to drinking water for 18,000 people though replacement of water pumps; and
- strengthen the disaster response and disaster preparedness capacity of the Red Crescent Society of Tajikistan and its branches through programme activities.

To ensure that humanitarian interventions contribute towards addressing root causes of food insecurity, aid programmers need to do at least two things:

- analyse the local context to ensure aid reinforces, rather than undermines, long-term recovery; and
- map the recovery initiatives of the government and other agencies to ensure aid explicitly complements and accelerates other efforts already under way to tackle root causes.

While aid may be intended as neutral alleviation of suffering, care should be taken to avoid its potentially negative impacts on the recovery process. As economist Robin Davies recently wrote in *Forum,* an International Committee of the Red Cross (ICRC) publication, "Humanitarian assistance has never been, and never will be, economically neutral for the host country... the more unstable the country and the more the local society and infrastructure have disintegrated, the greater the financial impact of the relief." Davies lists eight serious types of negative economic impact, which include boosting the 'shadow' or parallel economy and fuelling corruption.

Only more detailed analysis of the context within which humanitarian aid is delivered can determine the potential for both its positive and inadvertently negative effects. One approach being piloted by the International Federation is the 'Better Programming Initiative', which enables local and international actors to work together in analysing the aid context and designing programmes that support rather than undermine long-term recovery (see Box 6.2).

Mapping the road to recovery

Humanitarian agencies are not equipped to deal with macro-level recovery and structural reform. They lack the institutional expertise and access to the scale of resources required to engage effectively in this area. Moreover, the duration of such interventions usually requires a commitment far in excess of the typical humanitarian aid programme cycle. Such agencies' strength lies in their ability to deliver assistance to individuals, families and communities, based on identification of needs (see Box 6.3). Their success in alleviating suffering is made possible by their access to those affected by disaster. This access has generally been predicated on their adherence to the principle of neutrality.

As interventions move up the scale from individual, household and community level, to engage with provincial, regional and national actors, they become more obviously political in character. Political, racial, religious and, especially, ideological considerations are increasingly influential at higher levels. Equally, from a sectoral point of view, recovery programming in lifesaving sectors such as food, health, shelter, and water and sanitation is, in principle, less political in degree than institutional or macroeconomic reform. However, the neutrality of any action can never simply be counted upon. Aid at every level and of every kind demands an actively managed neutrality based on careful contextual analysis.

In order to develop a coherent humanitarian response, agencies must establish a delimited intervention within a broad, inter-agency strategy for recovery that clearly indicates whom the aid is intended to help. Isolated aid interventions planned in an information vacuum are prone to manipulation and failure. The use of a recovery mapping tool, or 'impact graph', can help frame an effective intervention strategy within which the roles and responsibilities of a broad range of local, national and international actors to assist specific individual and institutional beneficiaries, can be articulated (see Figure 6.1).

Mapping recovery interventions enables agencies to determine the most appropriate programming sector and level of engagement for their mandate and comparative advantage. The graph is designed to answer three questions: Where does our intervention sit in terms of all other agency strategies in-country? With whom do we work in partnership to extend our impact? Where can we expect the impact of our programming to be felt?

Box 6.2 The Better Programming Initiative

For the last two years, an International Federation team has been involved in the development and field testing of the Local Capacities for Peace Project (LCPP), a global initiative run by the US-based Collaborative for Development Action. The LCPP produced research demonstrating how humanitarian aid programmes may increase tensions between communities in conflict-prone areas.

The Better Programming Initiative (BPI) is an International Federation programme based on the LCPP't findings and born of the conviction that in communities affected by violence, well-planned humanitarian aid can support local capacities for recovery and reconciliation.

During 1999-2000, the International Federation introduced BPI to national Red Cross and Red Crescent societies programming in communities recovering from conflict in Bangladesh, Colombia, Côte d'Ivoire, Ethiopia, Kosovo, Liberia and Tajikistan.

In a series of training workshops, the BPI approach helped staff to analyse the impact of their aid programmes on the dynamics of conflict and to redesign programmes to avoid negative impacts on recovery and support local capacities for peace. The BPI approach applies five analytical steps:

- **Context analysis:** Identify and prioritize the factors of division ('dividers') and cohesion ('connectors') which characterize the post-conflict context.
- **Aid programme description:** Describe planned actions in detail – why, where, what, when, with whom, by whom, and (most importantly) how is aid being offered?
- **Impact identification:** Will aid reinforce or weaken dividers and connectors? Aid will make impacts through both its material consequences (e.g., how its distribution affects existing inequalities and divisions in society) and its symbolic effects (e.g., who does aid legitimize and delegitimize).
- **Options:** For each impact identified in the previous paragraph, brainstorm programming options that will decrease negative and reinforce positive impacts. Then check the options for their parallel effects on other dividers and connectors.
- **Repeat the analysis:** Contexts change rapidly, as do constraints and opportunities for aid programming. Analysis should be updated as frequently as the project cycle permits.

In Tajikistan, International Federation and staff from the Tajikistan Red Crescent have been piloting the BPI methodology since 1999. Initially, the approach was introduced in a sequence of workshops, before being applied to concrete programming in the food security sector.

The planning workshops used the BPI approach to build a detailed question guide for use by field assessment teams preparing drought response. Questioning went into greater detail than traditional needs assessment, for example, what is the nature of local land ownership, land privatization, water resource availability and control, and ethnic balance?

Accessing such detailed information enables aid programming to be fine-tuned to locally varying effects of disaster. Aid can then be implemented to alleviate suffering while not undermining local coping capacities, and can help link relief activities to long-term recovery.

In March 2001, staff from the American, British, Canadian, Danish, Norwegian, Sierra Leone, Spanish and Swedish Red Cross societies were trained as facilitators, and will conduct workshops to mainstream BPI methodology in other national Red Cross and Red Crescent societies working in post-conflict countries.

The root causes of food insecurity in Tajikistan are so complex that an impact graph is unlikely to provide a full picture of programming obstacles and solutions. Nevertheless, such a mapping tool can help to:
- **enable agencies to position interventions and define limits:** In the absence of a coherent recovery strategy, humanitarian aid is often expected to address causes of vulnerability rooted in political and economic systems – something it can never do. Positioning humanitarian aid within a broader recovery strategy enables agencies to clearly define its function and limits of impact;

Box 6.3 Complex contexts demand flexible responses

Tajikistan's post-conflict environment is highly complex. Food insecurity shows itself in 'micro-pockets' of hardship dotted across the country rather than blanket difficulties concentrated in one area, making effective relief targeting a challenge.

In the country's south, for example, irrigation breakdown is random and unpredictable: a leaky pipe here, a blocked canal there, producing often bizarre effects. In Beshkent II, near the Uzbek border, all but 650 people have left due to total lack of water. Factories and houses lie abandoned. The only drinking water is from a shallow, salty source – unsuitable for cattle, let alone humans. Yet, at the same time, houses in the north of the village are flooded and uninhabitable due to a leaking irrigation system nearby.

Ayvadj peasant association, on the Afghan border, is dry as dust. Agronomist Chorshan Chorekulov says the population of 7,000 depends on an irrigation canal which is nearly empty. A hole in the canal gapes where a pump was once mounted: since there is no electricity the pump is gone and water drains away through the hole. "There's been no rain between July and September," says Chorekulov, "and we can't count on rain for next year. How can we plan to use this land?" Ayvadj has had no crops for the last two seasons. Between 50 and 100 families left during 2000 for Kazakhstan, the Russian Federation or Uzbekistan.

In Shaartuz, workers on the collective farm say they are planting cotton, rather than wheat, because they hope to encourage the authorities to rehabilitate their irrigation, underlining the reality that priority across Tajikistan is given to cotton production at the expense of cereals. "There's no water here really, since there are

38 kilometres of canals leading to us and we are the last people at the end of the line."

Finally, in Shokh village, there's no water either. Most of the houses lie abandoned. Only 62 families remain; they began digging a channel from the existing irrigation canal (1.5 km from the village) to supply drinking water and irrigation. But work stopped for lack of funds needed to buy fuel and oil for the ditching machine.

Combine this kind of variation with extremely difficult logistics and communications in remoter parts of Tajikistan and clearly broad targeting of relief will leave significant pockets of suffering undetected. One solution, used successfully by the International Federation in the Balkans in the mid-1990s, is the use of mobile teams for targeting and implementation. As war in Bosnia and Herzegovina ended, humanitarian organizations phased out. But conditions for isolated, vulnerable people – the elderly and disabled, single mothers and the chronically ill – continued to deteriorate. Scattered amongst the regular population, they risked becoming invisible.

In response, the International Federation piloted mobile technical teams (MTTs) to target assistance directly where it was needed. Some 29 teams, comprising three or four individuals in their own vehicle, made exploratory house calls in remote areas to identify and help vulnerable individuals. Assistance included housing repairs, chopping fuelwood, and distribution of aid and hygiene parcels.

From 1996 to 1998, this flexible and proactive method of targeting in the Balkans proved highly effective in identifying near-invisible needs. For post-conflict contexts like Tajikistan, where needs can be equally hard to spot, similar targeting strategies may prove vital.

- clarify roles and responsibilities of a broad range of different actors in the recovery process: Humanitarian agencies are sometimes pressured to undertake activities that fall neither within their mandate nor their historical expertise, on the basis of addressing unmet needs. Recovery mapping helps to ensure agencies know the other actors involved in relief and recovery programming and in which sectors. Agencies need to be aware of the mandates, roles, activities and expertise of these actors to ensure complementarity of roles and coordination of efforts;
- identify potential impact of overall recovery process: Observers may express surprise that eight years of direct food aid to Tajikistan have failed to impact on the structural food deficit within the country. This may tempt donors to lose patience and prematurely shift from relief

to 'developmental' programming. However, without an overall map of the recovery process, encompassing which inputs are required to achieve recovery and an idea of how long that recovery may take, the impact of humanitarian aid cannot be gauged. Eight years of food aid may pale into insignificance when put in the context of a recovery strategy necessary to rebuild an economy which for 80 years was part of the integrated Soviet system;

- **facilitate coordination between organizations programming at different levels across sectors:** Sustainable recovery involves joint action by staff from relief and development agencies in data collection, situation analysis, assessment and planning. Recovery mapping allows the incorporation of relief and reconstruction into an overall recovery strategy shared by all actors in the process;

- **identify gaps in the recovery strategy not addressed by current efforts:** As a result of differing land and water availability throughout the country, the effect of severe drought will vary from relatively little impact in some areas to pockets of extreme suffering in others. These pockets will exist at micro level in isolated communities and may therefore be difficult to detect. The complexity of the disaster arising from the drought is such that no single organization working alone can hope to address all the needs of the affected population. By mapping the range of sectoral needs at community, district and national levels, gaps in aid provision can be identified and filled by the appropriate agencies;

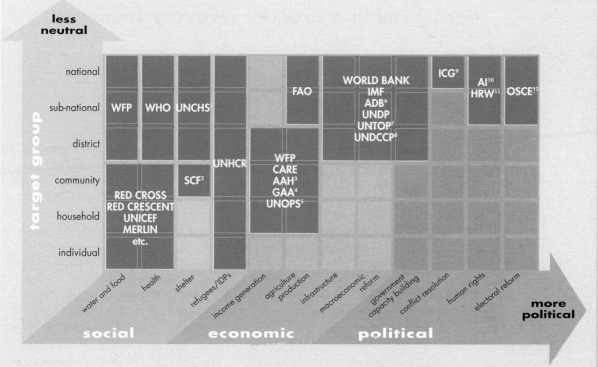

Figure 6.1:
Impact graph:
targeting recovery interventions
in Tajikistan
This graphic is for illustration purposes only

1 UN Centre for Human Settlements	7 UN Tajikistan Office of Peace Building
2 Save the Children	8 UN Office for Drug Control and Crime Prevention
3 Action against Hunger	9 International Crisis Group
4 German Agro Action	10 Amnesty International
5 UN Office for Project Services	11 Human Rights Watch
6 Asian Development Bank	12 Organisation for Security and Co-operation in Europe

■ **promote concurrent response and cross-sectoral thinking:** Without mapping the full range of ongoing recovery activities under way in Tajikistan, relief interventions may miss the opportunity to support longer-term solutions to food insecurity already elaborated by development agencies. The UN's consolidated appeal is a positive initiative in this area; and

■ **clarify political implications and identify neutral levels of engagement:** Assistance can be delivered at individual, household, community, district, sub-national and national levels. In a highly politicized environment such as Tajikistan's, questions may arise regarding the perceived neutrality of humanitarian aid. Mapping helps identify the optimal level at which agencies should target their intervention. The mapping tool presents a range of interventions ranging from apolitical programming (e.g., water and sanitation at the community level) to more political programming (e.g., electoral reform at the national level). Mapping the type of sector and level of engagement enables agencies to gauge how political they wish their interventions to be. For example, food security programming at household level may be perceived as a neutral, apolitical intervention that addresses suffering from malnutrition. However, the same sectoral intervention at district or national level may risk supporting political structures at the heart of food insecurity.

Placing aid in a broader recovery strategy

Confusion relating to the role of humanitarian aid in addressing structural causes of vulnerability and suffering has led to accusations of aid perpetuating food insecurity in Tajikistan. Only through more detailed contextual analysis will programmers be able to identify both the potentials and limits of humanitarian aid.

An analysis of Tajikistan's context suggests that the structural causes of food insecurity are deeply rooted in topographical, political and economic processes which cannot be resolved by relief alone. Political and economic actors must accept responsibility for the provision of long-term recovery strategies. At the same time, relief agencies must position their aid within a broader recovery strategy in order to clarify its limitations and relate it to other interventions by other agencies with different, complementary mandates. Recovery mapping is one tool suggested to further this process.

Relief programming will always have an impact on prospects for recovery. Emergency programmes either help to develop capacities for recovery in disaster-affected communities or they undermine them. Planning to address emergency needs should anticipate the negative as well as positive potential impacts of the proposed action. It is vital therefore that any intervention to address disaster-related needs be informed by the broader picture, in this case the real causes of chronic food insecurity.

Principal contributors to this chapter and boxes were Stephen Jackson, director of the International Famine Centre (a research endeavour of the National University of Ireland, Cork, which focuses on the political dimensions of hunger) and Sean Deely, senior officer in post-disaster recovery at the International Federation in Geneva.

Sources and further information

Abdoullaev, Kamoloudin. "The Civil War in Tajikistan" in *Peace & Policy*, Vol. 3, No.1 Spring 1998. Occasional journal of the Toda Institute for Global Peace and Policy Research.

Anderson, Mary B. *Do No Harm: How Aid Can Support Peace Or War.* Boulder, Colorado: Lynne Rienner, 1999.

Economist Intelligence Unit (EIU). *Tajikistan Country Report.* London: EIU, October 2000 and January 2001.

Falkingham, Jane. *A Profile of Poverty in Tajikistan.* Centre for Analysis of Social Exclusion (CASE), Economic and Social Research Council, CASE Paper 39. London: April 2000.

Freckleton, Ann. *Who's Needy: An Assessment of Household Food Insecurity in Tajikistan.* Brussels: European Community Humanitarian Office (ECHO), August 1997.

International Committee of the Red Cross (ICRC). *Forum – war, money and survival.* Geneva: ICRC, 2000.

International Crisis Group (ICG). *Central Asia: Crisis Conditions in Three States.* ICG Asia Report No. 7. Geneva, 7 August 2000.

Nourzhanov, Kirill. *Tajikistan: The History of an Ethnic State.* London: Hurst & Co., 2000.

Pannier, Bruce. *Central Asia: Water Becomes A Political Issue.* Radio Free Europe/Radio Liberty, August 2000.

Rubin, Barnett et al. *Calming the Ferghana Valley: Development and Dialogue in the Heart of Central Asia.* Washington, DC: Brookings Institution Press, 2000.

White, Philip and Cliffe, Lionel. "Matching Response to Context in Complex Emergencies: 'Relief', 'Development', 'Peace-Building' or Something In-Between?" in *Disasters*, Vol. 24, No. 4, pp. 314-340, 2000.

Web sites

Asian Development Bank **http://www.adb.org**

Food and Agriculture Organization **http://www.fao.org**

International Committee of the Red Cross **http://www.icrc.org**

International Federation **http://www.ifrc.org**

Radio Free Europe/Radio Liberty **http://www.rferl.org/nca/features/2000/08/ F.RU.000803122739.html**

United Nations Integrated Regional Information Network (IRIN) **http://www.reliefweb.int**

United Nations Development Programme **http://www.undp.org**

World Bank **http://www.worldbank.org**

World Food Programme **http://www.wfp.org**

Section Two

**Tracking
the system**

Habit of the heart: volunteering in disasters

"Too much help made a mess here," explained Sabre Ozcan, a manager at Istanbul's municipal water company. "But you can't stop people from coming," he told a reporter from the *New York Times*. Ozcan was one of tens of thousands of people who packed his truck and travelled to the city of Golcuk, Turkey, following a massive earthquake on 17 August 1999. The quake, which measured 7.4 on the Richter scale, killed over 17,000 people. Hoping to bring some relief to survivors, these spontaneous helpers created a 20-mile-long traffic jam obstructing emergency vehicles and rescue equipment. Even Ozcan found that once he arrived in the city, hundreds of other people had come in trucks loaded with bottled water and bread, far surpassing local needs.

Four years earlier, an earthquake of similar magnitude destroyed much of the port city of Kobe in Japan. The toll was catastrophic: 6,400 dead and an estimated US$ 130 billion of damage. "If we have to find, however, a hope even from one of the worst disasters, the quake created a surge of volunteerism around the nation, making 1995 the 'start year' of volunteerism in Japan," explains Aki Okabe, a researcher for the Ohdake Foundation. Government officials estimate that over 1 million Japanese spontaneously volunteered in response efforts during the first two months following the earthquake.

Those who volunteer their help during disasters may be either organized or disorganized – either way, many will have reacted spontaneously to the needs of those affected. They can come from the neighbourhood or abroad. They can be victims themselves, yet vital to international and national response efforts. They can be the first to respond or the last to leave, ensuring that recovery and reconstruction efforts are completed. And while they may not always be helpful during an emergency, ignoring their efforts can lead to greater confusion and chaos.

The story of volunteer response in Turkey, Japan or elsewhere following a disaster tells us about much more than the efforts of people trying to rebuild their city or country. A broader picture emerges of volunteering as a complex, dynamic and often misunderstood phenomenon. Numerous questions arise. Can we refer to those who spontaneously lend help during disasters as 'volunteers' at all? Coordinating such helpers is a key challenge in rapid-onset disasters. As emergencies become more protracted, does the spirit of volunteering come under threat from excessive per diem payments? Have organizations ignored the vulnerability of volunteers themselves in the face of disasters?

Is the traditional model of 'charitable' volunteering – where the organization defines needs and objectives, and the volunteer force delivers services to the less fortunate – adequate to combat the effects of today's recurrent disasters? Or is a combination of volunteer effort and community self-help a more sustainable approach? Finally, in this International Year of Volunteers (see Box 7.1), are we expecting too much from a largely unpaid workforce – can volunteers really pick up the tab as the effects of disasters deepen and donor pockets become ever shallower?

Photo opposite page: In the aftermath of disaster, volunteers offer an opportunity to invest more, not less, in tackling the root causes of suffering and disaster. Bangladesh Red Crescent volunteers set up and run a temporary kitchen for flood victims.

Torben-Lindberg/ International Federation, Bangladesh 1998

Box 7.1 A year for volunteers

The International Year of Volunteers 2001 (IYV2001) was officially launched at the United Nations in New York on 5 December 2000 – International Volunteer Day. The goal of this year-long celebration is to encourage the recognition, facilitation and promotion of voluntary activity.

First proposed back in the mid-1990s, the Japanese government, together with the Netherlands, Rotary Club International, and the International Association for Volunteer Effort (IAVE) spearheaded efforts within the UN to declare the year 2001 as the International Year of Volunteers. On 27 November 1997, the General Assembly adopted the initiative with the support of 122 countries.

UN Volunteers (UNV), with over 4,400 volunteers working around the world, is the focal point for the year. It has taken the lead in supporting over 100 IYV2001 national committees, using the Internet to coordinate national and local initiatives. Over 10,000 organizations are registered with the web site (http://www.iyv2001.org). By combining research and policy information with the personal accounts of volunteers in an interactive setting, the web site makes possible a global exchange of experiences, ideas and resources between volunteers.

As volunteering means different things in different cultural environments, the national committees have been established to reflect the local context in which volunteering takes place. Representatives from NGOs, community groups, government institutions and academia are all members. The committees are the force behind the year, directing efforts both nationally and locally to achieve the objectives of IYV2001. These include: assisting with the ongoing process of consultation on IYV2001; organizing numerous activities and events; and encouraging governments to adopt lasting measures to realize the aims of IYV2001 in each country.

Events organized during the year include: IAVE World Conference, the Young Asian Women Volunteers Congress, Conference On Civil Defence And Volunteerism and the Civicus World Assembly. Additionally each month, IYV2001 organizers will examine a different theme related to volunteering. For instance, May was devoted to considering the role of volunteers in emergency relief; August will examine youth, education and training; and December is given to looking at human rights.

To ensure that IYV2001 is more than just rhetoric, UNV organizers have established a series of indicators to measure the success of the year. These include: results of advocacy efforts to encourage countries to pass legislation promoting better conditions and prospects for volunteers; strengthened mechanisms for the recognition of volunteers through awards and documentation; increased and sustainable funding of volunteering efforts; a greater number of people volunteering; and the creation of an international network of volunteers acting locally but part of a global movement.

The overriding goal for IYV2001, as defined by all participants, is the need to recognize, promote and foster the continuing efforts of volunteers around the world. Kofi Annan, UN Secretary-General, in his opening message to participants at the IAVE World Conference in Amsterdam in January 2001, expressed this ambition and explained the value of volunteering in this way: "In these times marked by political and economic crises, and by disasters both natural and man-made, it is easy to be pessimistic about the future. But there are encouraging signs of progress in the human condition... Behind this progress lie many factors. One is the willingness of many individuals to donate their time, effort, resources and ideas to the well-being and advancement of all. We call them volunteers."

Solidarity among the ruins

Although the risk of earthquakes was well known in Japan prior to 1995's devastating strike on Kobe, relatively little investment had been made in earthquake preparedness, either by public organizations or residents. Most seismic mitigation efforts were orientated towards a more technical strategy of enhancing building construction and transportation facilities.

Organizationally, as contingency planning was considered the primary and exclusive domain of the state administration, there was no effort to develop the local population's capacity to manage an earthquake. This omission had tragic results.

When the earthquake struck, buildings and roads caved in. State-controlled plans couldn't cope with the scale of the disaster. A strong group of young volunteers assisted in disaster response, many of them students volunteering for the first time. And while they were no substitute for a coordinated and rapid government response, they proved very capable at saving lives, building shelters and distributing emergency medical and food supplies to affected areas.

Local authorities did little to encourage the volunteers' efforts. Volunteering in Japan, before 1995, was considered a concept irrelevant to the local context. This attitude is exemplified by the numerous bureaucratic attempts to discourage volunteers during the emergency response at Kobe.

European search-and-rescue dog teams were reportedly impounded. Qualified volunteer doctors from the US were turned away because they did not have certificates to practise medicine in Japan. According to the Kobe YMCA's post-quake report, two women from one of the city's hospitals asked local authorities for ten volunteers to help carry water. Water duty, they explained to the officials, diverted too many skilled nurses from more urgent medical duties. The officials turned them away. When they went back a second time to ask for more help, there were told to make a written request. Volunteer Japanese plumbers and electricians were also turned away since they were not certified to work in Kobe prefecture. But a year later they were invited back because infrastructure was taking so long to rebuild.

Kiyoyuki Kanemitsu, director of Kobe's international affairs division, in an interview with the magazine *Reason*, exemplified the government's hostile attitude towards volunteers, "In order to coordinate [the volunteers] it would take a lot of time… Also, we didn't know much about the people who volunteered. Frankly we couldn't verify the trustworthiness of the people who volunteered, so we could not take responsibility for them."

Activism at Kobe, however, had a profound impact on Japanese society. With numerous stories of bureaucratic bungling and trust in the government's ability to handle national crisis shattered, the success of the volunteer response launched an era of civic activity unheard of before in Japan. Legislation was quickly adopted to facilitate the growth of this emerging sector and new volunteer-based agencies were created to address a whole range of social, political and economic issues including disaster preparedness and mitigation.

Disaster volunteers – more harm than good?

The ability of volunteers in Kobe to organize themselves stands in marked contrast to the experience of Turkey. The spontaneous flood of helpers following August 1999's devastating earthquake quickly overwhelmed the capacity of the emergency services to effectively coordinate them. As the *New York Times* wrote, "In the absence of a coordinated plan or anything resembling a crisis-management centre, tens of thousands of volunteers from around Turkey arrived, outnumbering residents and promptly creating bedlam."

Many volunteer experts however would question whether such a disorganized crowd of helpers should be termed 'volunteers' at all. Christer Leopold, senior officer for local capacity building and volunteering at the International Federation, acknowledges that those who freely flood to the scene of disaster have the potential to become volunteers, but cannot be described as volunteers until they are organized, or organize themselves – 'spontaneous helpers' would be a more accurate description. While this may seem a technical point, the distinction Leopold draws between organized volunteers and disorganized helpers can clearly become a matter of life and death in a situation such as the Turkish quake.

When a second earthquake hit Turkey in November 1999, the response effort was better organized and managed. "We reached the point that had taken us one week to reach [during the first quake] in just one day," said Labour Minister Yasar Okuyan, 48 hours after the second disaster. While much of the necessary equipment was already in place and only a fraction of the death and destruction occurred, the government response was more rapid and efficient. This improved response meant fewer spontaneous helpers arrived trying to fill the gaps where the government had previously proved lacking, and enabled a more effective use of the skills and energies of those volunteers on hand.

The success of relief efforts by those spontaneously offering their help depends on the capacity of agencies and authorities to integrate them quickly and effectively into a coordinated strategy. One reason for the success of Kobe's volunteers was the way in which local authorities and volunteers eventually developed complementary functions. For example, while the government concentrated on repairing infrastructure, volunteers built and managed the day-to-day running of temporary shelters.

Caribbean national Red Cross societies have invested considerable energy in establishing systems to manage spontaneous helpers, offering a good example to other countries. Regionally, the priority is to ensure mechanisms are in place to integrate these people as quickly as possible into an operation by reviewing their skills and identifying a task and period of time when they can be absorbed into the relief effort. Usually these volunteers are brought in a few days after the emergency when the situation is moving into the recovery phase.

Rita Chick, director of volunteer resources for the San Francisco Bay area chapter of the American Red Cross, explains that the priority for managing spontaneous helpers is planning ahead, "Experience tells you that there are certain tasks spontaneous, untrained Red Cross volunteers can do." The most important element is to match these volunteers with the needs in affected areas. This requires considerable coordination and communication between volunteer managers and the damage assessment and logistics teams.

To do this, Chick and her colleagues have found that setting up a volunteer intake centre works best. They have devised a system whereby people can be interviewed in three minutes, providing information on availability and preferences for assigned tasks. They then receive any necessary training before being sent out. Chick believes in the value of spontaneous helpers and explains that the burden for using this force for good, rests with the agencies responsible for responding to the emergency. "There are many, many tasks they can do and I believe sometimes we're not creative enough to find tasks," she says.

Simply organizing volunteers may not in itself be enough to ensure they are useful – local knowledge and training are key elements of success. Following 1998's Hurricane Mitch in Central America, some first-time volunteers, especially those who arrived from abroad lacking the necessary language skills or training, had a negative impact on post-Mitch emergency and recovery efforts. While the majority of international volunteers who came to help made invaluable contributions, there was a large number of expatriate 'do-gooders' who proved more of a burden than a bonus, pulling essential resources away from the relief effort. The International Federation's operations manager Iain Logan clarifies: "It did create very real difficulties when major bilateral operators did not have enough sufficient trained personnel to implement their huge emergency programmes. So they sent 'volunteers' from their own countries who were not trained. They were in many cases, from the people I met, individuals from business and industry whose companies had donated to the appeal and wanted some of their people to go out and be humanitarians."

Logan found locals far more useful – the support they spontaneously offered to emergency operations undoubtedly prevented more lives being lost. Such volunteers, he says, made "a significant contribution to the search-and-rescue efforts, without which Red Cross performance would have been seriously limited". Logan adds, "It was extremely lucky that the disaster happened during university and school holidays. Because many of these people were students and were available."

Most major disasters bring out armies of people volunteering their time and skills and energy. Rapid-onset disasters in particular provoke spontaneous acts of compassion, which can save – and cost – lives. The critical element is to organize and train this human resource. To do this requires motivating people to turn these individual acts of courage into a sustained volunteer effort to reduce the effects of disasters and strengthen capacities to save as many lives and livelihoods as possible.

Vulnerability of volunteers to disaster

Volunteers who offer their services following a disaster can come from around the world but, more often than not, most come from disaster-affected communities. Frequently, these 'humanitarian foot soldiers' are themselves victims of the disaster. Whether it is offering psychosocial support or transporting food and medical items, they have to overcome their own personal grief and help others needing immediate assistance.

Often found on the front line of disaster response, volunteers are vulnerable as well. Organizations have a responsibility to protect the rights of their volunteers as victims and to do everything possible to support them, whether the emergency is short or long term. They must be provided with sufficient resources both to help others and to ensure their family's survival as well.

Bangladesh is one of the most disaster-prone countries in the world, best known for its cyclones and floods. But now, the insidious problem of river erosion causes even greater hardship, leaving an estimated half a million people landless and homeless each year – including Red Crescent volunteers. Neither humanitarian organizations nor the government have done much to alleviate the plight of victims, fearing perhaps that they may be drawn into a situation where there is no solution.

On Hatiya, one of countless threatened islands in the Bay of Bengal, a group of volunteers pleads: "Because of river erosion, 132 volunteers lost their houses and assets. For that reason they became homeless and helpless. In these circumstances and on humanitarian grounds they need help at this moment." By the end of 2000, nothing had been done to help these people as they struggled daily to find shelter and food.

Do not volunteer-based institutions have a moral obligation to do whatever is necessary to assist their volunteers devastated by this – or any other – catastrophe? Claims of helping the most vulnerable will ring hollow if the very people needed to deliver the care are ignored or forgotten when disaster strikes their families. Even from a purely pragmatic point of view, the efficiency of an organization depends on the ability of its individual constituents to play their full role. A key principle of first aid, after all, is to ensure first aiders avoid becoming casualties themselves.

Recent experience calls attention to the need for policies to ensure volunteers have equal protection to those they are working with. Juan Saenz, who was one of the contributors to the International Federation's review of operations in Central and South America published in December 2000, says, "A sad phenomenon observed during the review was that National Societies are not prepared to deal with their own volunteers who are affected by the disaster. Some volunteers in one country were told to wait when they requested plastic sheeting for their own houses. In another, no food was available for volunteers working at a distribution station. In many cases the National Society preferred not to deal with the situation in order to avoid any possible hint of conflict of interest, resulting in a situation where volunteers found themselves even more vulnerable than many of the people they are helping."

Based on his experience in the Caribbean and Central America, Iain Logan says, "One of the biggest complaints of volunteers is that they themselves and their families are very often victims, but because they are volunteers they are treated as second-class victims. We have had complaints of their not being allowed to go back to their families. Not being able to take food back to their families. But their families are victims. Their families are often in the shelters. People were in tears about how they felt that they were volunteering their time but being penalized for being a volunteer."

One person's expenses are another's wage

As disasters become bigger and more protracted, the difficult issue arises of whether to reward or pay those volunteers offering help. Iain Logan argues that the notion of reward depends on where you are operating. "You have to split it into two parts," he says. "One is: do you have a culture of what we would call true volunteerism, in which the most that a volunteer would get would be food, but they do not get paid. That would be the situation say in Canada, Britain, the G7. Once you move away from that, I think you get into a situation, in probably most of the countries that I can think of, where there is a short period of pure volunteerism, particularly in the search-and-rescue phase. Once that phase is over, you move rapidly to some form of payment."

In many disaster response operations, volunteer payment will often be termed an 'allowance' or 'per diem', yet frequently it is equivalent to a daily wage. Logan adds, "We [the Red Cross and Red Crescent] are often working in environments in which many of the volunteers are very poor people, have no jobs and are living on the margins. They have the ability to help us because they speak the language, know the communities and are hard physical workers. And for them it is a job."

Logan reflects the reality in which many relief coordinators operating in very poor countries find themselves: volunteers may only receive reimbursement for genuine expenses while their contribution is a few hours a week. But when disaster hits, and the relief coordinator urgently needs extra pairs of hands to work all day, then some form of payment is often an established and inevitable procedure.

An example from Ethiopia helps illuminate the dilemma. Bekele Mekonnen is 18 years old. His father is dead, but he has a mother, two brothers and three sisters. He attends high school and joined the Red Cross three years ago. He did a first-aid training course soon after joining and has worked as an ambulance volunteer for some time. He answers the phone and goes with the ambulance to the hospital. He works most evenings from 18h00 to 1h00 and for this he gets paid US$ 4 a month – 'expenses' money, as it is known.

Last year, Bekele was called upon to take part in a relief operation and worked in Wuchalie, one of the relief distribution points. He registered beneficiaries and helped with the distribution. For this he was given a temporary payment of US$ 1.20 a day. "It's called a 'lunch allowance'," says Richard May, the International Federation's head of delegation in Ethiopia, "but in reality it is more than the country's average wage, which is apparently just below a dollar a day." Adds May, "All the volunteers involved in relief operations in Ethiopia are paid. It is a very difficult, physical job. They sometimes work 12-15 hours a day. The volunteers used on relief programmes are generally those who have been through training and done other activities. So the relief allowance is seen as reward for this work. Monetary rewards certainly motivate these volunteers."

But given that financial motivation is not supposed to be part of the volunteering credo, can such work still be termed 'volunteering'? Richard Allen, a specialist in volunteering issues, acknowledges that many of the poorest volunteers regard their work as a job, but adds: "By calling these people 'volunteers' it both devalues the work of real volunteers who do things without expecting pay, and also disregards (potentially) labour laws, such as minimum wage requirements, disciplinary procedures, termination payments, and so on."

It would be fairer, argues Allen, to view these people as casual labourers who need payment whenever they work, for example during a food distribution for one day every two weeks. But, he points out, the advantage of calling them Red Cross or Red Crescent volunteers is that they often receive some form of training (e.g., in food distribution or the Movement's Fundamental Principles) and are listed on a reserve. Then, in case of future need, there is a ready supply of experienced and trained labourers, possibly with some loyalty to the Movement.

Failure to distinguish between volunteering and paid work may undermine the development of strong voluntary organizations, fears Leopold. "If you have introduced 'paid volunteers' as a concept in your work it is very difficult in the short term to change it," he says, adding that such practices are contrary to building a strong civil society.

Leopold suggests a sound guiding principle is that a volunteer should neither gain nor lose out financially due to time spent volunteering. This means not only reimbursement of 'out-of-pocket' expenses, but also – in the case of volunteers leaving their job temporarily to help out during a disaster – payment to cover any resultant loss in salary.

However, there is still a need to clarify exactly what are out-of-pocket expenses and define a policy which is applied equally, says Esther Okwanga, International Federation development delegate in eastern and southern Africa. She recounts the problem encountered by one secretary general in the region on this issue: "Following a forum at which volunteers were present, it took the intervention of the national governing body to avert a public demonstration. The volunteers saw 'unfair labour practice' by the National Society when they compared themselves with their counterparts in a neighbouring country. The latter were getting 'allowances' over and above bus fares whereas they were not even receiving the bus fares."

The use of language such as 'allowance' or 'honorarium' to refer to what is in effect a living, if temporary, wage, is not unique to the Red Cross and Red Crescent Movement. United Nations and American Peace Corps volunteers receive an honorarium often higher than the average monthly wage of the countries in which they are working – between US$ 750 and US$ 2,700 per month in the case of UN volunteers.

Clearly the levels of volunteer reimbursement vary enormously, and depend on the volunteer organization's policy, the country of operation and even the type of work. However, as Richard Allen points out: "The important thing is to label the work that is done and not the people. Work that is paid is paid employment or casual labour. Work that is not paid is volunteering. One person can do both paid work and volunteering work at different times."

Meaningful management

Experience shows there is a strong link between the quality of emergency response and the volunteer management systems in place – both before and after the event. International Federation delegates found that one issue which hindered National Society response following Hurricane Mitch was "the absence of volunteer management systems – systems which should include identification, recruitment, retention, involvement and recognition."

The coordination of spontaneous helpers and volunteers during a rapid-onset emergency is just part of the broader issue of managing all types of volunteers throughout the disaster management cycle. To guarantee the sustained involvement of communities and volunteers, the right structure must be in place to ensure that people receive the appropriate training and remain motivated.

Red Cross societies in the Caribbean are able to involve volunteers beyond the search-and-rescue phase, without payment, by having the appropriate management systems in place beforehand. Josephine Meyers of the Jamaica Red Cross explains, "Following a disaster we do not have much difficulty in retaining volunteers for longer periods because we have set up a shift system. For us it is a question of preparedness – getting people in place, knowing when they are available and when they are not and working around that."

Recruitment of volunteers, usually considered the first step, is just one element in a process which begins much earlier, with careful planning of programmes and a clear identification of the role of volunteers. Susan Ellis, an authority on volunteer issues in the US, has identified three steps to successful volunteer management:

- Understand exactly why your organization needs volunteers.
- Design meaningful volunteer assignments.
- Elaborate and implement a recruitment strategy.

"Volunteers are recruited to a specific task," adds Leopold. "It is the need and the task that attract them. Usually they cannot be moved from one task to another. First aid attracts a certain kind of people, visiting homes another kind. When planning for their activities in crisis situations this has to be remembered. In planning for disaster response, the most important thing is to train leaders and specialists. You can also train volunteers to do fast recruitment and training of potential volunteers."

The period between disasters provides an ideal chance to recruit and train volunteers to prepare for the next one. In the Americas, the Red Cross has initiated a more structured vehicle for disaster response, called RITS (regional intervention teams). Workshops are geared at training identified volunteers (and staff) to be available at 24-48 hours' notice, particularly in Central America and the Caribbean during the hurricane season. In previous disasters, while the resources were always there, the response had been uncoordinated. The RITS approach now provides the management strategy needed to integrate volunteers into any regional disaster response.

In addition, each American Red Cross chapter keeps a database of all volunteers available for emergencies, detailing their training and previous experience. If a national or overseas disaster happens and more resources are needed, the headquarters of the American Red Cross can appeal to each of its 2,000 or more chapters for volunteers with specific skills and generate a shortlist of candidates within hours. Matching the right volunteer to the right job in a disaster scenario is key to maintaining efficiency and motivation. Some potential volunteers use the Internet to match their skills and availability to the right organization or situation (see Box 7.2).

Another key management challenge is the relationship between temporary volunteers and permanent paid staff. According to Paul Jeffrey of CCD, a development agency involved in the response to Mitch, some non-governmental organization (NGO) staff "felt invaded by hordes of new people, mostly foreigners. Some staff felt their turf taken over, resisted, longed for the old days. In the long term, this persisted in resistance to new staff, physical changes in office space and so on. Some people just don't like change."

To implement a volunteer management strategy able to cope with all these challenges will, however, require investment. Volunteering does not come for free. But recent research suggests that investing in volunteers can provide up to eight times the value of that investment back in services to the community (see Box 7.3).

Sustaining commitment

Once volunteers are recruited, agencies need to commit further resources to retaining this much-needed human resource. At least that is what some people may assume. But Christer Leopold challenges this assumption: "Volunteers are attracted by needs and maintained by work and responsibility. When the disaster is over and the need is gone they leave. This is the

Box 7.2 Virtual volunteering

"Now you can save the world – in your pyjamas!" exclaimed a newspaper in the US. The article goes on to explain, "a growing number of do-gooders are using the Internet to do their bit for peace on earth, goodwill toward folks, all without having to leave the comfort of home or work computers."

The Internet is offering new opportunities for voluntary agencies, primarily in the US, seeking to recruit people too busy to take on traditional volunteering responsibilities. One cyber-service enthusiast, Jayne Cravens of the Virtual Volunteering Project, explains that there is nothing new in volunteering on the Internet, She says: "The Internet was built by virtual volunteers. The free information and advice that surfers have long provided each other in chat rooms and news groups come from a desire to help out."

Cyber-space volunteers are doing a variety of projects online from editing or writing publications to outreach programmes to building web sites. Chat rooms and e-mail are used as platforms for mentoring, tutoring or supporting projects. And another phenomenon, cyber philanthropy, is increasing in popularity as many voluntary agencies seek to strengthen and diversify funding avenues.

There are a growing number of web sites matching volunteers with organizations. The most notable are Global Volunteer Network, One World One Volunteer, Virtual Volunteering Project, and Vita.org. These sites are using the Internet to link the growing number of volunteers with organizations in need of freely given assistance. Vita.org is an American-based web site, which is specializing in linking disaster professionals and offering training in response issues. The hope of all these projects, as expressed by the Global Volunteer Network, is "to tap into the reservoir of voluntarism [with the aim of] improving not only the power within each organization, but also the quality of our world."

The United Nations is getting involved in bringing information technology to the developing world with the help of volunteers. Kofi Annan in his *Millennium Report* called upon member states to ensure their people are not denied "the opportunities offered by the digital revolution". As a result of his appeal, volunteers are being mobilized by the UN to help bridge the digital divide and train people in developing countries in the uses and opportunities of the information highway.

Some people have expressed concern about the limitations of new technology in the developing world and the usefulness of diverting resources like volunteers to such endeavours. They question the value of attempts to bridge the digital divide in countries where most people do not have electricity and illiteracy is widespread. As one magazine editorial commented, "It would make more sense to aim for universal literacy than universal Internet access."

nature of volunteering. If we want to keep them we must recruit them to other, more permanent tasks. If we have nothing important for them to do, we should let them go." So efforts to sustain volunteer commitment must be preceded by an understanding of exactly why the organization needs volunteers.

Clearly, agencies involved in both relief and development have no shortage of tasks which volunteers could potentially take on. But, as Leopold points out, how easily can volunteers recruited during the excitement of a crisis be inspired to continue contributing to, for example, health education activities?

Understanding what motivates people to volunteer in the first place is vital to sustain their commitment over the long term. Juan Saenz says that the National Societies examined in his Central American review suffered from an "inability to retain the volunteers offering their services immediately after the disaster. Furthermore, there were and are no formal mechanisms to systematically ensure that volunteers are recognized and valued as an important element in disaster preparedness and response."

Box 7.3 Invest to advance – is it worth it?

Volunteering does not come for free – management costs money. For many agencies, the expense of the management systems needed for a successful programme tends to discourage many from making a serious investment. Yet recent studies into the economics of volunteering provide conclusive evidence that the initial investment is well worth it.

These studies measure, through various methods, the monetary value of volunteering to communities. In 1995, the UK-based National Centre for Volunteering estimated the value of all volunteering in the UK as GB£ 41 billion. In the US, an NGO called the Independent Sector estimated that in 1998, "the volunteer workforce represented the equivalent of over 9 million full-time employees at a value of US\$ 225 billion." Beyond the industrialized world volunteering is an important economic factor as well. For example, volunteering in Colombia during 1995 has been calculated by Johns Hopkins University, based on the average agricultural Colombian wage, as worth the equivalent to US\$ 99.4 million or 2.1 per cent of Colombia's gross domestic product (see Figure 7.1).

The Danish Red Cross (DRC) participated in one such study with the Institute for Volunteering Research which found that every US dollar which the DRC invested in their own volunteers was leveraged into eight dollars' worth of community activity and assistance in return.

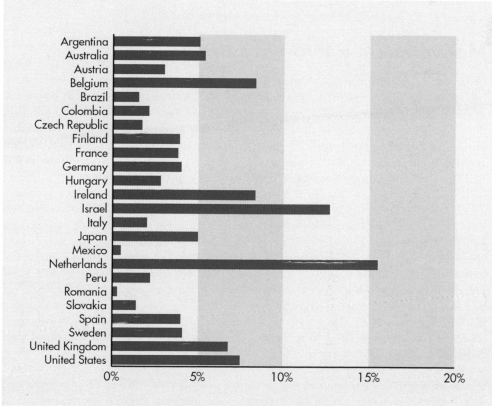

Figure 7.1: Volunteer input relative to the size of the national economy, as a percentage of 1995 gross domestic product.

Source: The Johns Hopkins Comparative Nonprofit Sector Project.

Many volunteers are motivated by the excitement of the moment and then go away when the emergency is over. It takes an enormous amount of effort on the part of agencies to keep in contact with these people and motivate them to continue helping. For Richard Allen, the answer is clear: "Attracting volunteers in non-emergency situations is simply a matter of reproducing the conditions for volunteering during emergencies – people see a pressing need, and they see that they can make a difference." Beyond that, most experts agree that to retain volunteers requires offering ongoing training, strong supervision, feedback and recognition.

Organizations like the Red Cross and Red Crescent have devised many ways to maintain volunteers' motivation and interest during non-crisis periods. One solution for a great number of National Societies is to provide those who volunteer for community development projects (such as health, social welfare or first aid) with training in disaster preparedness and response. This approach, writes Yasemin Aysan, acting chief of disaster reduction and recovery for the United Nations Development Programme (UNDP) in Geneva, "can enable the organization to maintain a structure for disaster response that is put into good use during 'normal' times, hence making it more feasible and useful to the public on a regular basis."

When it comes to recognition, volunteers may prefer their work to be celebrated by independent media, rather than in an organization's public-relations material. During the floods that devastated Mozambique in February-March 2000, around 4,000 Red Cross volunteers took part in rescue and relief activities, saving several thousand lives. Their work was publicly recognized in print by the Savana newspaper. Fernanda Teixera, secretary general of the Mozambique Red Cross, said: "It is always a great honour to be recognized for the work we carry out."

Motivation is a two-way street

Being able to 'make a difference' is often cited as the main motivation behind volunteering – but is it really that simple? To attract and motivate Jamaica Red Cross youth volunteers, Josephine Meyers organizes rallies, exchange programmes and summer camps. "In addition to that, they are seen as leaders in their schools when they are Red Cross youth, because they know first aid. So they get profile, a social life and they get to help. And they get to learn because they are always exposed to training." The strategy seems to be working – of the 50,000 Red Cross volunteers in the Caribbean, 65 per cent are under 18 years of age.

The motivation for some volunteers may derive from a spiritual influence. Whether that be a deity or perceived moral principles, it inspires people to commit to participating in something larger than themselves. This may offer people a link with, or comfort from, something beyond the material world. Jean Ayoub, director of the International Federation's disaster management and coordination division, reflects a commonly held belief when he says, "A Red Cross volunteer is a human being who still strongly believes in the seven principles [of the Red Cross and Red Crescent Movement] and acts based on that." On a somewhat less spiritual plane, Richard Allen says that, "Many National Societies that I have worked with in Africa suggest that people volunteer in emergencies because they want first chance to access food and relief items."

The disaster preparedness programmes, in which 33,000 Bangladesh Red Crescent volunteers and 50,000 Caribbean Red Cross volunteers are involved, provide some insight into motivation. These volunteers live in some of the poorest regions of the world. They are not given any financial compensation for their work, yet are on the front line of disaster response in their countries. Why do they do it?

Partly out of the desire to survive: each year, severe cyclones, storms and floods bring destruction to Bangladesh, so disaster preparedness is in everyone's best interest. But Red Crescent volunteers also take great pride in their role as a disaster preparedness squad member, disaster responder or first-aid provider. According to one evaluation of the Bangladesh Red Crescent's cyclone preparedness programme, "Through the work of almost 33,000 volunteers, cyclone warning and the response to it has become part of people's daily lives. In addition, the existing network of volunteers and radio systems affords a communication available immediately after a cyclone, thus being an important link during the relief and rehabilitation phase."

Survival, pride, peer recognition, training, spiritual solace. Many of the reasons why people volunteer today are bound up with the idea of reciprocity – contributing one thing in the expectation that you'll get something else back. Michael Taylor, a well-known American philosopher, explains that "reciprocity is usually characterized by a combination of what one might call short-term altruism and long-term self-interest."

The most successful form of volunteering may be less about charity and more a two-way street where both the volunteer and the recipient gain something positive. Indeed, volunteer and recipient may often be from the same community. Reciprocity thus forms the basis for strengthening social capital.

From charity to social capital

The examples above show that volunteering is no longer what it used to be – an act of charity by amateur do-gooders. In Europe and the United States, 19th-century notions of benevolence transformed volunteering into a class act whereby those who were richer gave their time and money to those who were poorer but deserving. However, as Margaret Bell, regional director of Civicus, an NGO supporting civil society initiatives globally, points out, "Well-meaning but patronizing and judgemental, it neither expresses the reason why people choose to volunteer nor does it provide a raison d'être for true service within the community." Richard Allen agrees: "The idea that volunteering is about one (favoured) group delivering something to another (less favoured) group is a 'Victorian' understanding of volunteering." But he finds this attitude still prevails in some National Societies.

For many in the disaster-prone world, the 'charitable' model of volunteering no longer meets their needs or describes reality on the ground. In Bangladesh, for example, volunteering is about communities taking responsibility for their own fates. In areas of life where the government has failed – or lacks the resources – to act, NGOs are making a significant impact, from micro-finance to disaster prevention. As Margaret Bell writes, "Volunteering [in Bangladesh] is at the cutting edge where change is needed and where it is truly making a difference."

In many poorer nations, points out David Peppiatt, disaster preparedness delegate for the British Red Cross, "There is often a fine line between volunteers and beneficiaries or affected people. And the vulnerability of volunteers is largely ignored. The issue, therefore, is much more about empowerment than volunteering – helping poor people as communities to manage risk and take action in crisis." And according to the Development Assistance Committee of the Organisation for Economic Co-operation and Development, it is essential "for people to become agents of their own development, and to promote the involvement and active participation of the general public and other stakeholders in a country's development".

Seen in this light, volunteering initiatives can form part of a broader investment in what is termed 'social capital' – a concept encompassing a range of social structures from churches and unions to local newspapers. Robert Putnam, a professor of public policy at Harvard University, has received considerable attention for his work showing that civic activity and norms of trust and reciprocity such as volunteering are important components of economic development. Social capital is a concept gathering ever-greater political and cultural recognition – institutions like the World Bank and the Inter-American Foundation are taking the concept very seriously and reviewing programmes to strengthen social capital components.

Encouraging disaster-affected communities to 'become agents of their own development' – in effect to manage their own disasters – may seem an obvious way forward. But is it compatible with the traditional 'service delivery' concept whereby volunteers are tasked to help other people, with the organization deciding what is to be done and how? According to such a volunteering model, volunteers and beneficiaries remain separate categories, and power rests firmly in the hands of the organization supplying the services.

But why should the defining of needs, tasks and means of delivery simply be the preserve of volunteer organizations? What about the perspective of volunteers themselves? One clear lesson from Hurricane George, says Iain Logan, is that "youth, who represented a very large percentage of volunteers, feel abused and misused. And they feel that they are not empowered.

Honduras Red Cross volunteers search for victims trapped in the debris caused by Hurricane Mitch.

Wilmer Antonio/ International Federation, Honduras 1998

They say, how can you develop a strategy for a disaster, which will ultimately depend on volunteers implementing it, if those same volunteers are not involved in its planning? They have got to be included in the planning." And that may mean long-term planning or getting involved in actually doing post-disaster needs-assessments.

Secondly, says Logan, organizations need to develop leadership within the community: "If you have a structure within the community in which there are youth leaders and volunteer leaders and you empower them, then they in turn will make the effort to keep their groups ready [for disaster response]." In a major disaster scenario, it is unrealistic to expect that humanitarian organizations alone can dictate the actions of all volunteers, so ways of empowering local communities to respond in a spontaneous yet coordinated way is surely essential. The experience of the Kobe and Turkey earthquakes made this clear.

Training leaders to encourage and enable their communities to take responsibility for their own problems is what Christer Leopold sees as the key contribution which volunteer organizations like the Red Cross and Red Crescent Movement can make to building social capital. Implicit in leadership is the ability to organize collective action – a form of social exchange that enables people to get beyond the isolated units of self and family. Such networks of voluntary action are an essential part of the structure of a strong civil society, he argues.

Margaret Bell adds, "The act of volunteering as it is practised today comes from a proactive model of behaviour borne out of the experience of empowerment." Sustainable volunteer effort, argues Bell, arises from people freely choosing to devote time and resources to developing their communities, because they want to make a positive change and believe it is possible.

Even volunteers have limits

Henry Dunant's volunteer force is shrinking. Dunant, founder of the Red Cross and Red Crescent Movement, dreamed over 140 years ago of forming cohorts of caregivers to help the wounded in wartime. He described these social soldiers as "zealous, devoted and thoroughly qualified volunteers". At its peak, over 200 million members and volunteers worldwide were estimated to have joined the Movement. But during the 1990s, this figure more than halved. Of the 97 million Red Cross and Red Crescent adherents remaining, around 20 million are believed to be volunteers. Today, National Societies from Russia to Bolivia are struggling to find ways of rebuilding their numbers.

International Federation staff list several reasons for the decline: the end of compulsory volunteering in the countries of the former Soviet Union and Eastern Europe, more accurate counting, changes in lifestyles and a proliferation of NGOs competing for volunteers. But these are not the only factors.

Volunteering as a phenomenon remains largely misunderstood and poorly managed as a resource within many organizations, both inside and outside the International Red Cross and Red Crescent Movement. Many agencies still consider the employment of volunteers as a way to save money rather than expand boundaries of action. This ignorance of the diversity and complexity of volunteering means that the recruitment and retention of them will continue to decline.

To reverse the trend, a better understanding of what motivates volunteers and a greater investment in their management are required. The Movement, faced with a diminishing number of volunteers and an increasing need for them, is renewing efforts to better understand and manage volunteers. Although numerous National Societies have devoted considerable resources to learning about and supporting their volunteer base, at many levels Red Cross and Red Crescent officials have not incorporated emerging volunteering trends into programmes.

A better understanding of volunteering may involve accepting that any attempt to impose a monolithic interpretation on volunteering is doomed to fail. As Justin Davis Smith, director of the UK-based Institute for Volunteering Research, points out, volunteering "takes on different forms and meanings in different settings. It is strongly influenced by the history, politics, religion and culture of a region. What may be seen as volunteering in one country may be dismissed as low paid or labour-intensive work (or even forced labour) in another."

At the World Conference on Volunteers in Amsterdam earlier this year, Dr Astrid Heiberg, president of the International Federation, argued: "We must build on local culture and traditions. In the past we did not pay enough attention to the fact that volunteering is different in different countries. Whatever model a National Society applies, it has to be based on local needs, on local vulnerabilities and local volunteers responding to them. The task for our organizational structures, and for our staff, is to enable those who work locally and voluntarily to do so as effectively as possible."

Focusing on volunteering during disasters helps to highlight the strengths and vulnerabilities of volunteers. Without appropriate systems to manage, train and motivate, most volunteer efforts will only end in frustration and deception. The failure by governments and organizations to recognize the true value of volunteers causes confusion and can even harm efforts to assist affected populations.

The examples of Kobe and Bangladesh have shown the crucial role volunteers can play in disaster reduction and recovery efforts. Governments have an obligation to ensure that their efforts are rooted at the centre of disaster management strategies rather than on the sidelines. At the same time, as disasters inflict ever-greater devastation, volunteers are increasingly being expected by humanitarian organizations to do more to reduce their impact.

Clearly, volunteer networks around the world offer an opportunity to invest more, not less, in tackling the root causes of suffering and disaster. But as the chorus of praise for volunteers increases during this celebration year, political and social leaders must be reminded that even volunteers have limits. The promotion of volunteer efforts should not be used as a cover for inaction, a cheap gap-filler to enable authorities to disengage from addressing the structural factors that drive disasters. For the truth is that what most victims of the pernicious cycle of crisis, poverty and risk need – better housing, access to education, more affordable health care, a living wage – volunteers alone cannot provide.

Major contributor to this chapter and boxes was Jean Milligan, a freelance writer based in Geneva.

Sources and further information

Anheier, Helmut and Salamon, Lester. *Volunteering in Cross-National Perspective: Initial Comparisons.* Paper presented at the 27th International Red Cross and Red Crescent Conference, November 1999.

Blacksell, Sarah and Phillips, David. *Paid to Volunteer. Voluntary Action Research* Third Series Paper 2. London, Volunteer Centre UK, 1994.

Civicus. *Civil Society at the Millennium.* Kumarian Press, 1999.

Davis Smith, Justin. *A Background Paper for Discussion at an Expert Group Meeting.* New York, United Nations Volunteers, November 1999.

Ellis, Susan. *From the Top Down.* Energize, Inc., 1996.

Ellis, Susan. The Volunteer Recruitment Book. Energize, Inc., 1996.

Gaskin, Katharine and Davis Smith, Justin. *A New Civic Europe? A Study of the Extent and Role of Volunteering.* London, The National Centre for Volunteering, 1995.

Lewis, David (ed.). *International Perspectives on Voluntary Action.* London: Earthscan Publications, 1999.

Oakes, Michael J. *A Shaky Recovery.* Reason Magazine. January 1998.

Okabe, Aki. *It All Started from Kobe.* Tokyo: Ohdake Foundation.

Putnam, Robert. *Bowling Alone.* New York: Simon and Schuster, 2000.

Volunteering Review Project: *Trend Report 2000.* Geneva: International Federation of Red Cross and Red Crescent Societies, January 2000.

Web sites

Energize, Inc. http://www.energizeinc.com

Independent Sector http://www.independentsector.org

Institute for Volunteering Research http://www.ivr.org

International Federation http://www.ifrc.org

International Year of Volunteers http://www.iyv2001.org

Johns Hopkins University Comparative Nonprofit Sector Project http://www.jhu.edu/~ccss/

Ohdake Foundation http://www.igc.org/ohdakefoundation/npo/kobe.htm

Soros Foundation Volunteer Development Programme http://www.soros.org/vdp

United Nations Volunteers http://www.unv.org

Virtual Volunteering Project http://www.serviceleader.org/vv

Volunteers in Technical Assistance http://www.vita.org

World Bank Social Capital Library http://www.worldbank.org/poverty/scapital/library/index.html

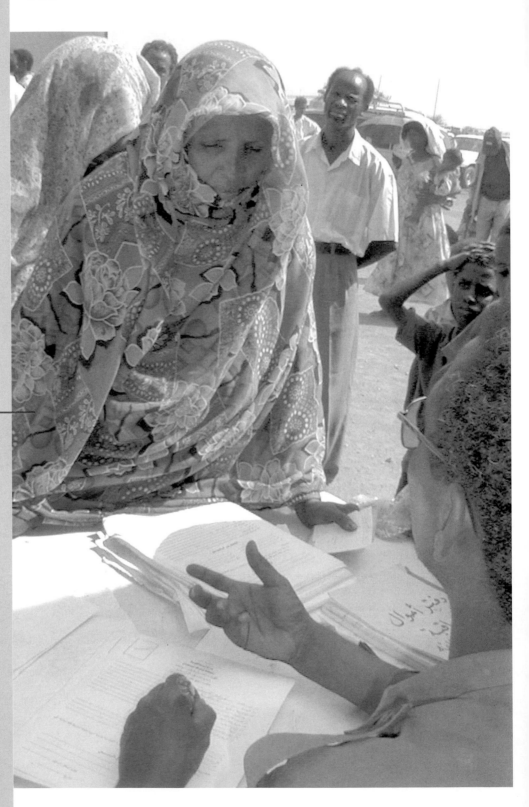

chapter 8

Tracking the system

Disaster data: key trends and statistics

This year's *World Disasters Report* features more data and analysis than before. In addition to the usual figures on natural and technological disasters, we have data on conflicts for the past decade. Natural disasters are now subdivided into hydro-meteorological and geophysical categories, to emphasize the effect on the decade's disasters of global warming.

Disaster data is analysed not only by continent and type of phenomenon, but for the first time by disasters' impact on countries categorized by the United Nations as being of high, medium and low human development. In addition, a new wall map included in the report presents the effect of disasters on nations by expressing the total numbers of people killed or affected as a percentage of each nation's total population. This analysis presents a clearer picture of the impact of disasters on the world's most vulnerable nations.

Another new set of data for *World Disasters Report 2001* is the combination of disaster and conflict data. These statistics combine the totals of those killed and affected by armed conflict and by natural or technological disasters – in effect, those people whose development is denied, either temporarily or permanently, by conflict and disaster. Along with data on refugees, internally displaced people and financial flows, this chapter provides a fuller picture than before for those responding to disasters. Key trends and statistics are identified in the first part of the chapter, while the second part presents data tables.

Disasters overview

More disasters were reported for 2000 than in any year over the last decade. Fortunately these disasters proved less deadly than in previous years: around 20,000 people lost their lives worldwide, compared to the decade's average of 75,250 deaths per year. However, last year 256 million people were reported affected by disasters, well above the decade's average of 210 million.

Natural disasters killed a reported 665,598 people from 1991-2000. This figure is probably an underestimate. Famine reportedly killed 280,000, but well-placed sources estimate that those who died just in the Democratic People's Republic of Korea's famine from 1995-98 may have numbered between 800,000 and 1.5 million. Of all those killed by natural disasters, 83 per cent were Asians. On average, natural disasters accounted for 88 per cent of all deaths from disasters over the last decade.

While the number of geophysical disasters reported over the last decade has remained fairly steady, the number of hydro-meteorological disasters since 1996 has more than doubled (see Figure 8.1). During the past decade, over 90 per cent of those killed by natural disasters lost their lives in hydro-meteorological events such as droughts, wind storms and floods.

Floods accounted for over two-thirds of the annual average of 211 million people affected by natural disasters, while famine affected nearly one-fifth. Yet floods proved less deadly,

Photo opposite page: Disaster data are numbers that matter: getting the numbers right helps improve the efficiency and effectiveness of disaster response

International Federation, Sudan 2000.

Figure 8.1
Source: CRED.

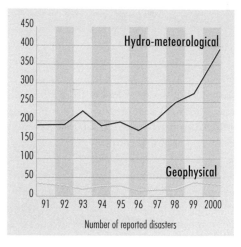

Number of reported disasters

accounting for 15 per cent of deaths from natural disasters, compared to famine's 42 per cent.

The cost of damage inflicted by disasters is notoriously difficult to estimate (see Boxes 8.1 and 8.2). Our data reflects only estimates of direct economic damage, not indirect or secondary effects. Statistics adjusted for inflation reveal that natural disasters worldwide inflict an average of US$ 78 billion per year in damage. The most expensive disasters are floods, earthquakes and wind storms. While earthquakes accounted for 30 per cent of estimated damage, they killed just 9 per cent of all those killed by natural disasters. Meanwhile, famine killed 42 per cent, but accounted for just 4 per cent of damage, over the past decade.

Analysing disasters by their impact on nations ranked by the United Nations Development Programme (UNDP) according to their level of human development reveals some unexpected trends. Of the 2,557 natural disasters reported over the last ten years, more than half were in countries of medium human development (MHD). However, two-thirds of those killed came from countries of low human development (LHD), while just 2 per cent came from highly developed nations. By comparing the totals reported killed with the total number of disasters, the effect of development on disasters becomes stark. On average, 22.5 people die per reported disaster in highly developed nations, 145 die per disaster in nations of medium human development, while each disaster in LHD countries claims an average of 1,052 people (see Figure 8.2).

When it comes to those affected by natural disaster, 88 per cent are from MHD nations, while just one-tenth are from countries of low human development. This may be explained by the

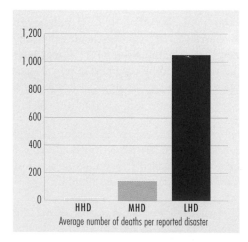

Average number of deaths per reported disaster

fact that the UN categorizes China and India, home to some of the world's biggest natural catastrophes, as nations of medium human development.

Estimated cost of damage tells a different story: 58 per cent of the direct costs of natural disasters is borne by highly developed countries, although these nations account for just 2 per cent of deaths. Meanwhile, LHD countries, which account for 67 per cent of deaths, bear just 4 per cent of the costs. Comparing estimated costs of natural disasters with the numbers reported, the average disaster costs highly developed nations

Figure 8.2
HHD = high human
development
MHD = medium
human development
LHD = low human
development
Source: CRED.

Box 8.1 Real economic costs of disasters remain hidden

Available data suggest that natural disasters can cause not only considerable physical damage, but also create potentially severe economic consequences. From 1991-2000, natural catastrophes are reported by CRED to have resulted in damage costing an estimated US$ 78.7 billion per annum (in 2000 prices). Meanwhile, reinsurance giant Munich Re has evidence to show that the costs of disasters have increased 14-fold between the 1950s and 1990s. Record damage amounting to US$ 190 billion worldwide was recorded in 1995, the year of Japan's Kobe earthquake – equivalent to 0.7 per cent of global GDP.

At country level, disasters can also take a heavy toll. For example, the estimated cost of the 1999 Izmit earthquake in Turkey was equivalent to 7 to 9 per cent of annual GDP. The impact of Hurricane Mitch in 1998 on the much-smaller Honduran economy was estimated at equivalent to three-quarters of annual GDP. For small island economies, the relative magnitude of losses can be higher again.

Such figures are dramatic. However, the full economic cost of a disaster is often even greater than ballpark figures suggest. Estimated costs are largely based on 'direct' physical impacts, or losses of fixed capital and inventory, including buildings, infrastructure, industrial plants, crops and materials. Meanwhile, many 'indirect' and 'secondary' effects on economic activity go unreported. Indirect costs refer to damage to the flow of goods and services, for example, lower output from damaged or destroyed assets and infrastructure. Secondary effects concern both the short- and long-term impacts of a disaster on overall economic performance, such as on external and government-sector balances, levels of debt and the thrust of government monetary and fiscal policies.

Direct losses can roughly be equated with stock losses whilst indirect costs and secondary effects both constitute flow losses. The various types of loss are not additive and any attempt to aggregate them would entail some double counting. The relative balance of direct costs, indirect costs and secondary effects also varies between disasters depending on the nature and extent of damage. However, in a number of cases, indirect and secondary costs may be substantially higher than direct ones.

Even figures on direct costs may be inaccurate as there are a number of difficulties associated with post-disaster damage assessments:

- Most countries **lack comprehensive guidelines** for estimating the costs of disasters. This can lead to discrepancies concerning the types of impact assessed. Different assessments may employ differing valuation methodologies. Some may value damaged property at replacement cost – correct if the aim is to estimate reconstruction costs. Others may value infrastructure at its remaining economic value, an appropriate methodology in estimating economic loss.
- Damage assessments are often undertaken by officials and volunteers on the ground, who have **little specialist training** or even experience in general survey techniques.
- Damage assessments are typically undertaken by a range of government and other agencies, each with their own **different objectives** and specific areas of concern. Some types of damage, for example to privately owned properties, may go unreported.
- Damage assessments are often **completed very rapidly,** before it is possible to assess the full economic cost of a disaster.

So it is not uncommon to see a wide range of estimates for the cost of the same disaster. Moreover, it is often difficult to identify the precise reasons underlying such differences or to reconcile the various figures.

It is important to promote more complete assessments of the economic impacts of disasters, because such information is needed to ensure that appropriate decisions are made concerning levels and forms of hazard mitigation. There is also considerable scope for greater integration of natural hazard risk reduction concerns into both economic policy formulation and the design of individual investment projects – but this, again, requires improved information.

Box 8.2 Natural disasters drain national budgets

Natural disasters can have potentially significant implications for public finance, creating additional demands on government resources to meet the costs of repair and rehabilitation and to provide support to victims. Simultaneously, they can reduce domestic revenue, as lower levels of economic activity (including possible net falls in imports and exports) imply reduced direct and indirect tax revenues. Although such losses may be partly offset by increased flows of external grant assistance, these flows are unlikely to compensate entirely for higher expenditure. Public enterprises may also experience disaster-related losses, placing an additional burden on government resources.

Perhaps surprisingly therefore, at first sight, data on aggregate national annual public revenue and expenditure typically suggest that disasters have relatively little budgetary impact, except for the most severe events in small economies. This engenders a dangerous perception, common to many governments, that it is not particularly important to take hazard risk reduction concerns into account when formulating social development and economic policy goals.

However, the impact of disaster is partly masked by governments' preference to reallocate existing budgetary resources in support of disaster relief and rehabilitation, rather than to sharply increase public expenditure. Such reallocations can then delay scheduled capital investment projects and reduce the flow of resources into non-essential services, including social sectors. Following Cyclone Kina in 1993, the Fiji government reduced its capital expenditure to only 75 per cent of the planned level, although total annual expenditure was just 0.5 per cent higher than had been forecast. Donors, as well as affected governments, may reallocate investment resources to support rehabilitation efforts.

These hidden costs of disasters may be substantial. Unplanned budgetary reallocations can force planned development off course and imply that targets are not met. Hidden costs may be exacerbated by the fact that post-disaster budgetary reallocations are typically not based on a careful and detailed review of their implications. More fundamentally, disasters can reduce the pace of public infrastructure development by reducing resources available for new investment. For example, in the small Caribbean island of Dominica, disasters have hampered the government's long-term efforts to extend and improve the island's infrastructure to such an extent that the government has continually identified the weakness of the island's infrastructure base as a critical constraint to economic growth.

To help meet disaster-related budgetary pressures and raise additional revenue, a government may also be obliged to increase the money supply, run down foreign-exchange reserves or increase levels of domestic and/or external borrowing. For example, to meet a significant budgetary shortfall following severe floods in 1998, the Bangladesh government resorted to bank borrowings totalling US$ 309 million during the financial year 1998-1999 and expanded its money supply. Such financing options have potentially significant knock-on effects. For instance, external borrowing places future strains on an economy via higher debt-servicing costs, limiting public resources available to meet domestic recurrent and capital needs.

Disasters can also impose more permanent pressures on public finance, through investment in disaster prevention, mitigation and preparedness measures – costs that governments in less disaster-prone countries do not face.

US$ 636 million, medium developed nations US$ 209 million, and nations of low human development US$ 79 million (see Figure 8.3).

Looking back over two decades, 1991-2000 proved less deadly than 1981-1990. The average number of those killed by natural and non-natural disasters fell from 86,328 to 75,252. The high mortality figures of the 1980s were largely due to major catastrophes in Ethiopia, Sudan and Mozambique. However more people were affected by disasters over the last decade – up from an average of 147 million per year (1981-1990) to 211 million per year (1991-2000). During 2000, Asia, Africa and Europe all reported statistics for those affected higher than the decade's average.

For the first time, the *World Disasters Report* has totalled the annual average (from 1991-2000) of those reported as killed and affected by natural and technological disasters, and expressed this figure as a percentage of each nation's total population (see wall map). This analysis of the 'proportional effect' of disasters on nations' populations creates some surprising results. The most affected nation is the Solomon Islands – exposed, as are many small island states, to recurrent natural hazards. The three hardest-hit nations (Solomon Islands, Malawi and Cambodia) are all classified as least developed countries (LDCs).

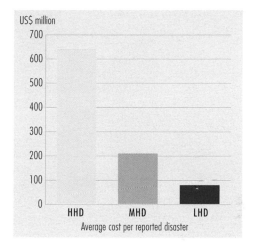

Figure 8.3
Source: CRED.

Denied development – the combined effects of conflict and disaster

Over the last decade, conflicts reportedly killed nearly 2.3 million people – over three times the 665,600 killed by natural disasters. Nations of low human development account for 76 per cent of the deaths reported due to conflicts.

Of the 2.3 million people reported as killed by conflict from 1991-2000, over three-quarters were from nations of low human development. Of the 665,600 reported killed by natural disasters over the same period, two-thirds were from LHD nations. Meanwhile, of the 86,923 deaths reported over the decade from technological disasters, 64 per cent were in nations of medium human development.

Combining the above figures, just over 3 million people reportedly lost their lives to conflict and both natural and technological disasters over the last decade. Conflict claimed the lion's share – killing over three times the number killed by natural disasters.

However, natural disasters reportedly affected on average 211 million people per year from 1991-2000. This is seven times more than the average of 31 million people annually affected by conflict.

When statistics over the last decade are totalled up, an average of 242 million people per year are killed and affected by disasters and conflicts. For all three categories of nation – low, medium and high human development – the total killed and affected by natural disasters is higher than the total killed and affected by conflict (see Figure 8.4).

Figure 8.4
Relative impact of
disasters and conflict:
percentages of total
numbers of people
killed and affected.
Source: CRED.

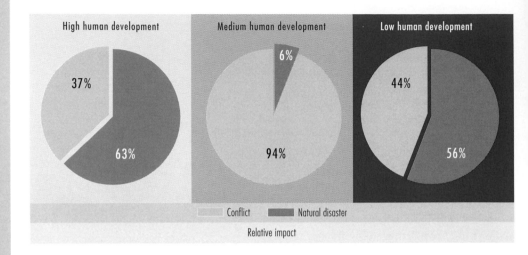

Many of these millions – whether refugees fleeing the fighting in Afghanistan and Angola, or Chinese and Bangladeshis fleeing annual floods – are affected by conflict and disaster year after year. For them, development hardly has a chance to take hold – it is denied by disaster.

Financial flows

For the second successive year, official development assistance (ODA) from members of the Organisation for Economic Co-operation and Development's (OECD) Development Assistance Committee (DAC) has risen, reaching US$ 55 billion in 1999, the latest year for which statistics are available (see Figure 8.5). This represents a rise of US$ 3 billion from 1998

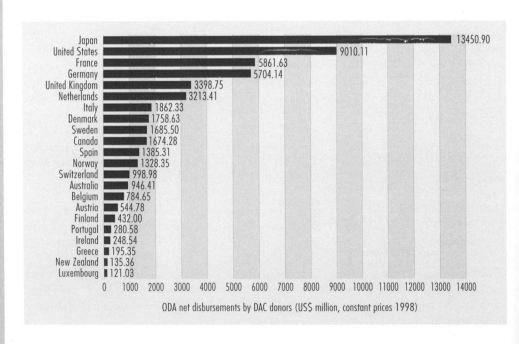

Figure 8.5
Source: CRED/OECD.

– in real terms, an increase of 5.6 per cent. Most of this increase is accounted for by Japan's increase of US\$ 2.8 billion between 1998 and 1999. Japan, the largest donor of ODA, has increased its giving 70 per cent in real terms since 1996. This is all the more remarkable considering the other big four donors (US, France, Germany, UK) have all reduced their giving by an average of nearly 10 per cent over the same period. Since 1991, ODA has fallen from US\$ 61.6 billion – a drop in real terms of 11 per cent. Over this period the US, which started the decade as the world's biggest giver, has reduced aid flows by 30 per cent (see Figure 8.6).

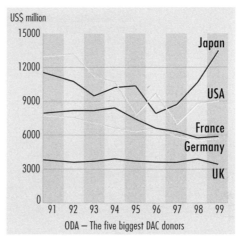

Figure 8.6
Source: CRED/OECD.

Expressed as a percentage of donor nations' gross national product (GNP), ODA has remained static at an average of 0.39 per cent – well below the UN's target of 0.7 per cent, and down from 1991's average of 0.48 per cent (see Figure 8.7). Only four nations out of the 22 DAC members make the UN target: Sweden (0.7), Netherlands (0.79), Norway (0.91), and Denmark (1.01). However, eight nations managed to increase their giving from 1998-1999 as a proportion of GNP.

Bilateral ODA to the 48 least developed countries continues to fall. At constant 1998 prices, its value was US\$ 16.8 billion in 1991 compared to just under US\$ 11 billion in 1999. As a share of 1999's bilateral ODA cake, the LDC slice was a little over one-quarter.

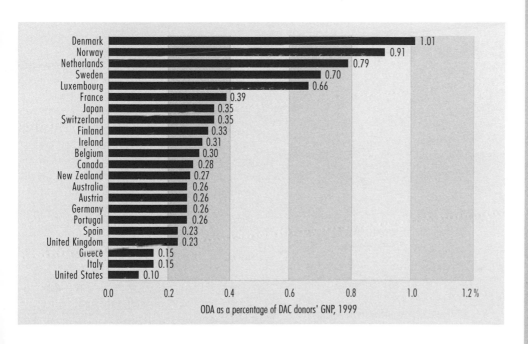

ODA as a percentage of DAC donors' GNP, 1999

Figure 8.7
Source: CRED/OECD.

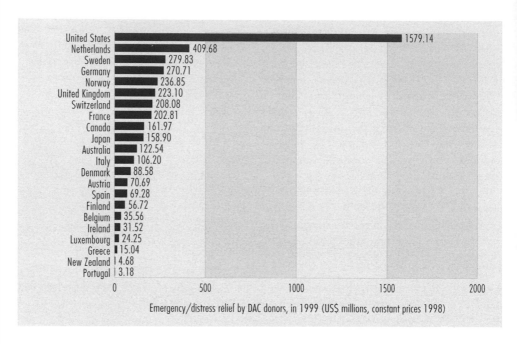

Figure 8.8
Source: CRED/OECD.

Emergency/distress relief by DAC donors, in 1999 (US$ millions, constant prices 1998)

Emergency relief from DAC donors shot up 56 per cent in real terms, from US$ 2.8 billion in 1998 to US$ 4.4 billion in 1999. Roughly one-third of this leap is accounted for by spending in the Balkans, which increased US$ 572 million between 1998 and 1999. All DAC donors, except Denmark, increased emergency spending. The US, notably, increased its relief donations by 76 per cent from US$ 898 million in 1998 to US$ 1,579 million in 1999 (at 1998 prices) (see Figure 8.8). However, the share of total bilateral emergency relief which goes to the LDCs has shrunk from 46 per cent in 1995 to just 28 per cent in 1999 (see Figure 8.9).

Disaster data: handle with care

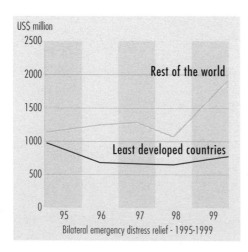

Bilateral emergency distress relief - 1995-1999

Figure 8.9
Source: CRED/OECD.

Data on disaster occurrence, its effect upon people and its cost to countries remain, at best, patchy. No single institution has taken on the role of prime providers of verified data, so the *World Disasters Report* draws upon two main sources (described in more detail below): the Centre for Research on the Epidemiology of Disasters (CRED) and the US Committee for Refugees (USCR). CRED has used the OECD's DAC database for ODA and emergency/distress relief statistics.

Key problems today with disaster data include the lack of standardized collection methodologies and definitions. Problems exist over such loose categories as 'internally displaced' people or even people 'affected' by disaster. Much of the data in this chapter, except that on DAC spending, is culled from a variety of public sources: newspapers, insurance reports, aid agencies, etc. The original information is not specifically gathered for statistical purposes and so, inevitably, even where the compiling organization applies strict definitions for disaster events and parameters, the original suppliers of the information may not. The figures therefore should be regarded as indicative. Relative changes and trends are more useful to look at than absolute, isolated figures.

Information systems have improved vastly in the last 25 years and statistical data is now more easily available. However, the lack of systematic and standardized data collection from disasters in the past is now revealing itself as a major weakness for any long-term planning. Despite efforts to verify and review data, the quality of disaster databases can only be as good as the reporting system. Fortunately, due to increased pressures for accountability from various sources, many donor and

Box 8.3 CRED: three decades of research

The Centre for Research on the Epidemiology of Disasters (CRED), established in 1973 as a non-profit institution, is located at the School of Public Health of the Louvain Catholic University in Brussels, Belgium. CRED became a World Health Organization (WHO) collaborating centre in 1980. Although CRED's main focus is on public health, the centre also studies the socio-economic and long-term effects of large-scale disasters.

Since 1988, CRED has maintained an Emergency Events Database (EM-DAT), sponsored by the International Federation, WHO, the United Nations Office for the Coordination of Humanitarian Affairs (OCHA) and the European Community Humanitarian Office (ECHO). USAID's Office of Foreign Disaster Assistance (OFDA) also collaborated in getting the database started, and a recent OFDA/CRED initiative has made a specialized, validated disaster database available on CRED's web site. The database's main objective is to assist humanitarian action at both national and international levels and aims at rationalizing decision-making for disaster preparedness, as well as providing an objective base for vulnerability assessment and priority setting.

Tables 1 to 19 in this chapter have been drawn from EM-DAT, which contains essential core data on the occurrence and effects of over 12,000 disasters in the world from 1900 to the present. The database is compiled from various sources, including UN agencies, NGOs, insurance companies, research institutes and press agencies. The entries are constantly reviewed for redundancies, inconsistencies and the completion of missing data.

CRED consolidates and updates data on a daily basis; a further check is made at three-monthly intervals; and revisions are made annually at the end of the calendar year. Priority is given to data from UN agencies, followed by OFDA, and then governments and the International Federation. This priority is not a reflection on the quality or value of the data, but the recognition that most reporting sources do not cover all disasters or have political limitations that may affect the figures.

CRED
School of Public Health
Catholic University of Louvain
30.94 Clos Chapelle-aux-Champs
1200 Brussels, Belgium
Tel.: (32)(2) 764 3369
Fax: (32)(2) 764 3441
E-mail: caroline.michellier@epid.ucl.ac.be
Web: http://www.cred.be

development agencies have started placing priority on data collection and its methodologies, but this has yet to result in any recognized and acceptable international system for disaster-data gathering, verification and storage.

Dates can be a source of ambiguity. For example, the declared date for a famine is both necessary and meaningless – famines do not occur on a single day. In such cases, the date the appropriate body declares an official emergency has been used. Changes in national boundaries also cause ambiguities in the data, most notably the break-up of the Soviet Union and Yugoslavia, and the unification of Germany.

Data can be skewed because of the rationale behind data gathering. Reinsurance companies, for instance, systematically gather data on disaster occurrence in order to assess insurance risk, but only in areas of the world where disaster insurance is widespread. Their data may therefore miss out poorer disaster-affected regions where insurance is unaffordable or unavailable.

Data on the numbers of people affected by a disaster can provide some of the most potentially useful figures, for planning both disaster preparedness and response, yet these are also some of the most loosely reported figures. The definition of 'affected' is open to interpretation, political or otherwise. In conflict, warring parties may wish to maximize sympathy for their causes and exaggerate the numbers of people under their control who are said to be affected. Even if political manipulation is absent, data is often extrapolated from old census information, with assumptions being made about percentages of an area's population affected.

Part of the solution to this data problem lies in retrospective analysis. Data is most often publicly quoted and reported during a disaster event, but it is only long after the event, once the relief operation is over, that estimates of damage and death can be verified. Some data gatherers do this, and this accounts for retrospective annual disaster figures changing one, two and sometimes even three years after the event.

Methodology and definitions

The *World Disasters Report* divides disasters into the following types:

Natural disasters

- *Hydro-meteorological:* avalanches/landslides; droughts/famines; extreme temperatures; floods; forest/scrub fires; wind storms; and other (insect infestation and waves/surges).
- *Geophysical:* earthquakes; volcanic eruptions.

Non-natural disasters

- *Industrial:* chemical spill, collapse of industrial structures, explosion, fire, gas leak, poisoning, radiation.
- *Miscellaneous:* collapse of domestic/non-industrial structures, explosion, fire.
- *Transport:* air, rail, road and water-borne accidents.

CRED uses the following definitions for disaster and conflict:

Disaster

A situation or event, which overwhelms local capacity, necessitating a request to national or international level for external assistance. In order for a disaster to be entered in EM-DAT at least one of the following criteria has to be fulfilled:

- 10 or more people reported killed;
- 100 people reported affected;
- a call for international assistance; and/or
- declaration of a state of emergency.

Killed: People confirmed dead, or missing and presumed dead.

Affected: People requiring immediate assistance during a period of emergency, i.e., requiring basic survival needs such as food, water, shelter, sanitation and immediate medical assistance. In EM-DAT, the total number of people affected include people reported injured, homeless, and affected.

Estimated damage: The economic impact of a disaster usually consists of direct damage (e.g., to infrastructure, crops, housing) and indirect damage (e.g., loss of revenues, unemployment, market destabilization). EM-DAT's estimates relate only to direct damage.

Conflict

The use of armed force between the military forces of two or more governments, or of government and at least one organized armed group, resulting in the battle-related deaths of at least 10 deaths or 100 affected in one year.

International conflict: includes border disputes, foreign invasion and other cross-border attacks.

Intrastate conflict or civil conflict: includes state control, state formation and state failure.

Refugees, asylum seekers and internally displaced people

Data concerning these populations, which is provided by USCR, are often controversial, because they involve judgements about why people have left their home areas. Differing definitions of the groups in question often promote confusion about the meaning of reported estimates.

USCR evaluates population estimates circulated by governments, UN agencies and humanitarian assistance organizations, and discerns which of the various estimates appear to be most reliable. The estimates reproduced in these tables are USCR's preliminary year-end figures for 2000. The quality of the data in these tables is affected by the less-than-ideal

Box 8.4 USCR: responding to the needs of the uprooted

USCR is the public information and advocacy arm of Immigration and Refugee Services of America, a non-governmental organization. USCR's activities are twofold: it reports on issues affecting refugees, asylum seekers and internally displaced people; and it encourages the public, policy-makers and the international community to respond appropriately and effectively to the needs of uprooted populations.

USCR travels to the scene of refugee emergencies to gather testimony from uprooted people, to assess their needs, and to gauge governmental and international response. It conducts public briefings to present its findings and recommendations, testifies before the US Congress, communicates concerns directly to governments, and provides first-hand assessments to the media. USCR publishes the annual *World Refugee Survey*, the monthly *Refugee Reports*, and issue papers.

US Committee for Refugees
1717 Massachusetts Avenue, NW, Suite 200
Washington, DC 20036, USA
Tel: (1)(202) 347-3507
Fax: (1)(202) 347-3418
E-mail: uscr@irsa-uscr.org
Web: http://www.refugees.org

conditions often associated with flight. Unsettled conditions, the biases of governments and opposition groups, and the need to use population estimates to plan for providing humanitarian assistance can each contribute to inaccurate estimates.

USCR considers refugees as people who are outside their home country and are unable or unwilling to return to that country because they fear persecution or armed conflict. Asylum seekers are people who claim to be refugees; many are awaiting a determination of their refugee status. While not all asylum seekers are refugees, they are nonetheless entitled to certain protections under international refugee law, at least until they are determined not to be refugees. Recognition of refugee status, however, does not *make* someone a refugee, but rather *declares* her or him to be one. Not all refugees are recognized as such by governments.

USCR includes people who have been admitted as refugees or granted asylum during the year, but thereafter regards them as having been granted permanent protection, even if they have not yet officially become citizens of their host country. This method of record-keeping differs from that employed by the Office of the UN High Commissioner for Refugees, which continues counting refugees until they gain citizenship.

Internally displaced people have fled their homes; unlike refugees and asylum seekers, however, they remain within their home country. No universally accepted definition of an 'internally displaced person' exists. USCR generally considers people who are uprooted within their country because of armed conflict or persecution – and thus would be refugees if they were to cross an international border – to be internally displaced. Broader definitions are employed by some agencies, which sometimes include people who are uprooted by natural or human-made disasters or other causes not directly related to human rights.

Most internally displaced persons are neither registered nor counted in any systematic way. Estimates of the size of internally displaced populations are frequently subject to great margins of error.

In the following tables, some totals may not correspond due to rounding.

This chapter and Boxes 8.3 and 8.4 were written by Jonathan Walter, editor of the World Disasters Report, *with contributions from CRED and USCR. Charlotte Benson, an economist, who has ten years' experience in research on the economic impacts of natural disasters and is currently a Senior Research Associate with the Overseas Development Institute, London, was principal contributor to Boxes 8.1 and 8.2.*

Table 1 Total number of reported disasters, by continent and by year (1991 to 2000)

	1991	1992	1993	1994	1995	1996	1997	1998	1999	2000	Total
Africa	52	54	48	57	57	59	55	84	143	195	**804**
Americas	116	88	94	81	97	93	99	112	135	142	**1,057**
Asia	210	162	220	182	171	173	193	202	238	284	**2,035**
Europe	62	51	46	69	62	53	60	65	78	118	**664**
Oceania	14	12	14	17	8	17	15	18	15	13	**143**
High human development	125	95	106	92	96	84	111	103	111	149	**1,072**
Medium human development	269	215	259	262	237	245	250	290	381	438	**2,846**
Low human development	60	57	57	52	62	66	61	88	117	165	**785**
Total	**454**	**367**	**422**	**406**	**395**	**395**	**422**	**481**	**609**	**752**	**4,703**

Source: EM-DAT, CRED, University of Louvain, Belgium

■ Between 1991 and 2000, Asia was the continent the most frequently hit by disasters, registering 43 per cent of the total number of events recorded in EM-DAT.
■ Nations of medium human development account for 60 per cent of the total number of events recorded in EM-DAT.
■ NOTE: CRED has recently revalidated and improved its data. This explains why there may be discrepancies between the numbers of disasters reported in this year's *World Disasters Report* and previous editions.
■ NOTE: Turkey and Cyprus are now included in Europe and not in Asia.

Table 2 Total number of people reported killed by disasters, by continent and by year (1991 to 2000)

	1991	1992	1993	1994	1995	1996	1997	1998	1999	2000	Total
Africa	2,660	4,981	1,637	3,104	2,932	3,484	3,903	7,092	2,675	5,610	**38,078**
Americas	2,208	1,748	4,606	2,925	2,622	2,530	2,753	22,944	33,948	1,757	**78,041**
Asia	163,758	13,414	22,769	13,362	74,975	69,679	71,113	82,274	75,890	11,056	**598,290**
Europe	1,160	2,089	1,159	2,340	3,366	921	1,166	1,429	19,448	1,417	**34,495**
Oceania	307	6	120	103	24	111	398	2,227	116	205	**3,617**
High human development	1,734	826	1,853	2,484	7,827	1,631	1,800	2,151	4,398	1,683	**26,387**
Medium human development	24,841	15,952	23,758	15,870	17,934	15,437	18,470	44,825	71,015	12,563	**260,665**
Low human development	143,518	5,460	4,680	3,480	58,158	59,657	59,063	68,990	56,664	5,799	**465,469**
Total	**170,093**	**22,238**	**30,291**	**21,834**	**83,919**	**76,725**	**79,333**	**115,966**	**132,077**	**20,045**	**752,521**

Source: EM-DAT, CRED, University of Louvain, Belgium

■ Of the total number of people reported killed by disasters from 1991 to 2000, 80 per cent are in nations of low human development.

■ 1991 was the year with the highest number of people reported killed, due mainly to a cyclone that devastated Bangladesh and caused some 139,000 deaths.

■ Hurricane Mitch, which killed 14,600 people in Honduras in October 1998, and the Venezuelan floods and mudslides, which killed 30,000 in December 1999, account for the high death tolls in the Americas in 1998 and 1999.

chapter 8

chapter 8

Table 3 Total number of people reported affected by disasters, by continent and by year (1991 to 2000) in thousands

	1991	1992	1993	1994	1995	1996	1997	1998	1999	2000	Total
Africa	16,748	21,697	9,500	11,234	9,533	6,982	7,036	10,738	14,087	23,043	**130,598**
Americas	1,190	3,429	1,970	2,722	1,027	2,200	2,088	18,180	13,746	1,342	**47,893**
Asia	264,988	50,894	162,254	168,268	245,787	207,140	56,177	314,992	188,605	229,118	**1,888,224**
Europe	3,274	372	1,380	909	6,519	30	679	621	6,549	2,906	**23,239**
Oceania	100	1,849	5,158	5,914	2,682	652	1,230	328	151	7	**18,071**
High human development	377	2,219	5,214	8,246	11,253	1,500	1,090	1,829	13,440	997	**46,165**
Medium human development	249,358	61,039	148,500	166,861	221,755	198,015	56,115	317,456	195,278	230,749	**1,845,126**
Low human development	36,565	14,984	26,548	13,939	32,540	17,491	10,004	25,574	14,419	24,670	**216,734**
Total	**286,300**	**78,242**	**180,262**	**189,047**	**265,548**	**217,005**	**67,210**	**344,858**	**223,138**	**256,416**	**2,108,025**

Source: EM-DAT, CRED, University of Louvain, Belgium

■ Globally, an average of 211 million people per year were affected by disasters between 1991 and 2000.

■ 90 per cent of those affected live in Asia, while just 2 per cent live in nations of high human development.

■ The number of people reported affected differs widely from one year to another. The two El Niño years of the decade (1991 and 1998) show the highest numbers of affected. But some 60 per cent of the number of people reported affected by disaster during these two years were due to floods in China (210 million in May 1991, and 239 million in August 1998).

Table 4 Total amount of disaster estimated damage, by continent and by year (1991 to 2000) in millions of US dollars (2000 prices)

	1991	1992	1993	1994	1995	1996	1997	1998	1999	2000	Total
Africa	26.7	280.8	10.6	495.9	139.4	122.1	7.5	347.6	747.8	149.5	**2,327.9**
Americas	8,642.2	56,063.2	26,231.7	36,258.7	25,261.3	13,561.0	9,326.9	19,585.3	14,740.8	3,259.4	**212,930.4**
Asia	27,159.0	17,076.3	17,688.3	32,183.3	175,908.9	31,605.5	27,610.7	30,289.2	27,470.4	16,469.6	**403,461.3**
Europe	77,769.7	2,995.1	1,843.7	24,771.0	13,518.4	186.5	10,375.8	2,634.2	36,932.6	8,272.1	**179,299.1**
Oceania	1,312.2	2,510.2	1,689.3	1,959.9	1,444.9	1,029.4	250.1	188.7	878.3	504.0	**11,767.1**
High human development	18,167.8	70,315.7	26,249.9	62,909.0	187,277.8	12,289.1	19,158.2	14,713.1	41,740.7	10,767.1	**463,588.3**
Medium human development	94,200.2	8,399.9	20,375.0	32,423.8	10,940.0	32,030.8	28,163.0	35,930.5	39,008.5	11,204.0	**312,674.9**
Low human development	2,541.9	209.8	839.7	336.0	18,055.2	2,184.6	249.6	2,401.3	20.9	6,683.5	**33,522.6**
Total	**114,909.9**	**78,925.4**	**47,463.6**	**95,668.8**	**216,273.0**	**46,504.5**	**47,570.9**	**53,044.9**	**80,770.0**	**28,654.6**	**809,785.8**

Source: EM-DAT, CRED, University of Louvain, Belgium

■ 57 per cent of estimated damage is reported in nations of high human development, due to higher value infrastructure and greater insurance penetration which leads to better reporting. Nations of low human development reported just 4 per cent of estimated damage.

■ Damage estimations are notoriously unreliable. Methodologies are not standard and coverage is not complete. Depending on where the disaster occurred and who is reporting, estimates will vary from none to billions of US dollars. In order to take into account inflation, estimated damages have been re-calculated at constant 2000 prices, using the US consumer prices index (US Department of Labor: http://stats.bls.gov/cpihome.htm).

chapter 8

chapter 8

Table 5 Total number of reported disasters, by type of phenomenon and by year (1991 to 2000)

	1991	1992	1993	1994	1995	1996	1997	1998	1999	2000	Total
Avalanches/landslides	11	14	22	8	15	24	13	22	15	29	**173**
Droughts/famines	19	30	13	9	15	9	18	34	30	46	**223**
Earthquakes	26	24	14	22	25	11	14	16	33	26	**211**
Extreme temperatures	8	7	4	10	13	5	13	13	8	31	**112**
Floods	82	57	82	80	86	69	77	90	112	153	**888**
Forest/scrub fires	6	8	2	13	6	5	15	16	22	30	**123**
Volcanic eruptions	10	5	6	6	4	5	4	4	5	5	**54**
Wind storms	62	74	100	67	59	62	67	73	85	99	**748**
Other natural disasters*	2	1	4	1	4	2	3	2	2	4	**25**
Subtotal hydro-meteorological disasters	*190*	*191*	*227*	*188*	*198*	*176*	*206*	*250*	*274*	*392*	*2,292*
Subtotal geophysical disasters	*36*	*29*	*20*	*28*	*29*	*16*	*18*	*20*	*38*	*31*	*265*
Total natural disasters	**226**	**220**	**247**	**216**	**227**	**192**	**224**	**270**	**312**	**423**	**2,557**
Industrial accidents	47	24	36	34	38	33	32	42	35	48	**369**
Miscellaneous accidents	31	13	25	29	26	36	30	25	50	47	**312**
Transport accidents	150	110	114	127	104	134	136	144	212	234	**1,465**
Total non-natural disasters	**228**	**147**	**175**	**190**	**168**	**203**	**198**	**211**	**297**	**329**	**2,146**
Total	**454**	**367**	**422**	**406**	**395**	**395**	**422**	**481**	**609**	**752**	**4,703**

*Insect infestation and waves/surges
Source: EM-DAT, CRED, University of Louvain, Belgium

■ NOTE: Epidemics have been removed from *World Disasters Report* statistics.

Table 6 Total number of people reported killed by disasters, by type of phenomenon and by year (1991 to 2000)

	1991	1992	1993	1994	1995	1996	1997	1998	1999	2000	Total
Avalanches/landslides	781	1,070	1,548	280	1,497	1,129	801	994	351	1,099	**9,550**
Droughts/famines	2,632	2,571	0	0	54,000	54,000	54,530	57,875	54,029	370	**280,007**
Earthquakes	2,863	3,936	10,113	1,242	7,966	582	3,076	7,412	21,870	189	**59,249**
Extreme temperatures	835	388	106	416	1,730	300	619	3,225	771	734	**9,124**
Floods	5,920	5,367	5,930	6,504	7,525	8,040	6,602	11,186	34,366	6,307	**97,747**
Forest/scrub fires	85	122	3	84	29	45	32	109	70	47	**626**
Volcanic eruptions	683	2	99	101	0	4	53	0	0	0	**942**
Wind storms	146,966	1,355	2,944	4,065	3,774	3,649	5,330	24,552	11,890	1,110	**205,635**
Other natural disasters*	10	0	59	31	0	32	400	2,182	3	1	**2,718**
Subtotal hydro-meteorological disasters	157,229	10,873	10,590	11,380	68,555	67,195	68,314	100,123	101,480	9,668	**605,407**
Subtotal geophysical disasters	3,546	3,938	10,212	1,343	7,966	586	3,129	7,412	21,870	189	**60,191**
Total natural disasters	**160,775**	**14,811**	**20,802**	**12,723**	**76,521**	**67,781**	**71,443**	**107,535**	**123,350**	**9,857**	**665,598**
Industrial accidents	1,603	1,385	1,244	779	513	660	955	1,925	729	1,613	**11,406**
Miscellaneous accidents	1,130	321	1,073	1,679	1,630	1,148	1,277	592	1,330	1,112	**11,292**
Transport accidents	6,585	5,721	7,172	6,653	5,255	7,136	5,658	5,914	6,668	7,463	**64,225**
Total non-natural disasters	**9,318**	**7,427**	**9,489**	**9,111**	**7,398**	**8,944**	**7,890**	**8,431**	**8,727**	**10,188**	**86,923**
Total	**170,093**	**22,238**	**30,291**	**21,834**	**83,919**	**76,725**	**79,333**	**115,966**	**132,077**	**20,045**	**752,521**

* Insect infestation and waves/surges
Source: EM-DAT, CRED, University of Louvain, Belgium

■ In 2000, non-natural disasters claimed more lives than natural disasters, for the first time in the decade.

chapter 8

Table 7 Total number of people reported affected by disasters, by type of phenomenon and by year (1991 to 2000) in thousands

	1991	1992	1993	1994	1995	1996	1997	1998	1999	2000	Total
Avalanches/landslides	89	79	80	298	1,122	9	34	214	15	208	**2,150**
Droughts/famines	27,118	39,944	12,132	15,515	30,431	8,536	8,450	24,647	38,372	176,457	**381,602**
Earthquakes	1,391	787	270	731	3,029	1,996	593	1,878	3,893	2,455	**17,023**
Extreme temperatures	0	16	3,001	1,108	535	0	615	36	725	28	**6,065**
Floods	227,529	23,421	149,341	129,688	184,726	180,113	43,700	291,725	150,167	62,111	**1,442,521**
Forest/scrub fires	7	52	0	3,067	12	6	53	167	19	39	**3,422**
Volcanic eruptions	1,193	357	174	236	23	7	7	8	34	119	**2,157**
Wind storms	28,833	13,563	15,209	38,368	45,619	26,302	13,594	26,077	29,891	14,944	**252,401**
Other natural disasters*	2	0	0	0	0	0	29	10	1	17	**60**
Subtotal hydro-meteorological disasters	283,579	77,075	179,763	188,045	262,446	214,966	66,475	342,876	219,190	253,804	**2,088,220**
Subtotal geophysical disasters	2,584	1,143	443	967	3,052	2,003	601	1,885	3,928	2,574	**19,180**
Total natural disasters	**286,163**	**78,219**	**180,207**	**189,012**	**265,498**	**216,969**	**67,076**	**344,761**	**223,118**	**256,378**	**2,107,401**
Industrial accidents	78	18	8	19	27	15	111	63	3	17	**360**
Miscellaneous accidents	56	3	45	11	19	18	20	30	12	15	**229**
Transport accidents	3	2	2	3	3	3	3	3	5	6	**35**
Total non-natural disasters	**137**	**23**	**56**	**34**	**50**	**36**	**134**	**97**	**20**	**38**	**624**
Total	**286,300**	**78,242**	**180,262**	**189,047**	**265,548**	**217,005**	**67,210**	**344,858**	**223,138**	**256,416**	**2,108,025**

* Insect infestation and waves/surges
Source: EM-DAT, CRED, University of Louvain, Belgium

■ Annual averages may be safer statistics to use than the decade's totals, since those affected by, for example, flood or drought one year may be counted again the following year

Table 8 Total amount of disaster estimated damage, by type of phenomenon and by year (1991 to 2000) in millions of US dollars (2000 prices)

	1991	1992	1993	1994	1995	1996	1997	1998	1999	2000	Total
Avalanches/landslides	19.4	531.5	845.8	72.3	11.6	0	17.4	0	0	168.4	**1,666.5**
Droughts/famines	2,612.0	3,066.4	1,315.2	1,419.6	6,527.5	1,320.0	437.6	475.9	7,056.5	6,305.1	**30,535.7**
Earthquakes	2,912.0	804.2	2,295.5	44,222.3	150,598.6	581.2	5,208.8	400.8	32,435.3	142.4	**239,601.2**
Extreme temperatures	1,224.7	3,628.5	0	2,586.8	942.8	0	3,214.3	3,922.0	1,030.0	124.1	**16,673.2**
Floods	90,684.6	6,892.7	29,083.4	22,315.7	29,019.1	26,045.8	12,432.6	31,961.6	13,712.9	10,670.5	**272,818.9**
Forest/scrub fires	2,007.4	518.1	1,190.0	176.3	152.0	1,893.4	18,199.8	597.9	505.4	1,052.4	**26,292.8**
Volcanic eruptions	286.0	0	0.6	464.0	0.8	18.1	8.6	0	0	0	**778.1**
Wind storms	14,792.6	62,414.7	10,510.2	10,118.6	27,536.8	13,748.9	8,016.3	15,497.6	25,819.8	9,640.2	**198,095.8**
Other natural disasters*	0	0	0	0	117.5	0	3.7	1.8	0.3	120.0	**243.3**
Subtotal hydro-meteorological disasters	111,340.7	77,051.8	42,944.6	36,689.3	64,307.3	43,008.2	42,321.9	52,456.9	48,124.8	28,080.7	**546,326.2**
Subtotal geophysical disasters	3,198.0	804.2	2,296.1	44,686.3	150,599.4	599.4	5,217.3	400.8	32,435.3	142.4	**240,379.3**
Total natural disasters	**114,538.8**	**77,856.1**	**45,240.7**	**81,375.6**	**214,906.7**	**43,607.5**	**47,539.2**	**52,857.7**	**80,560.1**	**28,223.1**	**786,705.6**
Industrial accidents	129.9	646.7	86.9	52.2	401.3	1,325.4	20.5	136.4	3.1	0	**2,802.3**
Miscellaneous accidents	189.3	33.9	1,378.0	13,662.5	204.6	1,344.3	0	19.8	2.3	431.5	**17,266.4**
Transport accidents	51.9	388.8	758.0	578.5	760.4	227.3	11.1	31.1	204.6	0	**3,011.6**
Total non-natural disasters	**371.1**	**1,069.4**	**2,222.9**	**14,293.2**	**1,366.3**	**2,897.0**	**31.7**	**187.2**	**209.9**	**431.5**	**23,080.3**
Total	**114,909.9**	**78,925.5**	**47,463.6**	**95,668.8**	**216,273.0**	**46,504.5**	**47,570.9**	**53,044.9**	**80,770.0**	**28,654.6**	**809,785.8**

*Insect infestation and waves/surges
Source: EM-DAT, CRED, University of Louvain, Belgium

■ Hydro-meteorological disasters accounted for 69 per cent of the decade's estimated damage from natural disasters

Table 9 Total number of reported disasters, by continent and type of phenomenon (1991 to 2000)

	Africa	Americas	Asia	Europe	Oceania	HHD[1]	MHD[2]	LHD[3]	Total
Avalanches/landslides	11	43	88	25	6	23	134	16	**173**
Droughts/famines	97	34	64	16	12	22	118	83	**223**
Earthquakes	9	47	111	37	7	37	158	16	**211**
Extreme temperatures	6	27	31	44	4	36	67	9	**112**
Floods	174	214	342	134	24	199	496	193	**888**
Forest/scrub fires	8	53	19	36	7	64	51	8	**123**
Volcanic eruptions	3	25	19	2	5	14	40	0	**54**
Wind storms	47	261	317	68	55	323	334	91	**748**
Other natural disasters*	4	5	14	0	2	1	18	6	**25**
Subtotal hydro-meteorological disasters	*347*	*637*	*875*	*323*	*110*	*668*	*1,218*	*406*	*2,292*
Subtotal geophysical disasters	*12*	*72*	*130*	*39*	*12*	*51*	*198*	*16*	*265*
Total natural disasters	**359**	**709**	**1,005**	**362**	**122**	**719**	**1,416**	**422**	**2,557**
Industrial accidents	31	62	208	66	2	73	265	31	**369**
Miscellaneous accidents	42	49	165	50	6	74	203	35	**312**
Transport accidents	372	237	657	186	13	206	962	297	**1465**
Total non-natural disasters	**445**	**348**	**1,030**	**302**	**21**	**353**	**1,430**	**363**	**2,146**
Total	**804**	**1,057**	**2,035**	**664**	**143**	**1,072**	**2,846**	**785**	**4,703**

* Insect infestation and waves/surges [1] High human development countries [2] Medium human development countries [3] Low human development countries

Source: EM-DAT, CRED, University of Louvain, Belgium

- Asia was the continent most affected from 1991-2000 by natural disasters (39 per cent of the total number reported) and by non-natural disasters (48 per cent of the total).
- Worldwide, floods and wind storms are the most reported disasters.
- Nations of medium human development accounted for 55 per cent of all reported natural disasters between 1991 and 2000.

Table 10 Total number of people reported killed by disasters, by continent and type of phenomenon (1991 to 2000)

	Africa	Americas	Asia	Europe	Oceania	HHD[1]	MHD[2]	LHD[3]	Total
Avalanches/landslides	274	2,172	5,754	1,071	279	566	7,941	1,043	**9,550**
Droughts/famines	6,326	0	273,583	0	98	0	3,795	276,212	**280,007**
Earthquakes	784	2,301	35,092	21,001	71	8,312	43,043	7,894	**59,249**
Extreme temperatures	105	1,941	5,745	1,310	23	1,777	6,516	831	**9,124**
Floods	8,163	35,687	52,437	1,438	22	2,121	82,566	13,060	**97,747**
Forest/scrub fires	101	130	238	150	7	188	300	138	**626**
Volcanic eruptions	0	70	863	0	9	82	860	0	**942**
Wind storms	1,274	23,187	180,206	715	253	3,154	57,618	144,863	**205,635**
Other natural disasters*	0	15	521	0	2,182	0	2,717	1	**2,718**
Subtotal hydro-meteorological disasters	16,243	63,132	518,484	4,684	2,864	7,806	161,453	436,148	**605,407**
Subtotal geophysical disasters	784	2,371	35,955	21,001	80	8,394	43,903	7,894	**60,191**
Total natural disasters	**17,027**	**65,503**	**554,439**	**25,685**	**2,944**	**16,200**	**205,356**	**444,042**	**665,598**
Industrial accidents	2,426	742	6,979	1,237	22	454	8,408	2,544	**11,406**
Miscellaneous accidents	1,016	1,433	7,728	1,057	58	1,933	8,520	839	**11,292**
Transport accidents	17,609	10,363	29,144	6,516	593	7,800	38,381	18,044	**64,225**
Total non-natural disasters	**21,051**	**12,538**	**43,851**	**8,810**	**673**	**10,187**	**55,309**	**21,427**	**86,923**
Total	**38,078**	**78,041**	**598,290**	**34,495**	**3,617**	**26,387**	**260,665**	**465,469**	**752,521**

* Insect infestation and waves/surges [1] High human development countries [2] Medium human development countries [3] Low human development countries

Source: EM-DAT, CRED, University of Louvain, Belgium

- In Africa, transport accidents were reported to kill more people from 1991-2000 than all natural disasters.
- Worldwide, of all people reported killed by disasters, droughts/famines claimed 37 per cent, wind storms 27 per cent and floods 13 per cent.

chapter 8

Table 11 Total number of people reported affected by disasters, by continent and type of phenomenon (1991 to 2000) in thousands

	Africa	Americas	Asia	Europe	Oceania	HHD[1]	MHD[2]	LHD[3]	Total
Avalanches/landslides	4	518	1,605	17	6	96	2,050	4	**2,150**
Droughts	108,781	14,730	240,297	9,210	8,583	13,000	277,899	90,702	**381,602**
Earthquakes	144	1,802	12,591	2,442	44	2,433	13,683	908	**17,023**
Extreme temperatures	0	78	638	748	4,601	4,647	1,383	34	**6,065**
Floods	16,267	9,593	1,413,095	3,335	230	5,819	1,344,397	92,306	**1,442,521**
Forest/scrub fires	6	132	3,105	123	56	182	3,185	56	**3,422**
Volcanic eruptions	10	618	1,369	7	154	218	1,939	0	**2,157**
Wind storms	5,293	20,302	215,147	7,284	4,374	19,620	200,168	32,613	**252,401**
Other natural disasters*	0	3	47	0	10	0	19	41	**60**
Subtotal hydro-meteorological disasters	*130,352*	*45,357*	*1,873,935*	*20,717*	*17,860*	*43,364*	*1,829,101*	*215,756*	*2,088,220*
Subtotal geophysical disasters	*153*	*2,420*	*13,960*	*2,449*	*198*	*2,651*	*15,622*	*908*	*19,180*
Total natural disasters	**130,505**	**47,776**	**1,887,895**	**23,167**	**18,058**	**46,014**	**1,844,724**	**216,663**	**2,107,401**
Industrial accidents	3	104	190	63	0	125	233	2	**360**
Miscellaneous accidents	82	5	124	5	12	16	150	64	**229**
Transport accidents	8	7	15	4	0	10	20	5	**35**
Total non-natural disasters	**93**	**116**	**329**	**72**	**12**	**151**	**403**	**71**	**624**
Total	**130,598**	**47,892**	**1,888,224**	**23,239**	**18,071**	**46,165**	**1,845,127**	**216,734**	**2,108,025**

*Insect infestation and waves/surges [1] High human development countries [2] Medium human development countries [3] Low human development countries

Source: EM-DAT, CRED, University of Louvain, Belgium

■ Of those reported affected by disasters, 90 per cent lived in Asia, while 88 per cent lived in nations of medium human development (MHD). This is probably because the UN defines China and India as MHD nations.

■ Worldwide, of all those reported affected by disasters, floods accounted for 68 per cent, droughts for 18 per cent, and wind storms for 12 per cent.

Table 12 Total amount of disaster estimated damage, by continent and by type of phenomenon (1991-2000) in millions of US dollars (2000 prices)

	Africa	Americas	Asia	Europe	Oceania	HHD[1]	MHD[2]	LHD[3]	Total
Avalanches/landslides	0	1,272.4	366.9	27.2	0	293.7	1,372.7	0	1,666.5
Droughts/famines	405.4	5,318.8	8,765.9	10,501.0	5,544.7	18,404.7	12,017.2	113.8	30,535.7
Earthquakes	329.9	34,284.6	178,211.4	26,471.8	303.4	209,923.4	29,563.9	114.0	239,601.2
Extreme temperatures	0.8	10,024.4	4,378.5	2,269.5	0	12,301.8	4,371.4	0	16,673.2
Floods	591.3	37,051.0	125,392.0	108,861.3	923.4	65,339.7	184,401.4	23,077.7	272,818.9
Forest/scrub fires	3.5	5,526.0	20,388	194.3	181.2	5,619.1	20,662.5	11.2	26,292.8
Volcanic eruptions	0	28.3	267.7	18.1	464.0	45.6	732.5	0	778.1
Wind storms	804.0	113,861.0	62,871.2	16,343.0	4,216.5	145,043.0	43,100.4	9,952.3	198,095.8
Other natural disasters*	5.5	117.5	0.3	0	120.0	120.0	119.6	3.7	243.3
Subtotal hydro-meteorological disasters	1,810.6	173,171.1	222,162.6	138,196.1	10,985.8	247,122.1	266,045.3	33,158.9	546,326.2
Subtotal geophysical disasters	329.9	34,312.9	178,479.1	26,489.9	767.4	209,969.0	30,296.4	114.0	240,379.3
Total natural disasters	**2,140.5**	**207,484.0**	**400,641.8**	**164,686.1**	**11,753.2**	**457,091.0**	**296,341.7**	**33,272.9**	**786,705.6**
Industrial accidents	33.3	1,635.2	673.2	446.6	13.9	819.5	1,957.4	25.5	2,802.3
Miscellaneous accidents	4.5	2,814.5	896.1	13,551.3	0	4,015.1	13,246.5	4.8	17,266.4
Transport accidents	149.6	996.7	1,250.2	615.1	0	1,662.7	1,129.4	219.5	3,011.6
Total non-natural disasters	**187.4**	**5,446.4**	**2,819.5**	**14,613.0**	**13.9**	**6,497.3**	**16,333.2**	**249.7**	**23,080.3**
Total	**2,327.9**	**212,930.4**	**403,461.3**	**179,299.1**	**11,767.1**	**463,588.3**	**312,674.9**	**33,522.6**	**809,785.8**

*Insect infestation and waves/surges   [1] High human development countries   [2] Medium human development countries   [3] Low human development countries

Source: EM-DAT, CRED, University of Louvain, Belgium

■ Nations of high human development accounted for 58 per cent of all estimated damage but just 2 per cent of deaths due to natural disasters.

■ Nations of low human development accounted for just 4 per cent of all estimated damage but 67 per cent of deaths due to natural disasters.

Table 13 Total number and annual average of people reported killed and affected by disasters, by country between 1981-1990, between 1991-2000, and in 2000

	Total number of people reported killed (1981-1990)	Total number of people reported affected (1981-1990)	Annual average of people reported killed (1981-1990)	Annual average of people reported affected (1981-1990)	Total number of people reported killed (1991-2000)	Total number of people reported affected (1991-2000)	Annual average of people reported killed (1991-2000)	Annual average of people reported affected (1991-2000)	Total number of people reported killed (2000)	Total number of people reported affected (2000)
Africa	**573,245**	**144,757,750**	**57,325**	**14,475,775**	**38,078**	**130,597,904**	**3,808**	**13,059,790**	**5,610**	**23,043,144**
Algeria	402	52,006	40	5,201	511	94,904	51	9,490	69	215
Angola	222	3,181,000	22	318,100	869	141,199	87	14,120	229	36,069
Benin	61	3,149,000	6	314,900	88	835,276	9	83,528	51	1,080
Botswana	8	4,067,847	1	406,785	23	244,276	2	24,428	3	138,776
Burkina Faso	16	5,335,396	2	533,540	28	164,350	3	16,435	n.a.	n.a.
Burundi	112	3,600	11	360	6	918,910	1	91,891	6	700,500
Cameroon	1,833	192,534	183	19,253	689	604,645	69	60,465	54	370
Cape Verde	64	119,722	6	11,972	18	16,306	2	1,631	n.a.	n.a.
Central African Rep.	31	1,850	3	185	19	76,543	2	7,654	12	10
Chad	3,054	4,182,198	305	418,220	41	813,206	4	81,321	n.a.	n.a.
Comoros	59	115,052	6	11,505	240	200	24	20	n.a.	n.a.
Congo, DR of[f]	476	327,848	48	32,785	1,138	114,392	114	11,439	169	275
Congo, PR of	23	0	2	0	643	78,581	64	7,858	11	31
Côte d'Ivoire	97	7,070	10	707	387	278	39	28	209	10
Djibouti	44	362,336	4	36,234	145	490,775	15	49,078	0	150,000
Egypt	1,054	163	105	16	2,696	204,096	270	20,410	164	246
Equatorial Guinea	15	313	2	31	1	100	0	10	1	100

Eritrea	–	–	0	0	133	1,950,709	13	195,071	0	335,000
Ethiopia	300,978	40,875,742	30,098	4,087,574	933	38,512,493	93	3,851,249	97	10,530,807
Gabon	0	10,300	0	1,030	102	0	10	0	n.a.	n.a.
Gambia, The	0	0	0	0	153	38,500	15	3,850	n.a.	n.a.
Ghana	138	12,504,300	14	1,250,430	389	1,029,111	39	102,911	13	n.a.
Guinea	292	26,436	29	2,644	562	6,107	56	611	74	16
Guinea Bissau	1	6,328	0	633	217	5,222	22	522	n.a.	n.a.
Kenya	332	617,114	33	61,711	1,906	10,613,090	191	1,061,309	317	4,212,804
Lesotho	40	680,000	4	68,000	0	501,750	0	50,175	n.a.	n.a.
Liberia	46	1,000,200	5	100,020	10	7,000	1	700	n.a.	n.a.
Libyan Arab Jam.	128	121	13	12	204	0	20	0	22	n.a.
Madagascar	517	1,974,523	52	197,452	833	3,797,555	83	379,756	132	1,337,499
Malawi	34	5,681,701	3	568,170	521	12,106,525	52	1,210,653	27	20,025
Mali	69	3,024,635	7	302,464	3,786	310,763	379	31,076	87	97
Mauritania	23	3,549,900	2	354,990	2,385	747,045	239	74,705	13	n.a.
Mauritius	161	37,358	16	3,736	5	10,800	1	1,080	n.a.	n.a.
Morocco	136	12,216	14	1,222	1,423	99,685	142	9,969	83	1,320
Mozambique	105,701	12,578,408	10,570	1,257,841	1,483	8,476,067	148	847,607	847	1,501,404
Namibia	0	0	0	0	20	443,200	2	44,320	0	5,000
Niger	191	6,293,000	19	629,300	119	144,746	12	14,475	2	4,159
Nigeria	1,259	3,307,530	126	330,753	5,591	811,508	559	81,151	1,989	6,131
Reunion	30	160,261	3	16,026	61	600	6	60	2	600
Rwanda	285	501,678	29	50,168	199	1,246,763	20	124,676	39	270,081
Senegal	0	93,000	0	9,300	369	441,518	37	44,152	13	210

	Total number of people reported killed (1981-1990)	Total number of people reported affected (1981-1990)	Annual average of people reported killed (1981-1990)	Annual average of people reported affected (1981-1990)	Total number of people reported killed (1991-2000)	Total number of people reported affected (1991-2000)	Annual average of people reported killed (1991-2000)	Annual average of people reported affected (1991-2000)	Total number of people reported killed (2000)	Total number of people reported affected (2000)
Seychelles	0	1,218,000	0	121,800	5	1,237	1	124	n.a.	n.a.
Sierra Leone	172	0	17	0	965	200,025	97	20,003	150	n.a.
Somalia	664	653,500	66	65,350	2,674	2,639,010	267	263,901	21	1,023,500
South Africa	1,745	6,569,212	175	656,921	1,999	382,275	200	38,228	254	11,232
Sudan	150,593	16,134,029	15,059	1,613,403	757	15,827,226	76	1,582,723	50	700,017
Swaziland	553	667,500	55	66,750	0	762,000	0	76,200	n.a.	272,000
Tanzania, UR of	272	2,366,577	27	236,658	1,645	8,947,986	165	894,799	93	1,301,525
Togo	0	400,000	0	40,000	3	281,905	0	28,191	n.a.	n.a.
Tunisia	441	163,549	44	16,355	34	89	3	9	13	n.a.
Uganda	242	947,580	24	94,758	624	1,250,752	62	125,075	209	204,015
Zambia	429	820,000	43	82,000	128	4,285,455	13	428,546	0	12,000
Zimbabwe	202	785,117	20	78,512	298	9,921,150	30	992,115	85	266,020
Americas	**65,956**	**63,218,981**	**6,596**	**6,321,898**	**78,041**	**47,893,095**	**7,804**	**4,789,310**	**1,757**	**1,341,521**
Anguilla	7	1	1	0	0	150	0	15	n.a.	n.a.
Antigua and Barbuda	2	83,030	0	8,303	5	76,684	1	7,668	n.a.	n.a.
Argentina	325	12,021,738	33	1,202,174	424	608,401	42	60,840	48	38,570
Bahamas	100	0	10	0	5	3,200	1	320	n.a.	n.a.
Barbados	0	330	0	33	0	0	0	0	n.a.	n.a.

Belize	0	273	0	27	36	125,170	4	12,517	14	62,570
Bermuda	28	40	3	4	18	0	2	0	18	n.a.
Bolivia	401	2,279,709	40	227,971	536	422,175	54	42,218	78	32,349
Brazil	5,162	29,421,777	516	2,942,178	2,267	11,055,183	227	1,105,518	265	228,270
Canada	834	70,856	83	7,086	505	573,605	51	57,361	11	840
Chile	690	2,112,275	69	211,228	435	515,599	44	51,560	16	195,494
Colombia	25,008	1,097,770	2,501	109,777	2,967	2,277,102	297	227,710	148	567,027
Costa Rica	61	161,284	6	16,128	173	1,013,222	17	101,322	34	200
Cuba	289	815,680	29	81,568	813	2,306,172	81	230,617	2	675
Dominica	2	10,710	0	1,071	12	3,716	1	372	n.a.	n.a.
Dominican Rep.	245	1,343,190	25	134,319	782	1,024,425	78	102,443	n.a.	n.a.
Ecuador	6,323	1,216,391	632	121,639	1,155	456,263	116	45,626	134	463
El Salvador	1,655	1,900,254	166	190,025	704	101,521	70	10,152	63	541
French Guiana	0	0	0	0	0	70,000	0	7,000	n.a.	n.a.
Grenada	0	1,000	0	100	0	210	0	21	n.a.	n.a.
Guadeloupe	5	12,084	1	1,208	4	899	0	90	n.a.	n.a.
Guatemala	944	128,806	94	12,881	837	154,547	84	15,455	86	3,844
Guyana	0	281	0	28	10	797,200	1	79,720	10	n.a.
Haiti	475	1,165,491	48	116,549	4,110	2,605,670	411	260,567	43	1,200
Honduras	409	114,137	41	11,414	15,237	2,814,095	1,524	281,410	0	1,125
Jamaica	166	882,703	17	88,270	13	556,512	1	55,651	n.a.	n.a.
Martinique	8	1,500	1	150	2	3,610	0	361	n.a.	n.a.
Mexico	11,961	753,887	1,196	75,389	4,902	2,851,231	490	285,123	324	73,498
Montserrat	11	12,000	1	1,200	32	13,000	3	1,300	n.a.	n.a.

chapter 8

chapter 8

	Total number of people reported killed (1981-1990)	Annual average of people reported killed (1981-1990)	Total number of people reported affected (1981-1990)	Annual average of people reported affected (1981-1990)	Total number of people reported killed (1991-2000)	Total number of people reported affected (1991-2000)	Annual average of people reported killed (1991-2000)	Annual average of people reported affected (1991-2000)	Total number of people reported killed (2000)	Total number of people reported affected (2000)
Netherlands Antilles	1	0	6	1	2	40,000	0	4,000	n.a.	n.a.
Nicaragua	424	42	714,239	71,424	3,494	1,878,888	349	187,889	9	15,487
Panama	72	7	96,732	9,673	145	47,566	15	4,757	22	1,000
Paraguay	76	8	305,000	30,500	101	530,664	10	53,066	45	15,010
Peru	3,703	370	6,143,631	614,363	2,289	2,704,606	229	270,461	84	15
Puerto Rico	818	82	4,200	420	71	106,483	7	10,649	n.a.	n.a.
St Kitts and Nevis	1	0	1,330	133	5	12,980	0	1,298	n.a.	n.a.
St Lucia	45	5	3,000	300	4	1,125	0	113	n.a.	n.a.
St Vincent & Grenadines	0	0	1,360	136	3	300	0	30	n.a.	n.a.
Suriname	169	17	0	0	0	0	0	0	n.a.	n.a.
Trinidad and Tobago	8	1	1,020	102	5	610	0	61	n.a.	n.a.
United States	0	0	770	77	5,175	11,440,494	518	1,144,049	280	70,839
Uruguay	4,800	480	187,037	18,704	116	24,587	12	2,459	7	5,500
Venezuela	0	0	18,500	1,850	30,636	665,222	3,064	66,522	16	27,004
Virgin Is. (UK)	728	73	124,959	12,496	0	3	0	0	n.a.	n.a.
Virgin Is. (US)	0	0	10,000	1,000	11	10,000	1	1,000	n.a.	n.a.

Asia	180,951	1,253,032,261	18,095	125,303,226	598,290	1,888,223,647	59,829	188,822,365	11,056	229,117,986
Afghanistan	7,614	251,369	761	25,137	11,060	3,274,589	1,106	327,459	42	2,580,015
Armenia[2]	–	–	0	0	106	1,604,810	11	160,481	0	297,000
Azerbaijan[2]	–	–	0	0	612	2,452,706	61	245,271	52	3,309
Bahrain	10	0	1	0	143	0	14	0	143	n.a.
Bangladesh	27,903	228,794,460	2,790	22,879,446	147,753	90,473,239	14,775	9,047,324	681	2,826,122
Bhutan	0	0	0	0	239	66,570	24	6,657	200	1,000
Cambodia	0	0	0	0	1,138	12,247,432	114	1,224,743	347	3,448,053
China, P. Rep.	20,232	282,789,695	2,023	28,278,970	35,289	1,124,008,730	3,529	112,400,873	2,448	30,740,753
Georgia[2]	15	45	2	5	627	963,270	63	96,327	n.a.	696,000
Hong Kong (China)	239	35,959	24	3,596	271	2,009,160	27	200,916	0	300
India	29,639	669,359,908	2,964	66,935,991	59,132	432,402,751	5,913	43,240,275	3,424	131,216,825
Indonesia	5,147	2,120,572	515	212,057	8,969	7,089,609	897	708,961	739	758,943
Iran, Islam Rep.	46,759	1,011,158	4,676	101,116	4,681	38,097,653	468	3,809,765	125	37,008,656
Iraq	776	0	78	0	133	808,507	13	80,851	15	7
Israel	62	398	6	40	115	1,912	12	191	3	410
Japan	2,066	3,223,833	207	322,383	6,695	2,840,222	670	284,022	35	590,920
Jordan	6	29	1	3	80	348,552	8	34,855	23	150,212
Kazakhstan[2]	–	–	0	0	244	640,536	24	64,054	0	2,500
Korea, DPR of	315	20,071	32	2,007	270,709	9,821,979	27,071	982,198	46	627,180
Korea, Rep. of	1,853	1,105,983	185	110,598	2,313	429,564	231	42,956	85	5,252
Kuwait	0	0	0	0	2	200	0	20	n.a.	n.a.
Kyrgyzstan[2]	–	–	0	0	266	264,328	27	26,433	11	n.a.

	Total number of people reported killed (1981-1990)	Total number of people reported affected (1981-1990)	Annual average of people reported killed (1981-1990)	Annual average of people reported affected (1981-1990)	Total number of people reported killed (1991-2000)	Total number of people reported affected (1991-2000)	Annual average of people reported killed (1991-2000)	Annual average of people reported affected (1991-2000)	Total number of people reported killed (2000)	Total number of people reported affected (2000)
Lao, PDR of	14	732,000	1	73,200	223	3,310,867	22	331,087	43	450,005
Lebanon	65	1,500	7	150	35	104,102	4	10,410	10	27
Macau	0	0	0	0	0	3,986	0	399	n.a.	n.a.
Malaysia	329	103,882	33	10,388	865	55,933	87	5,593	27	8,500
Maldives	0	300	0	30	10	23,849	1	2,385	n.a.	n.a.
Mongolia	87	500,000	9	50,000	180	1,110,912	18	111,091	4	1,005,850
Myanmar	1,219	272,398	122	27,240	607	777,063	61	77,706	n.a.	n.a.
Nepal	2,707	937,193	271	93,719	3,597	911,727	360	91,173	211	50,070
Oman	26	0	3	0	0	0	0	0	n.a.	n.a.
Pakistan	2,224	1,241,030	222	124,103	8,568	26,202,006	857	2,620,201	348	2,200,174
Palestine (West Bank)	0	0	0	0	14	20	1	2	n.a.	n.a.
Philippines	18,418	28,270,879	1,842	2,827,088	13,947	65,017,679	1,395	6,501,768	869	1,756,650
Saudi Arabia	1,570	5,098	157	510	1,172	3,938	117	394	48	2
Singapore	24	0	2	0	3	1,437	0	144	n.a.	n.a.
Sri Lanka	678	9,842,485	68	984,249	614	3,720,964	61	372,096	48	840,000
Syrian Arab Rep.	0	0	0	0	155	658,097	16	65,810	10	329,006
Taiwan (China)	966	22,539	97	2,254	3,154	112,986	315	11,299	184	3,150
Tajikistan[2]	–	–	0	0	1,874	3,399,304	187	339,930	0	3,017,000
Thailand	2,176	3,171,019	218	317,102	2,553	25,015,173	255	2,501,517	185	2,945,470

Turkmenistan[2]	–	–	0	0	40	420	4	42	n.a.	n.a.
United Arab Emirates	112	0	11	0	97	101	10	10	n.a.	n.a.
Uzbekistan[2]	4,355	18,111,958	436	1,811,196	141	574,388	14	57,439	0	500,000
Viet Nam	2,838	401,500	284	40,150	8,897	26,692,740	890	2,669,274	636	5,058,621
Yemen	507	705,000	51	70,500	967	679,636	97	67,964	14	4
Europe	**41,768**	**3,768,801**	**4,177**	**376,880**	**34,495**	**23,239,120**	**3,450**	**2,323,912**	**1,417**	**2,906,470**
Albania	126	12,807	13	1,281	75	3,246,500	8	324,650	n.a.	n.a.
Austria[2]	77	0	8	0	271	10,224	27	1,022	168	12
Azores[2]	172	0	17	0	74	1,215	7	122	n.a.	n.a.
Belarus[2]	–	–	0	0	61	63,468	6	6,347	n.a.	n.a.
Belgium	282	1,743	28	174	57	2,967	6	297	n.a.	n.a.
Bosnia & Herzegovina[2]	–	–	0	0	61	1,504	6	150	49	414
Bulgaria	94	3,160	9	316	42	6,759	4	676	12	167
Croatia[3]	–	–	0	0	137	2,225	14	223	41	200
Cyprus	0	0	0	0	59	4,307	6	431	5	400
Czech Republic[4]	–	–	0	0	47	102,111	5	10,211	n.a.	–
Czechoslovakia[4]	82	104	8	10	20	0	2	0	–	–
Denmark	224	0	22	0	7	100	1	10	n.a.	n.a.
Estonia[2]	–	–	0	0	912	140	91	14	n.a.	n.a.
Finland	0	0	0	0	11	33	1	3	n.a.	n.a.
France	768	507,279	77	50,728	808	3,844,907	81	384,491	124	2,519
German DR[5]	92	0	9	0	–	–	–	–	–	–

	Total number of people reported killed (1981-1990)	Annual average of people reported killed (1981-1990)	Total number of people reported affected (1981-1990)	Annual average of people reported affected (1981-1990)	Total number of people reported killed (1991-2000)	Total number of people reported affected (1991-2000)	Annual average of people reported killed (1991-2000)	Annual average of people reported affected (1991-2000)	Total number of people reported killed (2000)	Total number of people reported affected (2000)
Germany	–	0	–	0	305	247,283	31	24,728	31	121
Germany, FR of[5]	177	18	4,315	432	–	–	–	–	–	–
Greece	1,418	142	126,148	12,615	504	214,789	50	21,479	93	7,339
Hungary	4	0	0	0	107	135,774	11	13,577	1	2,000
Iceland	4	0	0	0	34	116	3	12	0	33
Ireland	396	40	129	13	46	4,200	5	420	n.a.	n.a.
Italy	785	79	58,983	5,898	837	244,519	84	24,452	63	46,022
Lithuania[2]	–	–	–	–	48	780,000	5	78,000	n.a.	n.a.
Luxembourg	0	0	0	0	0	0	0	0	n.a.	n.a.
Macedonia, FYR[3]	–	–	–	–	196	10,015	20	1,002	n.a.	n.a.
Malta	0	0	0	0	12	0	1	0	n.a.	n.a.
Moldova, Rep.[2]	–	–	–	0	59	2,654,537	6	265,454	0	2,600,000
Netherlands	0	0	0	0	144	265,691	14	26,569	22	964
Norway	236	24	0	0	270	4,630	27	463	19	630
Poland	708	71	17,794	1,779	468	225,767	47	22,577	28	n.a.
Portugal	406	41	6,697	670	107	1,410	11	141	4	70
Romania	218	22	2,700	270	480	240,087	48	24,009	29	63,831
Russia[2]	–	–	–	0	5,629	1,844,588	563	184,469	410	78,471
Serbia Montenegro[3]	–	0	–	0	118	83,185	12	8,319	3	6,082

Slovakia[4]	–	–	0	0	73	48,015	7	4,802	6	n.a.
Slovenia[3]	–	–	0	0	0	700	0	70	n.a.	n.a.
Soviet Union[2]	29,878	1,905,511	2,988	190,551	228	43,049	23	4,305	–	–
Spain	1,297	816,681	130	81,668	520	6,069,334	52	606,933	63	735
Sweden	223	100	22	10	76	184	8	18	n.a.	n.a.
Switzerland	173	2,190	17	219	72	6,711	7	671	26	1,500
Turkey	1,800	94,287	180	9,429	20,815	2,054,419	2,082	205,442	113	25,706
Ukraine[2]	1,428	206,907	143	20,691	407	481,864	41	48,186	91	48,110
United Kingdom	700	1,266	70	127	298	291,693	30	29,169	16	21,144
Oceania	**1,357**	**1,443,761**	**136**	**144,376**	**3,617**	**18,070,779**	**362**	**1,807,078**	**205**	**6,559**
American Samoa	10	0	1	0	15	0	2	0	n.a.	n.a.
Australia	431	20,371	43	2,037	409	15,641,620	41	1,564,162	182	1,559
Cook Is.	6	2,000	1	200	19	900	2	90	n.a.	n.a.
Fiji	79	606,201	8	60,620	80	430,730	8	43,073	4	n.a.
French Polynesia	17	5,050	2	505	13	511	1	51	n.a.	n.a.
Guam	0	502	0	50	229	12,033	23	1,203	n.a.	n.a.
Marshall Is.	0	0	0	0	0	6,000	0	600	n.a.	n.a.
Micronesia, Fed. States	5	203	1	20	0	84,000	0	8,400	n.a.	n.a.
New Zealand	6	2,000	1	200	0	28,800	0	2,880	n.a.	n.a.
Niue	41	29,433	4	2,943	0	0	0	0	n.a.	n.a.
Palau	0	200	0	20	4	3,365	0	337	n.a.	n.a.
Papua New Guinea	586	84,600	59	8,460	1	12,004	0	1,200	1	5,000
Solomon Is.	8	197,000	1	19,700	2,724	1,637,506	272	163,751	n.a.	n.a.

chapter 8

	Total number of people reported killed (1981-1990)	Total number of people reported affected (1981-1990)	Annual average of people reported killed (1981-1990)	Annual average of people reported affected (1981-1990)	Total number of people reported killed (1991-2000)	Total number of people reported affected (1991-2000)	Annual average of people reported killed (1991-2000)	Annual average of people reported affected (1991-2000)	Total number of people reported killed (2000)	Total number of people reported affected (2000)
Tokelau	101	181,850	10	18,185	13	88,000	1	8,800	n.a.	n.a.
Tonga	0	1,832	0	183	37	88,904	4	8,890	n.a.	n.a.
Tuvalu	8	149,617	1	14,962	0	6,571	0	657	18	n.a.
Vanuatu	0	700	0	70	18	150	2	15	n.a.	n.a.
Wallis & Futuna	58	157,702	6	15,770	50	29,665	5	2,967	n.a.	n.a.
Samoa	1	4,500	0	450	5	20	1	2	n.a.	n.a.
TOTAL	**863,277**	**1,466,221,554**	**86,328**	**146,622,155**	**752,521**	**2,108,024,545**	**75,252**	**210,802,455**	**20,045**	**256,415,680**

1 Formerly Zaire. 2 Prior to 1991, the Soviet Union is considered one country; after this date as separate countries: Belarus, Estonia, Latvia, Lithuania, Moldova, Russian Federation and Ukraine are included in Europe. Armenia, Azerbaijan, Georgia, Kazakhstan, Kyrgyzstan, Tajikistan, Turkmenistan and Uzbekistan are included in Asia. 3 Prior to 1992, Yugoslavia is considered one country; after this date as separate countries: Bosnia and Herzegovina, Croatia, Former Yugoslav Republic of Macedonia, Serbia Montenegro, Slovenia and Yugoslavia. 4 Prior to 1993, Czechoslovakia is considered one country; after this date as separate countries (Czech and Slovak Republics). 5 Prior to October 1990, Germany was divided into the Federal Republic of Germany and the German Democratic Republic; after this date, Germany is considered one country. n.a. Data for 2000 not available.

Source: EM-DAT, CRED, University of Louvain, Belgium

- The total number of people affected by disasters in 2000 (256 million people) is slightly above the decade's annual average (211 million people).
- The average number of people reported killed each year by disasters has fallen from 86,328 during 1981-1990 to 75,252 during 1991-2000.
- The average number of people reported affected each year by disasters has risen from 147 million during 1981-1990 to 211 million during 1991-2000.

chapter 8

Table 14 Total number of reported conflicts, by continent and by year (1991 to 2000)

	1991	1992	1993	1994	1995	1996	1997	1998	1999	2000	Total
Africa	20	18	18	24	23	16	16	18	18	17	**188**
Americas	3	3	4	6	5	3	2	2	2	2	**32**
Asia	16	18	17	21	25	18	19	19	20	15	**188**
Europe	7	8	4	4	6	2	2	2	3	4	**42**
Oceania	0	0	0	0	0	1	1	0	0	0	**2**
High human development	4	2	3	3	2	1	1	1	1	1	*19*
Medium human development	21	29	26	33	37	25	26	25	27	23	**272**
Low human development	21	16	14	19	20	14	13	15	15	14	**161**
Total	**46**	**47**	**43**	**55**	**59**	**40**	**40**	**41**	**43**	**38**	**452**

Source: EM-DAT, CRED, University of Louvain, Belgium

■ Nations of medium human development account for 60 per cent of the decade's reported conflicts.

■ Asia accounts for 45 per cent, and Africa for 42 per cent of the decade's reported conflicts.

Table 15 Total number of people reported killed by conflicts, by continent and by year (1991 to 2000)

	1991	1992	1993	1994	1995	1996	1997	1998	1999	2000	Total
Africa	83,000	344,800	373,933	572,248	15,621	35,477	122,978	103,870	70,935	49,050	1,771,912
Americas	8,700	10,000	5,009	2,017	100	2,450	6,200	3,117	2,560	400	40,553
Asia	95,439	52,350	49,975	42,262	16,510	14,219	14,820	9,390	12,788	8,710	316,463
Europe	11,876	24,100	15,630	10,225	46,100	26,500	6,000	4,100	10,250	1,300	156,081
Oceania	0	0	0	0	0	100	20	0	0	0	120
High human development	35,344	450	239	521	100	350	250	127	110	300	37,791
Medium human development	72,471	83,000	67,808	40,949	75,756	55,778	38,418	23,260	28,398	11,330	497,168
Low human development	91,200	347,800	376,500	585,282	2,475	22,618	111,350	97,090	68,025	47,830	1,750,170
Total	**199,015**	**431,250**	**444,547**	**626,752**	**78,331**	**78,746**	**150,018**	**120,477**	**96,533**	**59,460***	**2,285,129**

Source: EM-DAT, CRED, University of Louvain, Belgium

* Figures for 2000 may be underestimated since not all countries reported data at the time of going to press.

■ Nations of low human development account for 76 per cent of the deaths reported from the decade's conflicts. Less than 2 per cent of those killed live in nations of high human development.

■ Africa accounts for 77 per cent of the deaths reported from the decade's conflicts.

■ An average of nearly 4,400 people every week lost their lives in conflicts from 1991 to 2000.

chapter 8

Table 16 Total number of people reported affected by conflicts, by continent and by year (1991 to 2000, in thousands)

	1991	1992	1993	1994	1995	1996	1997	1998	1999	2000	Total
Africa	20,800	21,977	16,269	19,260	15,366	10,937	9,159	11,068	12,853	12,550	150,239
Americas	551	996	1,149	1,449	1,343	1,255	1,360	1,750	1,879	1,970	13,701
Asia	17,110	13,602	12,971	12,811	13,051	12,002	11,413	11,882	11,864	5,105	121,810
Europe	728	3,297	2,970	2,590	6,641	2,415	1,261	1,279	2,484	1,250	24,915
Oceania	0	0	0	0	0	0	0	0	0	0	0
High human development	2,545	2,658	2,801	3,137	265	3,719	3,743	3,816	4,156	0	26,840
Medium human development	11,302	14,755	14,946	13,320	18,715	8,624	6,748	8,047	9,421	8,090	113,966
Low human development	25,342	22,459	15,612	19,653	17,421	14,266	12,702	14,116	15,502	12,785	169,859
Total	**39,189**	**39,872**	**33,360**	**36,110**	**36,401**	**26,608**	**23,193**	**25,979**	**29,079**	**20,875**	**310,665**

Source: EM-DAT, CRED, University of Louvain, Belgium

■ Globally, an average of 31 million people per year were affected by conflicts between 1991 and 2000.
■ 48 per cent of those affected live in Africa, while 55 per cent live in nations of low human development. Less than 9 per cent of those affected by conflicts live in nations of high human development.

Table 17 Total number of people reported killed by disasters and conflicts, by continent and by year (1991 to 2000)

	1991	1992	1993	1994	1995	1996	1997	1998	1999	2000	Total
Africa	85,660	349,781	375,570	575,352	18,553	38,961	126,881	110,962	73,610	54,640	1,809,990
Americas	10,908	11,748	9,615	4,942	2,722	4,980	8,953	26,061	36,508	2,157	118,594
Asia	259,197	65,764	72,744	55,624	91,485	83,898	85,933	91,764	88,678	19,766	914,753
Europe	13,036	26,189	16,789	12,565	49,466	27,421	7,166	5,429	29,698	2,717	190,576
Oceania	307	6	120	103	24	211	418	2,227	116	205	3,737
High human development	37,078	1,276	2,092	3,005	7,927	1,981	2,050	2,278	4,508	1,983	64,178
Medium human development	97,312	98,952	91,566	56,819	93,690	71,215	56,888	68,085	99,413	23,893	759,833
Low human development	234,718	353,260	381,180	588,762	60,633	82,275	170,413	166,080	124,689	53,629	2,215,639
Natural disasters	160,775	14,811	20,802	12,723	76,521	67,781	71,443	107,535	123,350	9,857	665,598
Non-natural disasters	9,318	7,427	9,489	9,111	7,398	8,944	7,890	8,431	8,727	10,188	86,923
Conflicts	199,015	431,250	444,547	626,752	78,331	78,746	150,018	120,477	96,533	59,460	2,285,129
Total	**369,108**	**453,488**	**474,838**	**648,586**	**162,250**	**155,471**	**229,351**	**236,443**	**228,810**	**79,505**	**3,037,650**

Source: EM-DAT, CRED, University of Louvain, Belgium

■ Africa is the world's deadliest continent. Of the 3 million people reported killed by disasters and conflict over the last decade, 60 per cent came from Africa, while 31 per cent came from Asia.
■ Nations of low human development account for 73 per cent of all deaths from disasters and conflicts, while nations of high human development account for just 2 per cent.
■ Conflicts reportedly killed over three times more people during the last decade than natural disasters.

chapter 8

Table 18 Total number of people reported affected by disasters and conflicts, by continent and by year (1991 to 2000) in thousands

	1991	1992	1993	1994	1995	1996	1997	1998	1999	2000	Total
Africa	37,548	43,674	25,769	30,494	24,900	17,919	16,195	21,806	26,940	35,593	**280,837**
Americas	1,741	4,425	3,119	4,171	2,369	3,455	3,448	19,930	15,625	3,312	**61,594**
Asia	282,028	64,496	175,226	181,080	258,838	219,142	67,590	326,813	200,468	234,223	**2,010,034**
Europe	4,002	3,669	4,349	3,499	13,160	2,445	1,940	1,900	9,033	4,156	**48,154**
Oceania	100	1,849	5,158	5,914	2,682	652	1,230	328	151	7	**18,071**
High human development	2,922	4,877	8,016	11,383	11,518	5,218	4,833	5,645	17,596	997	**73,004**
Medium human development	260,659	75,794	163,446	180,181	240,469	206,638	62,863	325,503	204,699	238,839	**1,959,092**
Low human development	61,907	37,443	42,160	33,593	49,961	31,757	22,706	39,690	29,922	37,455	**386,593**
Natural disasters	286,163	78,219	180,207	189,012	265,498	216,969	67,076	344,761	223,118	256,378	**2,107,401**
Non-natural disasters	137	23	56	34	50	36	134	97	20	38	**624**
Conflicts	39,189	39,872	33,360	36,110	36,401	26,608	23,193	25,979	29,079	20,875	**310,665**
Total	**325,489**	**118,113**	**213,622**	**225,157**	**301,949**	**243,613**	**90,403**	**370,837**	**252,217**	**277,290**	**2,418,689**

Source: EM-DAT, CRED, University of Louvain, Belgium

■ Asia accounts for 83 per cent of those reported affected by disasters and conflicts, while nations of medium human development account for 81 per cent. Natural disasters account for 87 per cent of the total.

■ These figures are largely due to the enormous numbers of people reported affected by natural disasters (especially droughts, floods and windstorms) in China and India, the world's most populous nations and classified by the United Nations as nations of medium human development.

Table 19 Total number of people whose development has been denied by disasters and conflicts, by continent and by year (1991 to 2000) in thousands

	1991	1992	1993	1994	1995	1996	1997	1998	1999	2000	Total
Africa	37,633	44,024	26,145	31,069	24,918	17,958	16,322	21,917	27,013	35,648	**282,647**
Americas	1,752	4,437	3,129	4,176	2,372	3,460	3,457	19,956	15,661	3,314	**61,712**
Asia	282,357	64,562	175,229	181,135	258,929	219,226	67,676	327,965	200,557	234,243	**2,010,948**
Europe	4,015	3,696	4,366	3,511	13,209	2,473	1,947	1,905	9,063	4,159	**48,345**
Oceania	100	1,849	5,158	5,914	2,682	652	1,230	330	151	7	**18,075**
High human development	2,959	4,878	8,018	11,386	11,526	5,220	4,835	5,647	17,601	999	**73,069**
Medium human development	260,757	75,893	163,538	180,238	240,563	206,709	62,920	325,571	204,798	238,863	**1,959,849**
Low human development	62,142	37,796	42,541	34,182	50,022	31,839	22,877	39,856	30,047	37,508	**388,809**
Natural disasters	286,324	78,234	180,227	189,025	265,575	217,036	67,147	344,869	223,241	256,388	**2,108,067**
Non-natural disasters	146	30	65	43	57	45	142	105	29	48	**710**
Conflicts	39,388	40,303	33,804	36,737	36,479	26,687	23,343	26,099	29,177	20,934	**312,950**
Total	**325,858**	**118,567**	**214,097**	**225,805**	**302,111**	**243,768**	**90,632**	**371,074**	**252,446**	**277,370**	**2,421,727**

Source: EM-DAT, CRED, University of Louvain, Belgium

■ This table combines the totals of all those reported killed and affected by disasters and conflicts from 1991 to 2000 – in effect those people whose development is cut short or repeatedly denied by recurrent disasters and conflicts.

■ Over the past decade, an average of 242 million people each year were killed or affected by disasters and conflict.

chapter 8

Chapter 8 Disaster data

Table 20 Refugees and asylum seekers by country/territory of origin (1994 to 2000)

Africa	1994	1995	1996	1997	1998	1999	2000
	5,857,650	5,191,200	3,623,200	2,897,000	2,880,950	3,072,800	3,338,000
Algeria	–	–	–	–	3,000	5,000	8,000
Angola	344,000	313,000	220,000	223,000	303,300	339,300	400,000
Burundi	330,000	290,000	285,000	248,000	281,000	311,000	420,000
Chad	29,000	16,000	15,500	12,000	15,000	13,000	2,000
Congo, DR of[1]	56,000	58,600	116,800	132,000	136,000	229,000	350,000
Congo, PR of	–	–	–	40,000	20,000	25,000	17,000
Côte d'Ivoire	–	–	–	–	–	–	1,000
Djibouti	10,000	10,000	10,000	5,000	3,000	1,000	1,000
Egypt	–	–	–	–	–	3,000	–
Eritrea	384,500	342,500	343,100	323,000	323,100	323,100	380,000
Ethiopia	190,750	110,700	58,000	48,000	39,600	53,300	40,000
Ghana	–	–	10,000	12,000	11,000	10,000	10,000
Guinea	–	–	–	–	–	–	3,000
Guinea-Bissau	–	–	–	–	11,150	5,300	–
Kenya	–	–	–	–	8,000	5,000	–
Liberia	784,000	725,000	755,000	475,000	310,000	249,000	200,000
Mali	115,000	90,000	80,000	16,000	3,000	2,000	4,000
Mauritania	75,000	80,000	65,000	55,000	30,000	45,000	45,000
Mozambique	325,000	97,000	–	–	–	–	–
Namibia	–	–	–	–	–	1,000	2,000

Source: US Committee for Refugees

Niger	20,000	20,000	15,000	10,000	—	—	—
Nigeria	—	—	—	—	—	—	7,000
Rwanda	1,715,000	1,545,000	257,000	43,000	12,000	27,000	60,000
Senegal	17,000	17,000	17,000	17,000	10,000	10,000	10,000
Sierra Leone	260,000	363,000	350,000	297,000	480,000	454,000	400,000
Somalia	457,400	480,300	467,100	486,000	414,600	415,600	370,000
Sudan	510,000	448,100	433,700	353,000	352,200	423,200	430,000
Togo	140,000	95,000	30,000	6,000	3,000	3,000	3,000
Uganda	15,000	10,000	15,000	10,000	12,000	15,000	15,000
Western Sahara	80,000	80,000	80,000	86,000	100,000	105,000	110,000
East Asia and Pacific	**690,050**	**640,950**	**648,200**	**723,000**	**763,200**	**864,100**	**906,200**
Cambodia	30,250	26,300	34,400	77,000	51,000	15,100	16,000
China (Tibet)	139,000	141,000	128,000	128,000	128,000	130,000	130,000
East Timor	—	—	—	—	—	120,000	120,000
Indonesia	9,700	9,500	10,000	8,000	8,000	8,000	6,200
Laos	12,900	8,900	3,500	14,000	12,100	13,900	—
Myanmar	203,300	160,400	184,300	215,000	238,100	240,100	280,000
Philippines	—	—	—	45,000	45,000	45,000	57,000
Viet Nam	294,900	294,850	288,000	281,000	281,000	292,000	297,000
South and central Asia	**3,319,200**	**2,809,400**	**3,184,100**	**2,966,000**	**2,928,700**	**2,906,750**	**3,105,000**
Afghanistan	2,835,300	2,328,400	2,628,550	2,622,000	2,628,600	2,561,050	2,800,000
Bangladesh	48,300	48,000	53,000	40,000	—	—	—

Source: US Committee for Refugees

chapter 8

Bhutan	116,600	118,600	121,800	113,000	115,000	124,000
India	–	–	13,000	13,000	15,000	17,000
Sri Lanka	104,000	96,000	100,150	100,000	110,000	110,000
Tajikistan	165,000	170,400	215,600	32,000	15,100	62,500
Uzbekistan	50,000	48,000	52,000	46,000	45,000	33,200
Middle East	**3,826,950**	**3,958,500**	**4,373,100**	**4,304,000**	**3,987,050**	**4,659,000**
Iran	54,250	49,500	46,100	35,000	30,800	51,000
Iraq	635,900	622,900	608,500	526,000	534,450	565,000
Palestinians	3,136,800	3,286,100	3,718,500	3,743,000	3,931,400	4,043,000
Europe	**1,775,800**	**1,805,600**	**1,875,150**	**1,343,100**	**1,238,100**	**890,000**
Armenia	229,000	185,000	197,000	188,000	188,400	–
Azerbaijan	374,000	390,000	238,000	218,000	230,000	–
Bosnia and Herzegovina[2]	863,300	905,500	1,006,450	577,000	80,350	250,000
Croatia[2]	136,900	200,000	300,000	335,000	336,000	315,000
Georgia	106,800	105,000	105,000	11,000	2,800	25,500
Russian Federation	–	–	–	500	12,350	26,000
Turkey	13,000	15,000	15,000	11,000	11,800	23,500
Yugoslavia[2]	52,800	5,100	13,700	3,100	376,400	250,000
Americas & the Caribbean	**120,550**	**68,400**	**65,700**	**61,900**	**442,550**	**393,800**
Colombia	100	200	0	300	–	9,300
Cuba	30,600	4,000	850	600	850	1,200

Source: US Committee for Refugees

El Salvador	16,200	12,400	12,000	250,150	253,000	230,000
Guatemala	45,050	34,150	30,000	251,300	146,000	130,000
Haiti	5,850	1,500	—	600	23,000	20,000
Nicaragua	22,750	16,150	19,000	18,000	18,000	3,300
Peru	—	—	—	350	1,700	—
Total	**15,590,200**	**14,479,850**	**13,769,450**	**12,295,000**	**12,733,150**	**12,511,350**	**13,292,000**

Notes: — indicates zero or near zero; [1] formerly Zaire; [2] for 1992-93, refugees from Croatia and Bosnia included in Yugoslavia total, for 1994-95 Yugoslavia total includes only refugees from Serbia and Montenegro.

Source: US Committee for Refugees

- More than half of the world's refugees and asylum seekers in 2000 were either Palestinians or Afghans.

- The number of refugees in need of protection from Afghanistan, Burundi; the Democratic Republic of the Congo, Eritrea, the Philippines and other countries increased during the year, while the number of refugees from Bosnia and Herzegovina, the People's Republic of Congo, Kosovo (Yugoslavia), Liberia, Myanmar (Burma), Somalia and other countries declined during the year. In addition, people formerly counted as refugees from Armenia and Azerbaijan became eligible for citizenship in their host countries and were no longer considered by USCR to be refugees in need of protection.

- In part because asylum states do not always report country-of-origin data, this table understates the number of refugees and asylum seekers from many countries.

Table 21 Refugees and asylum seekers by host country/territory (1994 to 2000)

Africa	1994 5,879,700	1995 5,222,300	1996 3,682,700	1997 2,944,000	1998 2,924,000	1999 3,147,000	2000 3,287,000
Algeria	130,000	120,000	114,000	104,000	84,000	84,000	85,000
Angola	11,000	10,900	9,300	9,000	10,000	15,000	12,000
Benin	50,000	25,000	11,000	3,000	3,000	3,000	5,000
Botswana	–	–	–	–	–	1,000	3,000
Burkina Faso	30,000	21,000	26,000	2,000	–	–	1,000
Burundi	165,000	140,000	12,000	12,000	5,000	2,000	5,000
Cameroon	2,000	2,000	1,000	1,000	3,000	10,000	45,000
Central African Rep.	42,000	34,000	36,400	38,000	47,000	55,000	55,000
Chad	–	–	–	–	10,000	20,000	20,000
Congo, DR of [1]	1,527,000	1,332,000	455,000	255,000	220,000	235,000	230,000
Congo, PR of	16,000	15,000	16,000	21,000	20,000	40,000	125,000
Côte d'Ivoire	320,000	290,000	320,000	202,000	128,000	135,000	95,000
Djibouti	60,000	25,000	22,000	22,000	23,000	23,000	22,000
Egypt	10,700	10,400	46,000	46,000	46,000	47,000	45,000
Eritrea	–	–	–	3,000	3,000	2,000	1,000
Ethiopia	250,000	308,000	328,000	313,000	251,000	246,000	200,000
Gabon	–	1,000	1,000	1,000	1,000	15,000	15,000
Gambia	1,000	5,000	5,000	8,000	13,000	25,000	15,000
Ghana	110,000	85,000	35,000	20,000	15,000	12,000	13,000
Guinea	580,000	640,000	650,000	430,000	514,000	453,000	390,000

Source: US Committee for Refugees

Guinea-Bissau	16,000	15,000	15,000	4,000	5,000	5,000	5,000
Kenya	257,000	225,000	186,000	196,000	192,000	254,000	210,000
Liberia	100,000	120,000	100,000	100,000	120,000	90,000	70,000
Libyan A.J.	–	28,100	27,200	27,000	28,000	11,000	11,000
Malawi	70,000	2,000	–	–	–	–	3,000
Mali	15,000	15,000	15,000	17,000	5,000	7,000	7,000
Mauritania	55,000	35,000	15,000	5,000	20,000	25,000	25,000
Morocco	–	–	–	–	–	–	100
Mozambique	–	–	–	–	–	1,000	2,000
Namibia	1,000	1,000	1,000	1,000	2,000	8,000	20,000
Niger	3,000	17,000	27,000	7,000	3,000	2,000	1,000
Nigeria	5,000	8,000	8,000	9,000	5,000	7,000	10,000
Rwanda	–	–	20,000	28,000	36,000	36,000	30,000
Senegal	60,000	68,000	51,000	41,000	30,000	42,000	40,000
Sierra Leone	20,000	15,000	15,000	15,000	10,000	7,000	3,000
South Africa	200,000	90,000	22,500	28,000	29,000	40,000	30,000
Sudan	550,000	450,000	395,000	365,000	360,000	363,000	400,000
Swaziland	–	–	–	–	–	–	1,000
Tanzania	752,000	703,000	335,000	295,000	329,000	413,000	540,000
Togo	5,000	10,000	10,000	12,000	11,000	10,000	10,000
Tunisia	–	500	300	–	–	–	400
Uganda	323,000	230,000	225,000	185,000	185,000	197,000	230,000
Zambia	123,000	125,400	126,000	118,000	157,000	205,000	255,000
Zimbabwe	20,000	–	1,000	1,000	1,000	1,000	2,000

Source: US Committee for Refugees

chapter 8

East Asia and Pacific	**2,421,500**	**2,520,700**	**2,479,100**	**2,020,300**	**1,728,400**	**1,909,100**	**780,100**
Australia	5,300	7,500	7,400	18,000	15,000	17,000	16,800
Cambodia	–	–	–	–	200	100	–
China[2]	297,100	294,100	294,100	281,800	281,800	292,800	340,000
Hong Kong[2]	1,900	1,900	1,300	n.a.	n.a.	n.a.	n.a.
Indonesia	250	–	–	100	100	120,000	120,800
Japan	7,350	9,900	300	300	500	400	3,800
Malaysia[3]	6,100	5,300	5,200	5,200	50,600	45,400	57,400
Papua New Guinea	9,700	9,500	10,000	8,200	8,000	8,000	6,000
Philippines	250	450	50	100	300	200	200
Solomon Islands	3,000	1,000	1,000	800	n.a.	–	–
Thailand	83,050	98,200	95,850	205,600	187,700	158,400	216,000
Viet Nam	30,100	25,000	34,400	15,000	15,000	15,000	16,000
Europe	**2,421,500**	**2,520,700**	**2,479,100**	**2,020,300**	**1,728,400**	**1,909,100**	**1,205,400**
Albania	–	–	–	–	25,000	5,000	2,000
Armenia	295,800	304,000	150,000	219,150	229,000	240,000	–
Austria	59,000	55,900	80,000	11,400	16,500	16,600	5,000
Azerbaijan	279,000	238,000	249,150	244,100	235,300	222,000	3,700
Belarus	18,800	7,000	10,800	33,500	16,500	2,900	3,200
Belgium	19,400	16,400	18,200	14,100	25,800	42,000	40,000
Bosnia and Herzegovina	–	–	–	40,000	40,000	60,000	38,200

Source: US Committee for Refugees

Bulgaria	900	500	550	2,400	2,800	2,800	3,000
Croatia	188,000	189,500	167,000	50,000	27,300	24,000	22,500
Cyprus	–	–	–	200	200	300	200
Czech Republic	4,700	2,400	2,900	700	2,400	1,800	4,800
Denmark	24,750	9,600	24,600	13,000	6,100	8,500	10,300
Estonia	100	–	–	–	–	–	–
Finland	850	750	1,700	1,600	2,300	3,800	2,600
France	32,600	30,000	29,200	16,000	17,400	30,000	28,000
Georgia	–	–	–	100	300	5,200	7,600
Germany	430,000	442,700	436,400	277,000	198,000	285,000	180,000
Greece	1,300	1,300	5,600	2,100	2,800	7,500	7,000
Hungary	11,200	9,100	5,400	3,400	3,200	6,000	4,200
Iceland	–	–	–	–	–	100	–
Ireland	–	–	1,800	4,300	6,900	8,500	7,700
Italy	31,800	60,700	10,600	20,000	6,800	24,900	14,000
Latvia	150	150	–	–	–	–	–
Lithuania	–	400	–	100	100	100	200
Macedonia, FYR of	8,200	7,000	5,100	3,500	7,300	17,400	5,500
Netherlands	52,600	39,300	46,200	64,200	47,000	40,000	24,800
Norway	11,600	11,200	12,700	3,100	2,500	9,500	8,600
Poland	500	800	3,200	1,200	1,300	1,300	2,300
Portugal	600	350	200	150	1,400	1,700	1,700
Romania	600	1,300	600	2,000	900	900	1,000

Source: US Committee for Refugees

chapter 8

Russian Federation	451,000	500,000	484,000	324,000	161,900	104,300	102,000
Slovak Republic	2,000	1,600	2,000	100	300	400	400
Slovenia	29,000	24,000	10,300	5,300	7,300	5,000	12,000
Spain	14,500	4,300	7,200	3,300	2,500	4,500	1,100
Sweden	61,000	12,300	60,500	8,400	16,700	20,200	18,000
Switzerland	23,900	29,000	41,700	34,100	40,000	104,000	62,200
Turkey	30,650	21,150	13,000	5,000	12,000	9,100	4,100
Ukraine	5,000	6,000	8,000	4,900	8,600	5,800	5,500
United Kingdom	32,000	44,000	40,500	58,100	74,000	112,000	87,800
Yugoslavia[4]	300,000	450,000	550,000	550,000	480,000	476,000	483,800
Americas & the Caribbean	**297,300**	**256,400**	**232,800**	**616,000**	**739,950**	**737,000**	**560,000**
Argentina	–	–	400	10,700	1,100	3,300	1,050
Bahamas	–	200	–	50	100	100	100
Belize	8,800	8,650	8,700	4,000	3,500	3,000	1,700
Bolivia	600	600	550	300	350	400	350
Brazil	2,000	2,000	2,200	2,300	2,400	2,300	2,700
Canada	22,000	24,900	26,100	48,800	46,000	53,000	52,000
Chile	200	300	200	300	100	300	300
Colombia	400	400	200	200	200	250	200
Costa Rica	24,600	20,500	23,150	23,100	23,100	22,900	7,300
Cuba	–	1,800	1,650	1,500	1,100	1,000	1,000
Dominican Republic	1,350	900	600	600	600	650	500
Ecuador	100	100	200	200	250	350	1,600

Source: US Committee for Refugees

El Salvador	150	150	150	100	100	–	–
Guatemala	4,700	2,500	1,200	1,300	800	750	700
Honduras	100	50	–	–	100	100	–
Jamaica	–	–	–	–	50	50	–
Mexico	47,700	38,500	34,450	30,000	7,500	8,500	6,500
Nicaragua	300	450	900	700	150	500	300
Panama	900	800	650	300	1,300	600	1,300
Peru	700	700	300	–	–	700	700
United States	181,700	152,200	129,600	491,000	651,000	638,000	481,500
Uruguay	–	–	–	–	–	150	100
Venezuela	1,000	700	1,600	300	150	200	100
Middle East	**5,447,750**	**5,499,100**	**5,840,550**	**5,708,000**	**5,814,100**	**5,849,000**	**6,034,300**
Gaza Strip	644,000	683,600	716,900	746,000	773,000	798,400	824,600
Iran	2,220,000	2,075,500	2,020,000	1,900,000	1,931,000	1,835,000	1,900,000
Iraq	120,500	115,200	114,400	110,000	104,000	129,400	127,700
Israel	–	–	–	–	–	400	400
Jordan	1,232,150	1,294,800	1,362,500	1,413,800	1,463,800	1,518,000	1,580,000
Kuwait	25,000	55,000	42,000	90,000	52,000	52,000	52,000
Lebanon	338,200	348,300	355,100	362,300	368,300	378,100	383,300
Saudi Arabia	17,000	13,200	257,850	116,750	128,300	128,600	128,500
Syria	332,900	342,300	384,400	361,000	369,800	379,200	387,800
United Arab Emirates	150	400	400	500	200	–	–
West Bank	504,000	517,400	532,400	543,000	555,000	569,700	583,000

Source: US Committee for Refugees

Yemen	13,850	53,400	54,600	64,900	68,700	60,000	67,000
South and central Asia	**1,776,450**	**1,386,300**	**1,794,800**	**1,743,000**	**1,708,700**	**1,689,000**	**2,658,200**
Afghanistan	20,000	18,400	18,900	–	–	–	–
Bangladesh	116,200	55,000	40,000	40,100	53,100	53,100	121,600
India	327,850	319,200	352,200	323,500	292,100	292,000	290,000
Kazakhstan	300	6,500	14,000	14,000	4,100	14,800	20,000
Kyrgyzstan	350	7,600	17,000	15,500	15,000	10,900	10,600
Nepal	104,600	106,600	109,800	116,000	118,000	130,000	129,000
Pakistan	1,202,650	867,500	1,215,700	215,650	1,217,400	1,127,000	2,019,000
Tajikistan	2,500	2,500	2,200	3,800	5,500	4,700	15,400
Turkmenistan	–	–	22,000	13,000	500	18,500	14,200
Uzbekistan	2,000	3,000	3,000	1,250	3,000	38,000	38,400
Total	**16,182,050**	**16,266,800**	**15,337,650**	**14,479,550**	**13,566,400**	**13,988,000**	**14,526,000**

Notes: – indicates zero or near zero; n.a. not available, or reported estimates unreliable; [1]formerly Zaire; [2]as of 1997, figures for Hong Kong are included in total for China; [3]USCR reclassified as refugees 45,000 Filipino Muslims from the island of Mindanao previously regarded as "refugee-like". Malaysia regards them as refugees and permits them to reside legally, but temporarily, in Sabah. Another 450,000 are living in refugee-like conditions in Malaysia; [4]for 1993, refugees from Croatia and Bosnia included in Yugoslavia total, for 1994-95 Yugoslavia total includes only refugees from Serbia and Montenegro.

Source: US Committee for Refugees

■ The total number of refugees and asylum seekers increased by about 538,000 in 2000, reversing a decade-long downward trend for a second year, according to USCR. That downward trend was due to many factors, including refugee repatriations to several countries and to the unwillingness of many states, especially those in the developed world, to accept new refugees and asylum seekers.
■ The number of refugees and asylum seekers increased in Africa, east Asia, the Middle East, and south and central Asia during the year, largely because of ongoing or renewed conflicts. Almost half of the world's refugees and asylum seekers were found in just five countries or territories: Iran, Jordan, the Gaza Strip and the West Bank, Pakistan and Tanzania.

Table 22 Significant populations of internally displaced people

Africa	1994	1995	1996	1997	1998	1999	2000
	15,730,000	10,185,000	8,805,000	7,590,000	8,958,000	10,355,000	10,527,000
Algeria	–	–	10,000	n.a.	200,000	100,000	100,000
Angola	2,000,000	1,500,000	1,200,000	1,200,000	1,500,000	1,500,000	2,000,000
Burundi	400,000	300,000	400,000	500,000	500,000	800,000	600,000
Congo, DR[1]	550,000	225,000	400,000	100,000	300,000	800,000	1,500,000
Congo, PR	–	–	–	–	250,000	500,000	30,000
Côte d'Ivoire	–	–	–	–	–	–	2,000
Djibouti	50,000	–	25,000	5,000	–	–	–
Eritrea	–	–	–	–	100,000	250,000	310,000
Ethiopia	400,000	–	–	–	150,000	300,000	250,000
Ghana	20,000	150,000	20,000	20,000	20,000	–	–
Guinea	–	–	–	–	–	–	60,000
Guinea-Bissau	–	–	–	–	200,000	50,000	–
Kenya	210,000	210,000	100,000	150,000	200,000	100,000	100,000
Liberia	1,100,000	1,000,000	1,000,000	500,000	75,000	50,000	20,000
Mozambique	500,000	500,000	–	–	–	–	–
Nigeria	–	–	30,000	50,000	3,000	5,000	–
Rwanda	1,200,000	500,000	–	50,000	500,000	600,000	150,000
Senegal	–	–	–	10,000	10,000	–	5,000
Sierra Leone	700,000	1,000,000	800,000	500,000	300,000	500,000	700,000
Somalia	500,000	300,000	250,000	200,000	250,000	350,000	300,000

Source: US Committee for Refugees

South Africa	–	–	–	5,000	500,000	4,000,000
Sudan	4,000,000	4,000,000	4,000,000	4,000,000	4,000,000	4,000,000
Togo	–	–	–	–	–	100,000
Uganda	400,000	450,000	400,000	300,000	70,000	–
Americas & Caribbean	**2,176,000**	**1,886,000**	**1,755,000**	**1,624,000**	**1,220,000**	**1,280,000**
Colombia	2,100,000	1,800,000	1,400,000	1,000,000	600,000	600,000
Guatemala	–	–	–	250,000	200,000	200,000
Mexico	16,000	16,000	15,000	14,000	–	–
Peru	60,000	70,000	340,000	360,000	420,000	480,000
South and central Asia	**1,542,000**	**1,617,000**	**2,130,000**	**2,253,500**	**2,400,000**	**1,600,000**
Afghanistan	375,000	500,000	1,000,000	1,250,000	1,200,000	500,000
Bangladesh	60,000	50,000	50,000	–	–	–
India	507,000	507,000	520,000	200,000	250,000	250,000
Sri Lanka	600,000	560,000	560,000	800,000	900,000	850,000
Tajikistan	–	–	–	3,500	50,000	–
Europe	**3,539,000**	**3,993,000**	**3,685,000**	**3,695,000**	**4,735,000**	**5,080,000**
Armenia	–	–	60,000	70,000	50,000	75,000
Azerbaijan	575,000	568,000	576,000	550,000	550,000	670,000
Bosnia and Herzegovina	518,000	830,000	836,000	800,000	1,000,000	1,300,000
Croatia	34,000	50,000	61,000	110,000	185,000	240,000
Cyprus	265,000	265,000	265,000	265,000	265,000	265,000
Georgia	272,000	280,000	275,000	285,000	280,000	260,000

Source: US Committee for Refugees

chapter 8

Russian Federation	450,000	250,000	400,000	375,000	350,000	800,000	800,000
Turkey	2,000,000	2,000,000	2,000,000	1,250,000	1,000,000	600,000	600,000
Yugoslavia[2]	–	–	–	–	257,000	600,000	475,000
Middle East	**1,710,000**	**1,700,000**	**1,475,000**	**1,475,000**	**1,575,000**	**1,917,000**	**1,700,000**
Gaza Strip and West Bank	–	–	–	–	–	17,000	–
Iraq	1,000,000	1,000,000	900,000	900,000	1,000,000	900,000	700,000
Israel	–	–	–	–	200,000	200,000	200,000
Lebanon	600,000	400,000	450,000	450,000	450,000	350,000	350,000
Syria[3]	–	–	125,000	125,000	125,000	450,000	450,000
Yemen	110,000	300,000	–	–	–	–	–
East Asia and Pacific	**613,000**	**555,000**	**1,070,000**	**800,000**	**1,150,000**	**1,577,000**	**1,670,000**
Cambodia	113,000	55,000	32,000	30,000	22,000	–	–
East Timor	–	–	–	–	–	300,000	–
Indonesia	–	–	–	–	–	440,000	800,000
Korea, DPR of[1]	–	–	–	–	–	–	100,000
Myanmar	500,000	500,000	1,000,000	750,000	1,000,000	600,000	600,000
Papua New Guinea	–	–	70,000	20,000	6,000	5,000	–
Philippines	–	–	–	–	122,000	200,000	140,000
Solomon Islands	–	–	–	–	–	32,000	30,000
Total	**26,423,000**	**20,400,000**	**19,705,000**	**17,437,500**	**19,253,000**	**21,345,000**	**21,154,000**

Notes: – indicates zero or near zero; n.a. not available, or reported estimates unreliable; [1]formerly Zaire; [2]for 1993, refugees from Croatia and Bosnia included in Yugoslavia total, for 1994-95 Yugoslavia total includes only refugees from Serbia and Montenegro; [3]includes about 125,000 IDPs originally displaced from the Golan Heights in 1967 and their progeny.

Source: US Committee for Refugees

■ Estimates of the size of internally displaced populations are often imprecise. Where ranges are reported, USCR uses the lowest number in the range for compiling totals.

Section Two

**Tracking
the system**

chapter 9

International Federation overview

In 2000, the International Federation of Red Cross and Red Crescent Societies started putting into practice *Strategy 2010*, its guiding vision for the decade 2000-2010. *Strategy 2010* defines the International Federation's mission, which is to improve the lives of vulnerable people by mobilizing the power of humanity, and identifies three strategic directions to guide its actions:

- National Society programmes that are responsive to local vulnerability and focused on the areas where they have greatest impact.
- Well-functioning National Societies that can mobilize support and carry out their humanitarian mission, contributing to the building of civil society.
- The Red Cross and Red Crescent works more effectively with its partners, through programme coordination, long-term partnerships and funding, and more active advocacy.

Strategy 2010 also identifies four core areas which will be the focus of International Federation activities in the coming decade: disaster response; disaster preparedness; health and care in the community; and promotion of the International Red Cross and Red Crescent Movement's Fundamental Principles and humanitarian values.

During the 1990s, the number of beneficiaries targeted for International Federation support was ever increasing: from 5 million in 1990, 19 million in 1994, 22 million in 1997, to 30 million in 1999. The trend continued in 2000, with more than 50 million people affected by floods, droughts, earthquakes and displacement receiving assistance from the International Federation.

To assist these people in need, the International Federation launched relief appeals for 447 million Swiss francs, of which 305 million Swiss francs was sought for the annual appeal covering long-term operations and 142 million francs was requested for emergencies. The biggest emergency appeal of the year, for some 35 million francs, was in response to floods in southern Africa, which left 200,000 people homeless in Mozambique, the hardest-hit country.

The International Federation remains committed to improving the quality of humanitarian assistance and accountability. In 1994, along with seven other humanitarian agencies (Caritas Internationalis, Catholic Relief Services, International Committee of the Red Cross, International Save the Children Alliance, Lutheran World Federation, Oxfam and World Council of Churches), the International Federation developed the *Code of Conduct for the International Red Cross and Red Crescent Movement and Non-governmental Organizations (NGOs) in Disaster Relief.* The code sets out universal basic standards to govern the way signatory relief agencies should work in disaster assistance. It is a voluntary code and is applicable to any NGO, be it national or international, large or small. As of 31 March 2001, 193 NGOs had become signatories to the code, and had agreed to incorporate the code's ten points of principle into their work. For more information, visit the *Code of Conduct* page on the International Federation's web site at http://www.ifrc.org/publicat/conduct/

Photo opposite page: With the support of its 176 member Red Cross and Red Crescent societies, the International Federation coordinates and provides assistance to vulnerable people around the world.

Christopher Black/ International Federation, Mozambique 2001

The International Federation also continued its support to the Sphere project, an international inter-agency effort which provides humanitarian agencies with a new framework for rights-based humanitarian assistance and adherence to minimum standards. During 2000, the project was increasingly integrated into programming, particularly disaster response and disaster preparedness, and into basic training courses for International Federation delegates. More information about the Sphere project can be found at http://www.sphereproject.org/

A number of International Federation activities followed up on the issues raised in the *World Disasters Report 2000*, which focused on public health and included a chapter on the necessity for an international disaster response law (see Boxes 9.1 and 9.2).

Box 9.1 Developing an international disaster response law

The *World Disasters Report 2000* included a chapter written by Michael Hoffman, of the American Red Cross, entitled *Towards an international disaster response law*. The chapter prompted many positive reactions and, as a result, at its November 2000 session the International Federation's Governing Board declared the promotion of an international disaster response law (IDRL) one of its key issues for disaster preparedness.

Following consultations, the International Federation convened a meeting in Geneva with the aim of identifying a common position and agreeing on a concrete workplan. The meeting brought together legal and field experts from 18 national Red Cross and Red Crescent societies and representatives from the United Nations' Office for the Coordination of Humanitarian Affairs (OCHA), the International Committee of the Red Cross (ICRC) and academics.

The International Federation, and the International Red Cross and Red Crescent Movement, has had a long-standing role in helping to develop IDRL norms in the past (for example, resolution VI adopted at the 23rd International Conference of the Red Cross, Bucharest 1977), and its strategy for the decade 2000-2010, *Strategy 2010*, calls on active advocacy by National Societies to mobilize people and influence decisions in its core areas of disaster preparedness and response. The meeting agreed, therefore, that the International Federation, with the experience and expertise of its member national Red Cross and Red Crescent societies in disaster preparedness and relief in natural and technological disasters, is well suited to take a lead role in promoting IDRL and in ensuring its effective application.

One objective is to introduce the term "IDRL" into common usage by governmental authorities and intergovernmental and non-governmental actors in disaster relief. This will help ensure that, as a reference term for the legal framework, it will make them conscious of their obligations under existing law, and help them take the necessary steps to prepare for disasters.

A second objective is, after proper study and consultation with the relevant actors, to identify weaknesses or gaps in the present law, to propose improvements or develop new instruments where necessary, and to promote the faithful application of the law and the relevant norms.

The meeting recommended a 'needs-based' approach to these priorities. The International Federation's further action in this initiative will therefore focus on the areas identified by field experience as the most relevant to the beneficiaries of humanitarian relief.

A three-step action plan designed at the meeting provides for:

- the compilation and publication of all existing and relevant international rules, drawn from treaties and major instruments of less-than-treaty status, including regional and, where relevant, bilateral instruments;
- the collection of field experience, and an evaluation as to where existing rules do or do not respond effectively to the requirements of humanitarian actors in the field; and
- the identification of ways and means to improve the law, or to improve understanding of it, or to address recognized difficulties in non-legal ways.

Box 9.2 Is public health now on the map?

The *World Disasters Report 2000* focused on public health and asked the question, "Has public health fallen off the map?" Highlighting that up to 100,000 people die each year as a result of natural disasters, while some 13 million lose their lives to infectious diseases, the report showed how disasters destroy progress in public health and feed off weak public health infrastructures.

The United Nations Security Council made history in 2000 when it discussed AIDS, the first time a health issue has been considered there. Since then, AIDS has been debated in the Security Council three more times, and infectious diseases have been prominent in the discussions of world forums. The International Federation made AIDS and other health emergencies a key theme of its African regional conference held in Burkina Faso in 2000. The conference issued the Ouagadougou Declaration committing to massively scale up its public health interventions through its network of millions of volunteers. The declaration was later made an official United Nations document.

The year 2000 saw a record 550 million children under five immunized against polio in National Immunization Days organized by UNICEF and its partners including national Red Cross and Red Crescent societies. Nevertheless, there are still 30 million children born every year in the least developed countries who are not receiving the basic six vaccinations against tuberculosis, diphtheria, tetanus, polio, pertussis and measles. The Global Alliance for Vaccines and Immunizations (GAVI), launched in January 2000, is a significant step in the fight against vaccine-preventable childhood illness which claim 3 million lives annually. With the financial clout of the Bill & Melinda Gates Foundation in particular and the technical expertise of the World Health Organization and UNICEF, GAVI should be able to make significant strides in making vaccines available to children in developing countries and boosting vaccine research particularly for HIV/AIDS, malaria and tuberculosis.

In brief, 2000 saw understanding of public health broaden and the control of infectious diseases advance on the political and media agenda. However, the problems have continued to grow and, while resource mobilization has slightly improved, resources allocated by the international community remain grossly inadequate and nowhere near the levels required. The International Federation has seen its long-term health portfolio rise from representing 25 per cent of its appeal in 2000 to 31 per cent in 2001, consistent with the concerns expressed in the report. Health components of emergency response programmes take the figure to well over 50 per cent.

Much has been done to strengthen advocacy for health issues during the year. The current debate has largely focused on people of developing countries being denied access to treatment and on unacceptable pricing of drugs. The call of the report for "investing in people – not just in commodities" remains particularly pertinent. Service delivery and "demand creation" (for condoms, impregnated bed nets, voluntary counselling and testing, etc.) remain key challenges on which Red Cross and Red Crescent societies are working through scaled-up interventions. The International Federation's widely shared view that humanitarian concerns should take precedence over commercial interests seems to be prevailing on the issue of drug pricing and access to treatment following the settlement of the landmark court case brought by 39 pharmaceutical firms against the South African government. However, much needs to be done to ensure that systems are put in place for ensuring delivery and ensuring that it is done in a manner which does not lead to discrimination against people living with HIV/AIDS.

Focused partnerships were identified as key to moving forward. Progress has been made along these lines, with the International Federation now playing a more active role in, for example, the International Partnership against AIDS in Africa, Stop TB, the polio eradication initiative and the joint interventions that have been set up to fight Ebola and meningitis outbreaks.

Finally, chapters of the *World Disasters Report 2000* highlighted the need to focus health interventions following disasters not only in rehabilitating health infrastructure but on radically rebuilding the system in an appropriate manner. "We cannot just pack up and go home,... but pumping inadequate resources into dysfunctional systems is equally flawed," it read.

chapter 10

Section Two
Tracking
the system

The International
Federation's strength:
its global network
of national
Red Cross and
Red Crescent
societies.

Christopher Black/
International Federation,
Mozambique 2000

Reaching out around the world

Contact details for the members of the International Red Cross and Red Crescent Movement

THE INTERNATIONAL RED CROSS AND RED CRESCENT MOVEMENT

The International Federation of Red Cross and Red Crescent Societies
P.O. Box 372
1211 Geneva 19
SWITZERLAND
Tel. (41)(22) 7304222
Fax (41)(22) 7330395
Tlx (045) 412 133 FRC CH
Tlg. LICROSS GENEVA
E-mail secretariat@ifrc.org
Web http://www.ifrc.org

The International Committee of the Red Cross
19 avenue de la Paix
1202 Geneva
SWITZERLAND
Tel. (41)(22) 734 60 01
Fax (41)(22) 733 20 57
Tlx 414 226 CCR CH
Tlg. INTERCROIXROUGE GENEVE
E-mail icrc.gva@gwn.icrc.org
Web http://www.icrc.org

NATIONAL RED CROSS AND RED CRESCENT SOCIETIES

National Red Cross and Red Crescent Societies are listed alphabetically by International Organization for Standardization Codes for the Representation of Names of Countries, English spelling. Details correct as of 1 March 2001. Please forward any corrections to the International Federation's Information Resource Centre in Geneva (e-mail: irc@ifrc.org).

Afghan Red Crescent Society
Pul Artel
P.O. Box 3066
Shar-e-Now
Kabul
AFGHANISTAN
Tel. (873) (628)
          32357/33059/34288/32211

Albanian Red Cross
Rruga "Muhammet Gjollesha"
Sheshi "Karl Topia"
C.P. 1511
Tirana
ALBANIA
Tel. (355)(4) 225855/22037
Fax (355)(4) 225855/22037
Tlg. ALBCROSS TIRANA
E-mail: kksh01@albaniaonline.net

Algerian Red Crescent
15 bis, boulevard Mohammed V
Alger 16000
ALGERIA
Tel. (213) (2) 633155
Fax (213) (2) 634314/633690
Tlg. HILALAHMAR ALGER
E-mail: cra@algeriainfo.com

Andorra Red Cross

Prat de la Creu 22
Andorra la Vella
ANDORRA
Tel. (376) 825225
Fax (376) 828630
E-mail creuroja@creuroja.ad
Web http://www.creuroja.ad

Angola Red Cross

Rua 1° Congresso no 21
Caixa Postal 927
Luanda
ANGOLA
Tel. (244)(2) 336543/333991
Fax (244)(2) 391970
Tlx 3394 CRUZVER AN

Antigua and Barbuda Red Cross Society

Old Parham Road
P.O. Box 727
St. Johns, Antigua W.I.
ANTIGUA AND BARBUDA
Tel. (1)(268) 4620800/4609599
Fax (1)(268) 4609595
E-mail redcross@candw.ag

Argentine Red Cross

Hipólito Yrigoyen 2068
1089 Buenos Aires
ARGENTINA
Tel. (54)(114) 9511391/9511854
Fax (54)(114) 9527715
Tlg. ARGENCROSS
    BUENOS AIRES

Armenian Red Cross Society

21 Paronian Street
375015 Yerevan
ARMENIA
Tel. (374)(1) 538064
Fax (374)(1) 151129
Tlx 243345 ODER SU

Australian Red Cross

155 Pelham Street
P.O. Box 196
Carlton South VIC 3053
AUSTRALIA
Tel. (61)(3) 93451800
Fax (61)(3) 93482513
E-mail redcross@nat.redcross.org.au
Web http://www.redcross.org.au

Austrian Red Cross

Wiedner Hauptstrasse 32
Postfach 39
1041 Wien 4
AUSTRIA
Tel. (43)(1) 58900 0
Fax (43)(1) 58900 199
Tlx oerk a 133111
E-mail oerk@redcross.or.at
Web http://www.redcross.or.at

Red Crescent Society of Azerbaijan

Qizil Xac/Qizil Aypara Evi
First Magomayev Street 6 A
370004 Baku
AZERBAIJAN
Tel. (994)(12) 25792
Fax (994)(12) 97189
E-mail azerb.redcrescent@azdata.net
     azrc@ifrc.azerin.com

The Bahamas Red Cross Society

P.O. Box N-8331
Nassau
BAHAMAS
Tel. (1)(242) 3237370/3237371
Fax (1)(242) 3237404
Tlg. BAHREDCROSS NASSAU
E-mail redcross@bahamas.net.bs
Web http://www.bahamasrc.com

Bahrain Red Crescent Society

P.O. Box 882
Manama
BAHRAIN
Tel. (973) 293171
Fax (973) 291797
Tlg. HILAHAMAR MANAMA
E-mail hilal@baletco.com.bh

Bangladesh Red Crescent Society

684-686 Bara Maghbazar
G.P.O. Box 579
Dhaka – 1217
BANGLADESH
Tel. (880)(2) 9330188/9330189
Fax (880)(2) 831908
Tlg. RED CRESCENT DHAKA
E-mail bdrcs@bdonline.com

The Barbados Red Cross Society

Red Cross House
Jemmotts Lane
Bridgetown
BARBADOS
Tel. (1)(246) 4262052/4300646
Fax (1)(246) 4262052
Tlx 2201 P.U.B. T.L.X. W.B.
Tlg. REDCROSS BARBADOS
E-mail bdosredcross@caribsurf.com

Belarusian Red Cross

35, Karl Marx Str.
220030 Minsk
BELARUS
Tel. (375)(17) 2272620
Fax (375)(17) 2272620
Tlx 252290 KREST SU
E-mail redcross@un.minsk.by

Belgian Red Cross

Ch. de Vleurgat 98
1050 Bruxelles
BELGIUM
Tel. (32)(2) 6454411
Fax (32)(2) 6460439 (French);
6460441 (Flemish)
Tlx 24266 BELCRO B
E-mail info@redcross-fr.be (French)
documentatie@redcross-fl.be
(Flemish)
Web http://www.redcross.be

Belize Red Cross Society

1 Gabourel Lane
P.O. Box 413
Belize City
BELIZE
Tel. (501)(2) 73319
Fax (501)(2) 30998
Tlx BTL BOOTH 211
E-mail bzercshq@btl.net

Red Cross of Benin

B.P. No. 1
Porto-Novo
BENIN
Tel. (229) 212886
Fax (229) 214927
Tlx 1131 CRBEN

Bolivian Red Cross

Avenida Simón Bolívar No. 1515
Casilla No. 741
La Paz
BOLIVIA
Tel. (591)(2) 202930/202934
Fax (591)(2) 359102
Tlg. CRUZROJA – LA PAZ
E-mail cruzrobo@caoba.entelnet.bo
Web http://www.come.to/
cruzroja.org.bo

Botswana Red Cross Society

135 Independance Avenue
P.O. Box 485
Gaborone
BOTSWANA
Tel. (267) 352465/312353
Fax (267) 312352
Tlg. THUSA GABORONE
E-mail brcs@info.bw

Brazilian Red Cross

Praça Cruz Vermelha No. 10
20230-130 Rio de Janeiro RJ
BRAZIL
Tel. (55)(21) 2210658
Fax (55)(21) 5071538/5071594
Tlx (38) 2130532 CVBR BR
Tlg. BRAZCROSS RIO DE
JANEIRO

Brunei Darussalam Red Crescent Society

P.O. Box 3065
Bandar Seri Begawan BS 8675
BRUNEI DARUSSALAM
Tel. (673)(2) 339774/421948
Fax (673)(2) 382797

Bulgarian Red Cross

76, James Boucher Boulevard
1407 Sofia
BULGARIA
Tel. (359)(2) 650595
Fax (359)(2) 656937
Tlg. BULGAREDCROSS SOFIA
E-mail secretariat@redcross.bg
Web http://www.redcross.bg

Burkinabe Red Cross Society

01 B.P. 4404
Ouagadougou 01
BURKINA FASO
Tel. (226) 361340
Fax (226) 363121
Tlx LSCR 5438 BF
OUAGADOUGOU

Burundi Red Cross

18, Av. de la Croix-Rouge
B.P. 324
Bujumbura
BURUNDI
Tel. (257) 216246/218871
Fax (257) 211101
Tlx 5081 CAB PUB BDI

Cambodian Red Cross Society

17, Vithei de la Croix-Rouge
Cambodgienne
Phnom-Penh
CAMBODIA
Tel. (855)(23) 212876/362876
Fax (855)(23) 212875/362140
E-mail crc@camnet.com.kh

Cameroon Red Cross Society

Rue Henri Dunant
B.P. 631
Yaoundé
CAMEROON
Tel. (237) 224177
Fax (237) 224177
Tlx (0970) 8884 KN

The Canadian Red Cross Society

170 Metcalfe Street, Suite 300
Ottawa
Ontario K2P 2P2
CANADA
Tel. (1)(613) 7401900
Fax (1)(613) 7401911
Tlg. CANCROSS OTTAWA
E-mail cancross@redcross.ca
Web http://www.redcross.ca

Red Cross of Cape Verde

Rua Andrade Corvo
Caixa Postal 119
Praia
CAPE VERDE
Tel. (238) 611701/614169
Fax (238) 614174/613909
Tlx 6004 CV CV

Central African Red Cross Society

Avenue Koudoukou, Km 5
B.P. 1428
Bangui
CENTRAL AFRICAN
REPUBLIC
Tel. (236) 612223/502130
Fax (236) 613561
Tlx DIPLOMA 5213

Red Cross of Chad

B.P. 449
N'Djamena
CHAD
Tel. (235) 523434
Fax (235) 525218
Tlg. CROIXROUGE
    N'DJAMENA
E-mail croix-rouge@intnet.td

Chilean Red Cross

Avenida Santa María No. 150
Correo 21, Casilla 246 V
Santiago de Chile, CHILE
Tel. (56)(2) 7771448
Fax (56)(2) 7370270
Tlg. "CHILECRUZ"
E-mail cruzroja@rdc.cl

Red Cross Society of China

53 Ganmian Hutong
100010 Beijing
CHINA
Tel. (86)(10) 65124447/65135838
Fax (86)(10) 65124169
Tlg. HONGHUI BEIJING
E-mail hq@chineseredcross.org.ac.cn
Web http://www.chineseredcross.
    org.cn

Colombian Red Cross Society

Avenida 68 No. 66-31
Apartado Aéreo 11-110
Bogotá D.C.
COLOMBIA
Tel. (57)(1) 4376339/ 4289423
Fax (57)(1) 4281725/4376301
Tlg. CRUZ ROJA BOGOTA
E-mail inter@andinet.com
Web http://www.crcol.org.co/

Congolese Red Cross

Place de la Paix
B.P. 4145
Brazzaville
CONGO
Tel. (242) 824410
Fax (242) 828825
Tlx UNISANTE 5364
E-mail: sjm@ficr.aton.cd

Red Cross of the Democratic Republic of the Congo

41, Avenue de la Justice
B.P. 1712
Kinshasa I
CONGO, D.R. OF THE
Tel. (243)(12) 34897
Fax (243) 8804551
E-mail: secretariat@crrdc.aton.cd

Costa Rican Red Cross

Calle 14, Avenida 8
Apartado 1025
San José 1000
COSTA RICA
Tel. (506) 2337033/2553761
Fax (506) 2237628
Tlg. COSTACRUZ SAN JOSÉ
E-mail bcrcsn@sol.racsa.co.cr
Web http://www.cruzrojahumanidad.
    org/costarica/

Red Cross Society of Côte d'Ivoire

P.O. Box 1244
Abidjan 01
CÔTE D'IVOIRE
Tel. (225) 22321335
Fax (225) 22225355
Tlx 24122 SICOGI CI

Croatian Red Cross

Ulica Crvenog kriza 14
10000 Zagreb
CROATIA
Tel. (385)(1) 4655814
Fax (385)(1) 4550072
E-mail redcross@hck.hr
Web http://www.hck.hr/

Cuban Red Cross

Calle Calzada No. 51 Esquina
C.P. 10400
CUBA
Tel. (53)(7) 552555 /552556
Fax (53)(7) 662057
Tlg. CRUROCU HABANA
E-mail crsn@infomed.sld.cu

Czech Red Cross

Thunovska 18
CZ-118 04 Praha 1
CZECH REPUBLIC
Tel. (420)(2) 51104111
Fax (420)(2) 57532113
Tlg. CROIX PRAHA
E-mail cck.zahranicni@iol.cz

Danish Red Cross

Blegdamsvej 27
P.O. Box 2600
DK-2100 Köbenhavn Ö
DENMARK
Tel. (45) 35259200
Fax (45) 35259292
Tlg. DANCROIX KÖBENHAVN
E-mail drc@redcross.dk
Web http://www.redcross.dk

Red Crescent Society of Djibouti

B.P. 8
Djibouti
DJIBOUTI
Tel. (253) 352451/353552
Fax (253) 351505
Tlx 5871 PRESIDENCE DJ

Dominica Red Cross Society

Federation Drive
Goodwill
DOMINICA
Tel. (1)(767) 4488280
Fax (1)(767) 4487708
Tlg. DOMCROSS
E-mail redcross@cwdom.dm

Dominican Red Cross

Calle Juan E. Dunant No. 51
Ens. Miraflores
Apartado Postal 1293
Santo Domingo, D.N.
DOMINICAN REPUBLIC
Tel. (1)(809) 6823793/6897344
Fax (1)(809) 6822837
E-mail cruz.roja@codetel.net.do

Ecuadorian Red Cross

Antonio Elizalde E 4-31 y Av.
Colombia (esq.)
Casilla 1701 2119
Quito
ECUADOR
Tel. (593)(2) 582481/582480
Fax (593)(2) 570424
E-mail difusio@attglobal.net

Egyptian Red Crescent Society

29, El Galaa Street
Cairo
EGYPT
Tel. (20)(2) 5750558/5750397
Fax (20)(2) 5740450
Tlx 93249 ERCS UN
Tlg. 124 HELALHAMER
E-mail erc@brainyl.ie-eg.com

Salvadorean Red Cross Society

17 C. Pte. y Av. Henri Dunant
Apartado Postal 2672
San Salvador
EL SALVADOR
Tel. (503) 2227743/2227749
Fax (503) 2227758
Tlx 20550 cruzalva
E-mail crsalvador@vianet.com.sv
Web http://www.cruzrojahumanidad.
org/elsalvador/

Red Cross of Equatorial Guinea

Alcalde Albilio Balboa 92
Apartado postal 460
Malabo
EQUATORIAL GUINEA
Tel. (240)(9) 3701
Fax (240)(9) 3701
Tlx 099/1111 EG.PUB MBO

Estonia Red Cross

Lai Street 17
EE0001 Tallinn
ESTONIA
Tel. (372) 6411643
Fax (372) 6411641
Tlx 173491
E-mail epr@online.ee

Ethiopian Red Cross Society

Ras Desta Damtew Avenue
P.O. Box 195
Addis Ababa
ETHIOPIA
Tel. (251)(1) 519364/159074
Fax (251)(1) 512643
Tlx 21338 ERCS ET
E-mail ercs@padis.gn.apc.org

Fiji Red Cross Society

22 Gorrie Street
GPO Box 569
Suva
FIJI
Tel. (679) 314133/314138
Fax (679) 303818
Tlx 2279 Red Cross
Tlg. REDCROSS SUVA

Finnish Red Cross

Tehtaankatu 1 a
P.O. Box 168
FIN-00141 Helsinki
FINLAND
Tel. (358)(9) 12931
Fax (358)(9) 1293326
Tlg. FINCROSS HELSINKI
E-mail forename.surname@redcross.fi
Web http://www.redcross.fi

French Red Cross

1, Place Henry-Dunant
F-75384 Paris Cedex 08
FRANCE
Tel. (33)(1) 44431100
Fax (33)(1) 44431101
Tlg. CROIROUGE PARIS 086
E-mail cr@croix-rouge.fr
Web http://www.croix-rouge.fr

Gabonese Red Cross Society

Boîte Postale 2274
Libreville
GABON
Tel. (241) 766160/766159
Fax (241) 766160
E-mail gab.cross@internetgabon.com

The Gambia Red Cross Society

Kanifing Industrial Area – Banjul
P.O. Box 472
Banjul
GAMBIA
Tel. (220) 392405/393179
Fax (220) 394921
Tlg. GAMREDCROSS BANJUL
E-mail redcrossgam@delphi.com

Red Cross Society of Georgia

15, Krilov St.
38002 Tbilisi
GEORGIA
Tel. (995)(32) 954282/951386
Fax (995)(32) 953304
E-mail grc@caucasus.net

German Red Cross

Carstennstrasse 58
D-12205 Berlin
GERMANY
Tel. (49) (30) 85404-0
Fax (49) (30) 85404470
Tlx 886619 DKRB D
E-mail drk@drk.de
Web http://www.rotkreuz.de

Ghana Red Cross Society

Ministries Annex Block A3
Off Liberia Road Extension
P.O. Box 835
Accra
GHANA
Tel. (233)(21) 662298
Fax (233)(21) 667226
Tlg. GHANACROSS ACCRA
E-mail grcs@ghana.com

Hellenic Red Cross

Rue Lycavittou 1
Athens 106 72
GREECE
Tel. (30)(1) 3621681/3615606
Fax (30)(1) 3615606
Tlg. HELLECROIX ATHENES
E-mail hrc@nermode.ntua.gr
Web http://www.redcross.gr

Grenada Red Cross Society

Upper Lucas Street
P.O. Box 551
St. George's
GRENADA
Tel. (1)(473) 4401483
Fax (1)(473) 4401829
E-mail grercs@caribsurf.com

Guatemalan Red Cross

3a Calle 8 – 40, Zona 1
Guatemala, C.A.
GUATEMALA
Tel. (502)(2) 322026/532027
Fax (502)(2) 324649
E-mail crg@guate.net

Red Cross Society of Guinea

B.P. 376
Conakry
GUINEA
Tel. (224) 404344/402887
Fax (224) 414255
Tlx 22101

Red Cross Society of Guinea-Bissau

Avenida Unidade Africana, No. 12
Caixa postal 514-1036 BIX, Codex
Bissau
GUINEA-BISSAU
Tel. (245) 202408
Tlx 251 PCE BI

The Guyana Red Cross Society

Eve Leary
P.O. Box 10524
Georgetown
GUYANA
Tel. (592)(2) 65174
Fax (592)(2) 77099/67852
Tlx 2226 FERNA GY
E-mail redcross@sdnp.org.gy
Web http://www.sdnp.org.gy/
redcross/

Haitian National Red Cross Society

1, rue Eden Bicentenaire
CRH, B.P. 1337
Port-Au-Prince
HAITI
Tel. (509) 2231035
Fax (509) 2231054
E-mail croroha@haitiworld.net

Honduran Red Cross

7a Calle
entre 1a. y 2a. Avenidas
Comayagüela D.C.
HONDURAS
Tel. (504) 2378876/2374628
Fax (504) 2380185/2374558
Tlx 1437 CRUZ R HO
E-mail honducruz@datum.hn

Hungarian Red Cross

Arany János utca 31
Magyar Vöröskereszt
1367 Budapest 5, Pf. 121
HUNGARY
Tel. (36)(1) 3313950/3317711
Fax (36)(1) 1533988
Tlg. REDCROSS BUDAPEST
E-mail intdept@hrc.hu

Icelandic Red Cross

Efstaleiti 9
103 Reykjavik
ICELAND
Tel. (354) 5704000
Fax (354) 5704010
E-mail central@redcross.is
Web http://www.redcross.is/

Indian Red Cross Society

Red Cross Building
1 Red Cross Road
New Delhi 110001
INDIA
Tel. (91)(11) 3716441/3716442
Fax (91)(11) 3717454
Tlg. INDCROSS NEW DELHI
E-mail indcross@nde.vsnl.net.in

Indonesian Red Cross Society

Jl. Jenderal Datot Subroto Kav. 96
P.O. Box 2009
Jakarta 12790
INDONESIA
Tel. (62)(21) 7992325
Fax (62)(21) 7995188
Tlx 66170 MB PMI IA
Tlg. INDONCROSS JKT

Red Crescent Society of the Islamic Republic of Iran

Ostad Nejatolahi Ave.
Tehran
IRAN, ISLAMIC REPUBLIC OF
Tel. (98)(21) 8849077/8808155
Fax (98)(21) 8849079
Tlx 224259 RCIA-IR
E-mail helal@mail.dci.co.ir

Iraqi Red Crescent Society

Al-Mansour
P.O. Box 6143
Baghdad
IRAQ
Tel. (964)(1) 8862191
Fax (964)(1) 5372519
Tlx 213331 HELAL IK
Tlg. REDCRESCENT
BAGHDAD

Irish Red Cross Society

16, Merrion Square
Dublin 2
IRELAND
Tel. (353)(1) 6765135/6765136
Fax (353)(1) 6614461
Tlx 32746 IRCS F.I
E-mail redcross@iol.ie
Web http://www.redcross.ie

Italian Red Cross

Via Toscana, 12
I – 00187 Roma – RM
ITALY
Tel. (39)(06) 47591
Fax (39)(6) 44244534
Tlx 613421 CRIROM I
Tlg. CRIROM 00187
Web http://www.cri.it/

Jamaica Red Cross

Spanish Town, St. Catherine
76 Arnold Road
Kingston 5
JAMAICA WEST INDIES
Tel. (1)(876) 98478602
Fax (1)(876) 9848272
Tlg. JAMCROSS KINGSTON
E-mail jrcs@infochan.com
Web http://www.infochan.com/
ja-red-cross/

Japanese Red Cross Society

1-3 Shiba Daimon, 1-Chome,
Minato-ku
Tokyo-105-8521
JAPAN
Tel. (81)(3) 34381311
Fax (81)(3) 34358509
Tlg. JAPANCROSS TOKYO
E-mail rcjpn@ppp.bekkoame.or.jp
Web http://www.sphere.ad.jp/
redcross/

Jordan National Red Crescent Society

Madaba Street
P.O. Box 10001
Amman 11151
JORDAN
Tel. (962)(64) 773141/773142
Fax (962)(64) 750815
Tlg. HALURDON AMMAN
E-mail jrc@index.com.jo

Kenya Red Cross Society

Nairobi South "C"
(Belle Vue), off Mombasa Road
P.O. Box 40712
Nairobi
KENYA
Tel. (254)(2) 503781/503789
Fax (254)(2) 503845
Tlg. KENREDCROSS NAIROBI
E-mail kenyarc@africaonline.co.ke

Kiribati Red Cross Society

P.O. Box 213
Bikenibeu
Tarawa
KIRIBATI
Tel. (686) 28128
Fax (686) 21416

Red Cross Society of the Democratic People's Republic of Korea

Ryonwa 1, Central District
Pyongyang
KOREA, DEMOCRATIC
PEOPLE'S REPUBLIC OF
Tel. (850)(2) 18333/18444
Fax (850)(2) 3814644/3814410
Tlg. KOREACROSS
PYONGYANG

The Republic of Korea National Red Cross

32 – 3ka, Namsan-dong
Choong-Ku
Seoul 100 – 043
KOREA, REPUBLIC OF
Tel. (82)(2) 37053705/37053661
Fax (82)(2) 37053667
E-mail knrc@redcross.or.kr
Web http://www.redcross.or.kr

Kuwait Red Crescent Society

Al-Jahra St.
P.O. Box 1359
13014 Safat
KUWAIT
Tel. (965) 4815478/ 4814793
Fax (965) 4839114
Tlx 22729
E-mail krcs@kuwait.net

Red Crescent Society of Kyrgyzstan

10, prospekt Erkindik
720040 Bishkek
KYRGYZSTAN
Tel. (996)(312) 222414/222411
Fax (996)(312) 662181
E-mail redcross@imfiko.bishkek.su

Lao Red Cross

Avenue Sethathirath
B.P. 650
Vientiane
LAO PEOPLE'S DEMOCRATIC
REPUBLIC
Tel. (856)(21) 222398/216610
Fax (856)(21) 212128
Tlx 4491 TE via PTT LAOS
Tlg. CROIXLAO VIENTIANE

Latvian Red Cross

1, Skolas Street
RIGA, LV-1010
LATVIA
Tel. (371)(7) 310902/2275635
Fax (371)(7) 310902/2275635

Lebanese Red Cross

Rue Spears
Beyrouth
LEBANON
Tel. (961)(1) 372802/372803
Fax (961)(1) 378207/371391
Tlg. LIBACROSS BEYROUTH
E-mail lrc-comm@dm.net.lb
Web http://www.dm.net.lb/redcross/

Lesotho Red Cross Society

23 Mabile Road
P.O. Box 366
Maseru 100
LESOTHO
Tel. (266) 313911
Fax (266) 310166
Tlg. LESCROSS MASERU
E-mail lesoff@lesred.co.za

Liberian Red Cross Society

107 Lynch Street
P.O. Box 20-5081
1000 Monrovia 20
LIBERIA
Tel. (231) 225172/227521
Fax (231) 226231/227521
Tlx 44210/44211

Libyan Red Crescent

P.O. Box 541
Benghazi
LIBYAN ARAB JAMAHIRIYA
Tel. (218)(61) 9095202/9095152
Fax (218)(61) 9095829
Tlx 40341 HILAL PY
Tlg. LIBHILAL BENGHAZI

Liechtenstein Red Cross

Heiligkreuz 25
FL-9490 Vaduz
LIECHTENSTEIN
Tel. (41)(75) 2322294
Fax (41)(75) 2322240
Tlg. ROTESKREUZ VADUZ

Lithuanian Red Cross Society

Gedimino ave. 3a
2600 Vilnius
LITHUANIA
Tel. (370)(2) 628037
Fax (370)(2) 619923
E-mail redcross@tdd.lt
Web http://www.tdd.lt/lrk.redcross.lt/

Luxembourg Red Cross

Parc de la Ville
B.P. 404
L – 2014 LUXEMBOURG
Tel. (352) 450202/450201
Fax (352) 457269
Web http://www.croix-rouge.lu/

The Red Cross of The Former Yugoslav Republic of Macedonia

No. 13 Bul. Koco Racin
91000 Skopje
MACEDONIA, THE FORMER
YUGOSLAV REPUBLIC OF
Tel. (389)(91) 114355
Fax (389)(91) 230542

Malagasy Red Cross Society

1, rue Patrice Lumumba
B.P. 1168
Antananarivo
MADAGASCAR
Tel. (261)(20) 2222111
Fax (261)(20) 2235457
E-mail crm@dts.mg

Malawi Red Cross Society

Red Cross House
(along Presidential Way)
P.O. Box 30096
Lilongwe 3
MALAWI
Tel. (265) 775590
Fax (265) 775590
E-mail mrcs@eomw.net

Malaysian Red Crescent Society

JKR 32, Jalan Nipah
Off Jalan Ampang
55000 Kuala Lumpur
MALAYSIA
Tel. (60)(3) 4578122/4578236
Fax (60)(3) 4533191
Tlx MACRES MA 30166
E-mail mrcs@po.jaring.my
Web http://www.redcrescent.org.my/

Mali Red Cross

Route Koulikoro
B.P. 280
Bamako
MALI
Tel. (223) 224569
Fax (223) 240414
Tlx 2611 MJ

Malta Red Cross Society

104 St Ursula Street
Valletta VLT 05
MALTA
Tel. (356) 222645/226010
Fax (356) 243664
E-mail redcross@waldonet.net.mt
Web http://www.redcross.org.mt/

Mauritanian Red Crescent

Avenue Gamal Abdel Nasser
B.P. 344
Nouakchott
MAURITANIA
Tel. (222)(2) 51249
Fax (222)(2) 54784
Tlx 5830 CRM

Mauritius Red Cross Society

Ste. Thérèse Street
Curepipe
MAURITIUS
Tel. (230) 6763604
Fax (230) 6748855
Tlg. MAUREDCROSS
CUREPIPE
E-mail redcross@intnet.mu

Mexican Red Cross

Calle Luis Vives 200
Colonia Polanco
México, D.F. 11510
MEXICO
Tel. (52)(5) 3950606/5575270
Fax (52)(5) 3951598/3950044
Tlg. CRUZROJA MEXICO
E-mail cruzroja@mexporta.com
Web http://www.cruz-roja.org.mx/

Red Cross of Monaco

27, Boulevard de Suisse
Monte Carlo
MONACO
Tel. (377)(97) 976800
Fax (377)(93) 159047
Tlg. CROIXROUGE
MONTECARLO
E-mail redcross@monaco.mc
Web http://www.red-cross.mc

Mongolian Red Cross Society

Central Post Office
Post Box 537
Ulaanbaatar 13
MONGOLIA
Tel. (976) (1) 321864
Fax (976) (1) 321864
E-mail redcross@magicnet.mn

Moroccan Red Crescent

Palais Mokri Takaddoum
B.P. 189
Rabat
MOROCCO
Tel. (212)(7) 650898/651495
Fax (212)(7) 759395
Tlx ALHILAL 319-40 M RABAT
Tlg. ALHILAL RABAT

Mozambique Red Cross Society

Avenida Agostinhoaero 284
Caixa Postal 2488
Maputo
MOZAMBIQUE
Tel. (258)(1) 490943/497721
Fax (258)(1) 497725
Tlx 6-169 CV MO
E-mail cvm@mail.tropical.co.mz

Myanmar Red Cross Society

Red Cross Building
42 Strand Road
Yangon
MYANMAR
Tel. (95)(1) 296552/295238
Fax (95)(1) 296551
Tlx 21218 BRCROS BM
Tlg. MYANMARCROSS
YANGON

Namibia Red Cross

Erf 2128, Independence Avenue
P.O. Box 346
Windhoek
NAMIBIA
Tel. (264)(61) 235216/235226
Fax (264)(61) 228949
E-mail namcross@iafrica.com.na
Web http://www.members.xoom.
com/namcross/

Nepal Red Cross Society

Red Cross Marg, Kalimati
P.O. Box 217
Kathmandu
NEPAL
Tel. (977)(1) 270650/270167
Fax (977)(1) 271915
Tlg. REDCROSS KATHMANDU
E-mail nrcs@nhqs.wlink.com.np

The Netherlands Red Cross

Leeghwaterplein 27
P.O. Box 28120
2502 KC The Hague
NETHERLANDS
Tel. (31)(70) 4455666/4455755
Fax (31)(70) 4455777
Tlg. ROODKRUIS THE HAGUE
E-mail hq@redcross.nl
Web http://www.redcross.nl/

New Zealand Red Cross

69 Molesworth Street
P.O. Box 12-140
Thorndon
Wellington 6038
NEW ZEALAND
Tel. (64)(4) 4723750
Fax (64)(4) 4730315
E-mail national.office@redcross.
org.nz
Web http://www.redcross.org.nz/

Nicaraguan Red Cross

Reparto Belmonte
Carretera Sur, Km 7
Apartado 3279
Managua
NICARAGUA
Tel. (505)(2) 651307/651517
Fax (505)(2) 651643
Tlg. NICACRUZ-MANAGUA
E-mail nicacruz@ibw.com.ni
Web http://www.cruzrojahumanidad.
org/nicaragua/

Red Cross Society of Niger

B.P. 11386
Niamey
NIGER
Tel. (227) 733037
Fax (227) 732461
Tlx CRN GAP NI 5371
E-mail crniger@intnet.ne

Nigerian Red Cross Society

11, Eko Akete Close
South West Ikoyi
P.O. Box 764
Lagos
NIGERIA
Tel. (234)(1) 2695188/2695189
Fax (234)(1) 2691599
Tlx 21470 NCROSS NG
Tlg. NIGERCROSS LAGOS

Norwegian Red Cross

Hausmannsgate 7
Postbox 1. Gronland
0133 Oslo
NORWAY
Tel. (47) 22054000
Fax (47) 22054040
Tlg. NORCROSS OSLO
E-mail documentation.
        center@redcross.no
Web http://www.redcross.no/

Pakistan Red Crescent Society

Sector H-8
Islamabad
PAKISTAN
Tel. (92)(51) 9257404/9257405
Fax (92)(51) 9257408
Tlg. HILALAHMAR
        ISLAMABAD
E-mail hilal@comsats.net.pk

Palau Red Cross Society

P.O. Box 6043
Koror
REPUBLIC OF PALAU 96940
Tel. (680) 4885780/4885781
Fax (680) 4884540
E-mail palredcross@palaunet.com

Red Cross Society of Panama

Albrook, Areas Revertidas
Calle Principal
Edificio # 453, Apartado 668
Zona 1 Panamá
PANAMA
Tel. (507) 2325589/2325559
Fax (507) 2327450
Tlg. PANACRUZ PANAMA
E-mail cruzroja@pan.gbm.net
Web http://www.cruzroja.org.pa/

Papua New Guinea Red Cross Society

Taurama Road
Port Moresby
P.O. Box 6545
Boroko
PAPUA NEW GUINEA
Tel. (675) 3258577/3258759
Fax (675) 3259714

Paraguayan Red Cross

Brasil 216 esq. José Berges
Asunción
PARAGUAY
Tel. (595)(21) 222797/208199
Fax (595)(21) 211560
Tlg. CRUZ ROJA PARAGUAYA
E-mail cruzroja@pla.net.py

Peruvian Red Cross

Av. Arequipa No. 1285
Lima
PERU
Tel. (51)(1) 4710701
Fax (51)(1) 4710701
Tlg. CRUZROJA PERUANA
        LIMA
E-mail scrperu@mail.iaxis.com.pe

The Philippine National Red Cross

Bonifacio Drive, Port Area
P.O. Box 280
Manila 2803
PHILIPPINES
Tel. (63)(2) 5270866/5270856
Fax (63)(2)5270857
Tlg. PHILCROSS MANILA
E-mail secgen_pnrc@email.com

Polish Red Cross

Mokotowska 14
P.O. Box 47
00-950 Warsaw
POLAND
Tel. (48)(22) 6285201/6285202
Fax (48)(22) 6284168
Tlg. PECEKA WARSZAWA
E-mail pck@atomnet.pl
Web http://www.pck.org.pl/

Portuguese Red Cross

Jardim 9 de Abril, 1 a 5
1293 Lisboa Codex
PORTUGAL
Tel. (351)(1) 3905571/3905650
Fax (351)(1) 3951045
Tlg. CRUZVERMELHA
E-mail cvp.sede@mail.telepac.pt

Qatar Red Crescent Society

P.O. Box 5449
Doha
QATAR
Tel. (974) (4) 435111
Fax (974) (4) 439950
Tlg. hilal doha

Romanian Red Cross

Strada Biserica Amzei, 29
Sector 1
Bucarest
ROMANIA
Tel. (40)(1) 6593385/6506233
Fax (40)(1) 3128452
Tlx 10531 romcr r
Tlg. ROMCROIXROUGE
        BUCAREST

The Russian Red Cross Society

Tcheryomushkinski Proezd 5
117036 Moscow
RUSSIAN FEDERATION
Tel. (7)(095) 1265731
Fax (7)(095) 3107048
Tlg. IKRESTPOL MOSKWA
Web http://www.redcross.ru/

Rwandan Red Cross

B.P. 425
Kigali
RWANDA
Tel. (250) 74402
Fax (250) 73233
Tlx 22663 CRR RW

Saint Kitts and Nevis Red Cross Society

Horsford Road
P.O. Box 62
Basseterre
SAINT KITTS AND NEVIS
Tel. (1)(869) 4652584
Fax (1)(869) 4668129
E-mail skbredcr@caribsurf.com

Saint Lucia Red Cross

Vigie
P.O. Box 271
Castries St. Lucia, W.I.
SAINT LUCIA
Tel. (1)(758) 4525582
Fax (1)(758) 4537811
Tlx 6256 MCNAMARA
E-mail sluredcross@candw.lc

Saint Vincent and the Grenadines Red Cross

Halifax Street
Ministry of Education Compound
Kingstown
P.O. Box 431
SAINT VINCENT AND
THE GRENADINES
Tel. (1)(784) 4561888
Fax (1)(784) 4856210
E-mail svgredcross@caribsurf.com

Samoa Red Cross Society

P.O. Box 1616
Apia
SAMOA
Tel. (685) 23686
Fax (685) 22676
Tlx 779 224 MORISHED SX
"Attention Red Cross"

Red Cross Republic of San Marino

Via Scialoja, Cailungo
REPUBLIC OF SAN MARINO
47031
Tel. (37)(8) 994360
Fax (37)(8) 994360
Tlg. CROCE ROSSA
REPUBBLICA DI
SAN MARINO
Web http://www.tradecenter.sm/crs/

Sao Tome and Principe Red Cross

Avenida 12 de Julho No. 11
B.P. 96
Sao Tome
SAO TOME AND PRINCIPE
Tel. (239)(12) 22305/22469
Fax (239)(12) 22305
Tlx 213 PUBLICO ST
"Pour Croix-Rouge"
E-mail cvstp@sol.stome.telepac.net

Saudi Arabian Red Crescent Society

General Headquarters
Riyadh 11129
SAUDI ARABIA
Tel. (966)(1) 4740027
Fax (966)(1) 4740430
Tlx 400096 HILAL SJ
E-mail redcrescent@zajil.net

Senegalese Red Cross Society

Boulevard F. Roosevelt
B.P. 299
Dakar
SENEGAL
Tel. (221) 8233992
Fax (221) 8225369

Seychelles Red Cross Society

Place de la République
B.P. 53, Victoria
Mahé
SEYCHELLES
Tel. (248) 324646
Fax (248) 321663
E-mail redcross@seychelles.net
Web http://www.seychelles.net/
redcross/

Sierra Leone Red Cross Society

6 Liverpool Street
P.O. Box 427
Freetown
SIERRA LEONE
Tel. (232)(22) 229082/229854
Fax (232)(22) 229083
Tlg. SIERRA RED CROSS
E-mail slrcs@sierratel.sl

Singapore Red Cross Society

15 Penang Lane
SINGAPORE 238486
Tel. (65) 3360269
Fax (65) 3374360
E-mail tplsrcs@singnet.com.sg
Web http://www.redcross.org.sg/

Slovak Red Cross

Grösslingova 24
814 46 Bratislava
SLOVAKIA
Tel. (421)(7) 52925305/5292357/6
Fax (421)(7) 52923279

Slovenian Red Cross

Mirje 19
P.O. Box 236SI
61000 Ljubljana
SLOVENIA
Tel. (386)(61) 2414300
Fax (386)(61) 2414344
E-mail rdeci.kriz-slo@guest.arnes.si

The Solomon Islands Red Cross

P.O. Box 187
Honiara
SOLOMON ISLANDS
Tel. (677) 22682
Fax (677) 25299
Tlx 66347 WING HQ
E-mail sirc@solomon.com.sb

Somali Red Crescent Society

c/o ICRC Box 73226
Nairobi
KENYA
Tel. (871 or 873)
131 2646 (Mogadishu)/
(254)(2) 723963 (Nairobi)
Fax 1312647 (Mogadishu)/
715598 (Nairobi)
Tlx 25645 ICRC KE

The South African Red Cross Society

P.O. Box 50696, Waterfront
ZA Cape Town
SOUTH AFRICA 8002
Tel. (27)(21) 4186640
Fax (27)(21) 4186644
E-mail sarcs@cybertrade.co.za

Spanish Red Cross

Rafael Villa, s/n (Vuelta Ginés Navarro)
28023 El Plantio, Madrid
SPAIN
Tel. (34)(91) 3354444/3354545
Fax (34)(91) 3354455
Tlg. CRUZ ROJA ESPANOLA
E-mail informa@cruzroja.es
Web http://www.cruzroja.es/

The Sri Lanka Red Cross Society

307, T.B. Jaya Road
P.O. Box 375
Colombo 10
SRI LANKA
Tel. (94)(1) 699935
Fax (94)(1) 695434
Tlg. RED CROSS COLOMBO
E-mail slrc@sri.lanka.net

The Sudanese Red Crescent

P.O. Box 235
Khartoum
SUDAN
Tel. (249)(11) 772011
Fax (249)(11) 772877
Tlg. EL NADJA KHARTOUM
E-mail srcs@sudanmail.net

Suriname Red Cross

Gravenberchstraat 2
Postbus 2919
Paramaribo
SURINAME
Tel. (597) 498410
Fax (597) 464780
E-mail surcross@sr.net

Baphalali Swaziland Red Cross Society

104 Johnstone Street
P.O. Box 377
Mbabane
SWAZILAND
Tel. (268) 4042532
Fax (268) 4046108
Tlg. BAPHALALI MBABANE
E-mail bsrcs@redcross.sz

Swedish Red Cross

Östhammarsgatan 70
Box 27316
SE-102 54 Stockholm
SWEDEN
Tel. (46)(8) 4524600
Fax (46)(8) 4524761
E-mail postmaster@redcross.se
Web http://www.redcross.se/

Swiss Red Cross

Rainmattstrasse 10
Postfach
3001 Bern
SWITZERLAND
Tel. (41)(31) 3877111
Fax (41)(31) 3877122
Tlx 911102 CRSB CH
E-mail info@redcross.ch
Web http://www.redcross.ch/

Syrian Arab Red Crescent

Al Malek Aladel Street
Damascus
SYRIAN ARAB REPUBLIC
Tel. (963)(11) 4429662/4441366
Fax (963)(11) 4425677
Tlx 412857 HLAL
E-mail SARC@net.sy

Red Crescent Society of Tajikistan

120, Omari Khayom St.
734017, Dushanbe
TAJIKISTAN
Tel. (7)(3772) 240374
Fax (7)(3772) 245378
E-mail rcstj@rcstj.td.silk.org

Tanzania Red Cross National Society

Upanga Road
P.O. Box 1133
Dar es Salaam
TANZANIA, UNITED
REPUBLIC OF
Tel. (255)(51) 116514/151236
Tlx TACROS 41878
E-mail redcross@unidar.gn.apc.org
Web http://www.cats-net.com/
        Tanzaniaredcross/

The Thai Red Cross Society

Terdprakiat Building
1871, Henry Dunant Road
Bangkok 10330
THAILAND
Tel. (66)(2) 2564037/2564008
Fax (66)(2) 2553064
E-mail wmaster@redcross.or.th
Web http://www.redcross.or.th/

Togolese Red Cross

51, rue Boko Soga
Amoutivé
B.P. 655
Lome
TOGO
Tel. (228) 212110
Fax (228) 215228
Tlg. CROIX-ROUGE
        TOGOLAISE LOME
E-mail crtogol@syfed.tg.refer.org

Tonga Red Cross Society

P.O. Box 456
Nuku'Alofa
South West Pacific
TONGA
Tel. (676) 21360/21670
Fax (676) 24158
Tlx 66222 CW ADM TS
Tlg. REDCROSS TONGA

The Trinidad and Tobago Red Cross Society

7A, Fitz Blackman Drive
Wrightson Road
P.O. Box 357
Port of Spain
TRINIDAD AND TOBAGO
Tel. (1)(868) 6278215/6278128
Fax (1)(868) 6278215
Tlg. TRINREDCROSS
E-mail ttrcs@carib-link.net

Tunisian Red Crescent

19, Rue d'Angleterre
Tunis 1000
TUNISIA
Tel. (216)(1) 320630/325572
Fax (216)(1) 320151
Tlx 12524 HILAL TN
Tlg. HILALAHMAR TUNIS

Turkish Red Crescent Society

Atac Sokak 1 No. 32
Yenisehir, Ankara
TURKEY
Tel. (90)(312) 4302300/4311158
Fax (90)(312) 4300175
Tlg. KIZILAY ANKARA
Web http://www.kizilay.org.tr/

Red Crescent Society of Turkmenistan

48 A. Novoi str.
744000 Ashgabat
TURKMENISTAN
Tel. (993)(12) 395511
Fax (993)(12) 351750
E-mail nrcst @online.tm

The Uganda Red Cross Society

Plot 97, Buganda Road
P.O. Box 494
Kampala
UGANDA
Tel. (256)(41) 258701/258702
Fax (256)(41) 258184
Tlx (0988) 62118 redcrosug
Tlg. UGACROSS KAMPALA

Ukrainian Red Cross Society

30, Pushkinskaya St.
252004 Kiev
UKRAINE
Tel. (380)(44) 2350157/2293484
Fax (380)(44) 2351096/2465658
E-mail redcross@ukrpack.net
Web http://www.redcross.org.ua

Red Crescent Society of the United Arab Emirates

P.O. Box 3324
Abu Dhabi
UNITED ARAB EMIRATES
Tel. (9)(712) 6219000
Fax (9)(712) 6212727
Tlx 23582 RCS EM
Tlg. HILAL AHMAR ABU
DHABI

British Red Cross

9 Grosvenor Crescent
London SW1X 7EJ
UNITED KINGDOM
Tel. (44)(207) 2355454
Fax (44)(207) 2456315
Tlx 918657 BRCS G
E-mail information@redcross.org.uk
Web http://www.redcross.org.uk

American Red Cross

431 18th N.W. Street, 2nd Floor
Washington, DC 20006
UNITED STATES
Tel. (1)(202) 6393400/6393410
Fax (1)(202) 6393595
Tlx ARC TLX WSH 892636
E-mail postmaster@usa.redcross.org
Web http://www.redcross.org/

Uruguayan Red Cross

Avenida 8 de Octubre, 2990
11600 Montevideo
URUGUAY
Tel. (598)(2) 4802112
Fax (598)(2) 4800714
Tlg. CRUZ ROJA URUGUAYA
E-mail cruzroja@adinet.com.uy

Red Crescent Society of Uzbekistan

30, Yusuf Hos Hojib St.
700031 Tashkent
UZBEKISTAN
Tel. (988)(712) 563741
Fax (988)(712) 561801
E-mail rcuz@uzpak.uz
Web http://www.redcrescent.uz/

Vanuatu Red Cross Society

P.O. Box 618
Port Vila
VANUATU
Tel. (678) 27418
Fax (678) 22599
Tlg. VANRED

Venezuelan Red Cross

Avenida Andrés Bello, 4
Apartado 3185
Caracas 1010
VENEZUELA
Tel. (58)(2) 5714380/5712143
Fax (58)(2) 5761042
Tlx 27237 CRURO VC
Tlg. CRUZ ROJA CARACAS
E-mail dirnacsoc@cantv.net
Web http://www.cruzrojahumanidad.
org/venezuela/

Red Cross of Viet Nam

82, Nguyen Du Street
Hanoï
VIET NAM
Tel. (844)(8) 225157/266283
Fax (844)(8) 266285
Tlg. VIETNAMCROSS HANOI
E-mail vnrchq@netnam.org.vn
Web http://www.vnrc.org.vn

Yemen Red Crescent Society

26 September Street
P.O. Box 1257
Sanaa
YEMEN
Tel. (967)(1) 283132/283133
Fax (967)(1) 283131
Tlg. SANAA HELAL AHMAR

Yugoslav Red Cross

Simina 19
11000 Belgrade
YUGOSLAVIA
Tel. (381)(11) 623564
Fax (381)(11) 622965
Tlg. YUGOCROSS BELGRADE
E-mail jckbg@jck.org.yu
Web http://www.jck.org/yu

Zambia Red Cross Society

2837 Los Angeles Boulevard
P.O. Box 50001 (Ridgeway 15101)
Lusaka
ZAMBIA
Tel. (260)(1) 250607/253661
Fax (260)(1) 252219
Tlg. REDRAID LUSAKA
E-mail zrcs@zamnet.zm

Zimbabwe Red Cross Society

98 Cameron Street
P.O. Box 1406
Harare
ZIMBABWE
Tel. (263)(4) 775416/773912
Fax (263)(4) 751739
Tlg. ZIMCROSS HARARE
E-mail zrcs@harare.iafrica.com
Web http://users.harare.
iafrica.com/~zrcs/

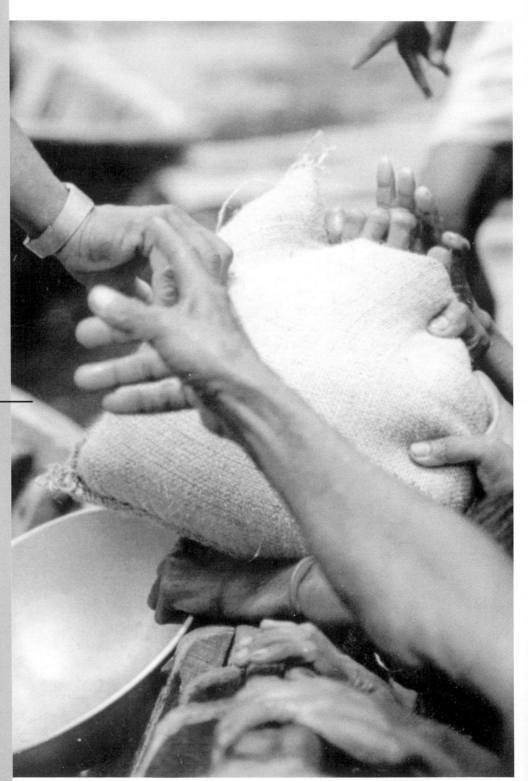

chapter 11

Section Two
Tracking the system

The International Federation coordinates global disaster response in support of the actions of National Societies.

Bjorn Otto Eder/ International Federation, Bangladesh 1998

A worldwide presence

Contact details for regional and country offices of the International Federation of Red Cross and Red Crescent Societies. Information correct as of 1 March 2001.

THE INTERNATIONAL FEDERATION OF RED CROSS AND RED CRESCENT SOCIETIES

P.O. Box 372
1211 Geneva 19
SWITZERLAND
Tel. (41)(22) 7304222
Fax (41)(22) 7330395
Tlx (045) 412 133 FRC CH
Tlg. LICROSS GENEVA
E-mail secretariat@ifrc.org
Web http://www.ifrc.org

Red Cross/EU Office

Rue Belliard 65, bte 7
1040 - Brussels
BELGIUM
Tel. (32)(2) 2350680
Fax (32)(2) 2305465
E-mail infoboard@redcross-eu.net

International Federation of Red Cross and Red Crescent Societies at the United Nations

630 Third Avenue
21st floor
Suite 2104
New York NY 10017
UNITED STATES
Tel. (1)(212) 3380161
Fax (1)(212) 3389832

International Federation regional offices

Buenos Aires

Lucio V. Mansilla 2698 2o
1425 Buenos Aires
ARGENTINA
Tel. (541)(14) 9638659 / 9636866
Fax (541)(14) 9613320
E-mail ifrcbue@satlink.com

Yaounde

Rue Mini-Prix (Bastos)
BP 11507
Yaounde
CAMEROON
Tel. (237) 217437 / 217438
Fax (237) 217439
E-mail ifrccm04@ifrc.org

Beijing

Apt. 4-2-51 (Building 4,
Entrance 2, Floor 5, Apt.1)
Jianguomenwai Diplomatic
Compound,
Chaoyang District,
Beijing 100600,
CHINA
Tel. (8610) 65327162 / 65327163
Fax (8610) 65327166

Abidjan

rue C 43 CHU Cocody Nord
04 PO Box 2090
Abidjan, 04
CÔTE D'IVOIRE
Tel, (225) 22404450 / 22404466
Fax (225) 22404459
E-mail fedecr-r@africaonline.co.ci

Santo Domingo

C/Juan E. Dunant, 51
Ensanche Miraflores
P.O. Box 5358
Santo Domingo
DOMINICAN REPUBLIC
Tel. (1)(809) 6869612
Fax (1)(809) 6869495
E-mail ifrc01@codetel.net.do

Suva

P.O. Box 2507
Government Building
Suva
FIJI
Tel. (679) 311855 / 311665
Fax (679) 311406
E-mail ifrcrds@is.com.fj

Guatemala City

19 Calle 1-26, Zona 14
Av. de las Américas
Pl. Uruguay
Ciudad de Guatemala 01014
GUATEMALA
Tel. (502) 3371686/3335425
Fax (502) 3631449
E-mail fedecruz@guate.net

Budapest

Zolyomi Lepcso Ut 22
1124 Budapest
HUNGARY
Tel. (36)(1) 3193423 /25
Fax (36)(1) 3193424
E-mail ifrc01@ifrc.org

New Delhi

F-25A Hauz Khas Enclave
New Delhi 110 016
INDIA
Tel. (9111) 6561669 / 6858672
Fax (9111) 6857567
E-mail ifrcin01@ifrc.org

Amman

Al Shmeisani
Maroof Al Rasafi Street
Building No. 19
P.O. Box 830511 / Zahran
Amman
JORDAN
Tel. (962)(6) 5681060 / 5694911
Fax (962)(6) 5694556
E-mail ifrc@index.com.jo

Almaty

86, Kunaeva Street
480100 Almaty
KAZAKHSTAN
Tel. (7)(3272) 918838 / 914156
Fax (7)(3272) 9142 67
E-mail ifrckz01@ifrc.org

Nairobi

Chaka Road (off Argwings Kodhek)
P.O. Box 41275
Nairobi
KENYA
Tel. (254)(2) 714255 / 714313
Fax (254)(2) 718415
E-mail ifrcke01@ifrc.org

Bangkok

Ocean Tower 2, 18th Floor
75/26 Sukhumvit 19
Wattana
Bangkok 10110
THAILAND
Tel. (662) 6616933
Fax (662) 6616937
E-mail ifrcth01@ifrc.org

Harare

9, Coxwell Road
Milton Park
Harare
ZIMBABWE
Tel. (263)(4) 720315 / 720316
Fax (263)(4) 708784
E-mail ifrczw01@ifrc.org

International Federation country offices

Afghanistan

43D S. Jamal-ud-Din Afghani Rd.
University Town
Peshawar
PAKISTAN
Tel. (873) 382280530
Fax (873) 382280534
E-mail kabul@wireless.ifrc.org

Albania

c/o Albanian Red Cross
Rruga "Muhamet Gjollesha"
Sheshi "Karl Topia"
Tirana
ALBANIA
Tel. (355) 4256708
Fax (355) 4256707
E-mail irfcal02@ifrc.org

Angola

Caixa Postal 3324
Rua Emilio M'Bidi 51–51A
Bairro Alvalade
Luanda
ANGOLA
Tel. (244)(2) 322001 / 325211
Fax (244)(2) 320648
E-mail ifrcao01@ifrc.org

Armenia
Gevorg Chaush St. 50/1
Yerevan 375088
ARMENIA
Tel. (3741) 354649 / 341708
Fax (3741) 151072
E-mail kelemu@ifrc.org

Azerbaijan
First Magomayev Street 6A
370004 Baku
AZERBAIJAN
Tel. (99)(412) 925792 / 927430
Fax (99)(412) 971889
E-mail office@ifrc.azerin.com

Bangladesh
c/o Bangladesh Red Crescent
Society
684-686 Bara Magh Bazar
Dhaka – 1217
BANGLADESH
Tel. (880)(2) 8315401 / 8315402
Fax (880)(2) 9341631
E-mail ifrcbd@citechco.net

Belarus
Ulitsa Mayakovkosgo 14
Minsk 220006
BELARUS
Tel. (375)(172) 217273
Fax (375)(172) 213446
E-mail ifrcby01@ifrc.org

Belize
c/o Belize Red Cross
PO Box 413
BELIZE CITY
Tel. (501) 272 107
Fax (501) 230998
E-mail bzercshq@btl.net

Bosnia and Herzegovina
Titova 7
71000 Sarajevo
BOSNIA AND HERZEGOVINA
Tel. (387)(33) 666003
Fax (387)(33) 666010
E-mail ifrc_sar@bih.net.ba

Burundi
Avenue des Etats-Unis 3674A
B.P. 324
Bujumbura
BURUNDI
Tel. (257) 229524 / 229525
Fax (257) 229408

Cambodia
53 Deo, Street Croix-Rouge
Central Post Office/P.O. Box 620
Phnom Penh
CAMBODIA
Tel. (855)(23) 210162 / 362690
Fax (855)(23) 210163
E-mail ifrckh01@ifrc.org

Colombia
Av. 68 No. 66-31
Bogotá
COLOMBIA
Tel. (571) 4285144
Fax (571) 4299328
E-mail ifrcbogota@
        sncruzroja.org.co

**Congo, Democratic
Republic of the**
21 Avenue Flamboyant
(Place de Sefoutiers)
Gombe
Kinshasa
DEMOCRATIC REPUBLIC
OF THE CONGO
Tel. (243) 1221495
Fax (243) 1234059
E-mail: hod@ficr.aton.cd

Congo, Republic of
60, Av. de la Libération de Paris
B.P. 88
Brazzaville
CONGO, REPUBLIC OF
Tel. (242) 667564
Fax (242) 815044

El Salvador
c/o Salvadorean Red Cross Society
17 Calle Pte. y Av. Henri Dunant
Apartado postal 2672
San Salvador
EL SALVADOR
Tel. (50)(3) 2811932
Fax (50)(3) 2811932
E-mail ifrc@vianet.com.sv

Eritrea
c/o Red Cross Society of Eritrea
Andnet Street
P.O. Box 575
Asmara
ERITREA
Tel. (291)(1) 150550
Fax (291)(1) 151859
E-mail ifrc@eol.com.er

Ethiopia
Ras Destra Damtew Avenue
P.O. Box 195
Addis Ababa
ETHIOPIA
Tel. (251)(1) 514571 / 514317
Fax (251)(1) 512888
E-mail ifrcet04@ifrc.org

Georgia
7, Anton Katalikosi Street
Tbilisi
GEORGIA
Tel. (995)(32) 950945
Fax (995)(32) 985976
E-mail ifrcge01@ifrc.org

Guinea

Coleah, route du Niger
Près de l'Ambassade
de Yougoslavie
B.P. 376
Conakry
GUINEA
Tel. (224) 413825
Fax (224) 414255

Honduras

Colonia Florencia Norte segunda
calle casa No 1030
contigua al edificio Tovar Lopez
Tegucigalpa
HONDURAS
Tel. (504) 2320707
Fax (504) 2390718

Indonesia

c/o Indonesian Red Cross Society
P.O. Box 2009
Jakarta
INDONESIA
Tel. (6221) 79191841
Fax (6221) 79180905
E-mail ifrcid01@ifrc.org

Iran

c/o Red Crescent Society of the
Islamic Republic of Iran
Taleghani Avenue, Gharani Corner
Tehran
IRAN
Tel. (9821) 8890568
Fax (9821) 8849079
E-mail helai@www.dci.co.ir

Iraq

c/o Iraqi Red Crescent Society
P.O. Box 6143
Baghdad
IRAQ
Tel. (964)(1) 5434184 / 8844036
Fax (964)(1) 5434184

Kenya

South "C" Belle Vue
Off Mombasa Road
P.O. Box 41275
Nairobi
KENYA
Tel. (254)(2) 602465
Fax (254)(2) 602467
E-mail ifrcke31@ifrc.org

Korea, Democratic People's Republic of

c/o Red Cross Society of the DPR
Korea
Ryonwa 1, Central District
Pyongyang
KOREA, DEMOCRATIC
PEOPLE'S REPUBLIC OF
Tel. (850)(2) 3813490 / 3814350
Fax (850)(2) 3813490

Laos

c/o Lao Red Cross
P.O.Box 2948
Setthatirath Road, Xiengnhune
Vientiane
LAO PEOPLE'S DEMOCRATIC
REPUBLIC
Tel. (856) 21215762
Fax (856) 21215935
E-mail laoifrc@laotel.com

Latvia

c/o Latvian Red Cross
Skolas Street 1
Riga LV – 1010
LATVIA
Tel. (3717) 333058
Fax (3717) 333058

Lebanon

N. Daher Building
Mar Tacla
Beirut
LEBANON
Tel. (9611) 424851
Fax (9615) 459658
E-mail ifrc@cyberia.net.lb

Liberia

c/o Liberian Red Cross Society
107, Lynch Street
P.O. Box 5081
Monrovia
LIBERIA
Tel. (231) 227485 / 226231
Fax (231) 226363
E-mail ifrc.org.li@libnet.net

Macedonia

Bul. Koco Racin 13
Skopje 9100
MACEDONIA, FORMER
YUGOSLAV REPUBLIC OF
Tel. (38991) 114271 / 212818
Fax (38991) 115240
E-mail ifrcmk01@ifrc.org

Madagascar

c/o Croix-rouge Malgasy
1, rue Patrice Lumumba
Tsaralana B.P. 1168
Antananarivo
MADAGASCAR
Tel. (261) 320790635
Fax (261) 202222111
E-mail ifrcmg01@ifrc.org

Moldova

c/o Moldovan Red Cross
'67-A Uéitsa Asachi
Chisinau 277028
MOLDOVA
Tel. (3732) 735781
Fax (3732) 729700

Mongolia

c/o Red Cross Society of Mongolia
Central Post Office,
Post Box 537
Ulaanbaatar,
MONGOLIA
Tel. (97611) 320171
Fax (97611) 321684
E-mail ifrcmongol@magicnet.mn

Mozambique

Avenida Agostinho Neto, No 284
Caixa postal 2488
Maputo
MOZAMBIQUE
Tel. (258)(1) 492277
Fax (258)(1) 492278
E-mail ifrcmz01@ifrc.org

Myanmar

c/o Myanmar Red Cross Society
Red Cross Building
42 Strand Road
Yangon
MYANMAR
Tel. (95)(1) 297877
Fax (95)(1) 297877
E-mail ifrc@mptmail.net.mm

Namibia

IFRC Office
P.O. Box 346
Katatura 2128
Windhoek
NAMIBIA
Tel. (264)(61) 218210
E-mail ifrcnm01@ifrc.org

Nicaragua

c/o Nicaraguan Red Cross
Reparto Belmonte, Carretera Sur
Apartado Postal 3279
Managua
NICARAGUA
Tel. (505) 2650186 / 2650377
Fax (505) 2652069

Nigeria

c/o Nigerian Red Cross Society
11, Eko Akete Close
Off St. Gregory's Road
South West Ikoyi
P.O. Box 764
Lagos
NIGERIA
Tel. (234)(1) 2695228
Fax (234)(1) 2695229
E-mail fedcross@infoweb.abs.net

Pakistan

c/o Pakistan Red Crescent Society
National Headquarters
Sector H-8
Islamabad
PAKISTAN
Tel. (925)(1) 9257122 / 9257123
Fax (925)(1) 4430745
E-mail ifrc@isb.comsats.net.pk

Palestine

c/o Palestine Red Crescent Society
P.O. Box 3637
Al Bireh / West Bank
PALESTINE
Tel. (9722) 2400484
Fax (9722) 2406518
E-mail ifrc@palnet.com

Papua New Guinea

c/o Papua New Guinea Red Cross
Society
P.O. Box 6545
Boroko
PAPUA NEW GUINEA
Tel. (675) 3112277
Fax (675) 3230731
E-mail ifrcpg@ifrc.org

Russian Federation

c/o Russian Red Cross Society
Tcheryomushkinski Proezd 5
117036 Moscow
RUSSIAN FEDERATION
Tel. (7502) 9375267 / 9375268
Fax (7502) 9375263
E-mail moscow@ifrc.org

Rwanda

c/o Rwandan Red Cross
B.P. 425, Nyamiranbo
Kigali
RWANDA
Tel. (250) 73232 / 73874
Fax (250) 73233
E-mail ifrcrw02@ifrc.org

Sierra Leone

c/o Sierra Leone Red Cross Society
6, Liverpool Street
P.O. Box 427
Freetown
SIERRA LEONE
Tel. (23)(222) 227772
Fax (23)(222) 228180
E-mail ifrc@sierratel.sl

Somalia

Chaka Road
(off Argwings Kodhek)
P.O. Box 41275
Nairobi
KENYA
Tel. (254)(2) 715249
Fax (254)(2) 729070

Sri Lanka

3rd floor, 307 T B Jayah Mawatha
Colombo 10
Sri Lanka
Tel. (9474) 7155977
Fax (9474) 571275
E-mail ifrclk01@srilanka.net

Sudan

Al Mak Nimir Street/
Gamhouria Street
Plot No 1, Block No. 4
P.O. Box 10697
East Khartoum
SUDAN
Tel. (249)(11) 771033
Fax (249)(11) 770484
E-mail flora@sudanmail.net

Tajikistan

c/o Tajikistan Red Crescent Society
120, Omar Khayom St.
734017 Dushanbe
TAJIKISTAN
Tel. (992)(372) 244296 / 245981
Fax (992)(372) 248520
E-mail ifrcdsb@ifrc.org

Tanzania

Ali Hassan Mwinyi Road
Plot No. 294/295
P.O. Box 1133
Dar es Salaam
TANZANIA, UNITED
REPUBLIC OF
Tel. (255)(51) 116514 / 135526
Fax (255)(51) 117308
E-mail ifrctz01@ifrc.org

Tunisia

Residence "Les Deux Lacs"
Les Berges du Lac
2045 Tunis
TUNISIA
Tel. (2)(161) 862485
Fax (2)(161) 862971
E-mail ifrc.tu01@ifrc.org

Turkey

c/o Turkish Red Crescent Society
Nuzheitiye Caddesi Derya Dil
Sokak
No. 1 Besiktas
Istambul
TURKEY
Tel. (902)(12) 2367902 / 2367903
Fax (902)(12) 2367711

Uganda

c/o Uganda Red Cross Society
Plot 97, Buganda Road
P.O. Box 494
Kampala
UGANDA
Tel. (256)(41) 234968 / 343742
Fax (256)(41) 258184
E-mail ifrc@imul.com

Ukraine

c/o Red Cross Society of Ukraine
30 Ulitsa Pushkinskaya
Kyiv 252004
UKRAINE
Tel. (38044) 2286110
Fax (38044) 2345082
E-mail federation@ukrpack.net

Venezuela

2da Avenida de Campo Alegre
Quinta Villa Carlota
Municipio Chacao
Estado Miranda
Caracas
VENEZUELA
Tel. (582) 2655423/2650976
E-mail ifrcven@telcel.net.ve

Viet Nam

19 Mai Hac De Street
Hanoï
VIET NAM
Tel. (84)(4) 9438250
Fax (84)(4) 9436177
E-mail ifrc@hn.vnn.vn

Yugoslavia

Simina Ulica Broj 21
11000 Belgrade
YUGOSLAVIA
Tel. (381)(11) 3282202
Fax (381)(11) 3281791
E-mail telecom@ifrc.org.yu

Zambia

c/o Zambia Red Cross
2837 Los Angeles Boulevard
P.O. Box 50001
Ridgeway 15101
Lusaka
ZAMBIA
Tel. (2601) 254074 / 251599
Fax (2601) 251599
E-mail ifrczmb01@ifrc.org

Index